CHOOSING TO LEAD

by
KENNETH E. CLARK
and
MIRIAM B. CLARK

A Center for Creative Leadership Book

Published by Leadership Press Ltd.

Authors
Kenneth E. Clark and Miriam B. Clark

Managing Editor
Judy Rock Allen

Production Coordinator
Don J. Beville

Typesetting
Thomas McDaniel

Dust Jacket Design
Dennis Michael Stredney

Library of Congress Cataloging-in-Publication Data
ISBN 0-9638301-0-4

CIP 93-79886

Any inquires should be directed to the Distributor:
Iron Gate Press
P.O. Box 32753
Charlotte, NC 28232
1-804-276-4662

Table of Contents

Acknowledgments

We gratefully acknowledge the cooperation of the following persons and organizations who have given permission for reproduction of copyrighted materials in this book:

The Consulting Psychologists Press, Inc. for special permission to reproduce the instructions for completing the FIRO-B®, the Myers Briggs Type Indicator®, and the California Psychological Inventory®. FIRO-B®, Myers Briggs Type Indicator®, MBTI®, California Psychological Inventory®, and CPI® are trademarks owned by the Consulting Psychologists Press, Inc., Palo Alto, CA 94303.

David P. Campbell for permission to reproduce four charts from the manuals of The Campbell Organizational Survey™ (COS)™ (National Computer Systems, Inc., P.O. Box 1416, Minneapolis, MN 55440, 1990). Campbell Organizational Survey™ and COS™ are trademarks owned by David P. Campbell, Ph.D.

Dow Jones & Company, Inc. for selections reprinted by permission of *The Wall Street Journal* © 1991, 1992, and 1993 Dow Jones & Company, Inc. All Rights Reserved Worldwide.

Fortune and Alan Farnham for permission to reprint part of "The TRUST GAP" © 1989 Time Inc. All Rights Reserved.

The University of Michigan Press for permission to reprint the description by Jyuji Misumi of his early work in leadership from *The Behavioral Science of Leadership*, © 1985, Ann Arbor.

Lexington Books, an imprint of Macmillan, Inc., for permission to reprint material excerpted from Figure 1–2 and Figure 1–3 of *The Lessons of Experience: How Successful Executives Develop on the Job* by Morgan W. McCall, Jr., Michael M. Lombardo, and Ann M. Morrison. Copyright © 1988 by Lexington Books.

FOREWORD

Choosing to Lead

The latter half of the twentieth century has been so packed with change, conflict, and discovery that future historians will be hard pressed to characterize neatly these tumultuous years. Three decades ago there were tendencies to identify this era as the nuclear age or the space age. Such labels have become notably inadequate.

Given that technological advances have been the catalyst for changing the tone and tempo of our lives, the larger reality is that the collective influence of humans on other humans remains the lead story. Political, social, and family structures have emerged in new forms. A generalized and continuing redistribution of power represents the true hallmark of our times: from the king to the legislature, the bishop to the parishioners, the industrial baron to the stockholders, and from the central committee to the collectives.

These changes toward a more democratic, distributed, egalitarian, and humanistic world have not gone smoothly. Only in rare instances has there been a cadre of individuals in place with the skills, insights, and discipline essential for the acceptance of the additional responsibilities that attend a decentralization of power. We are, of course, talking about that wonderful and complex human activity known as "leadership." The essence of "leadership" is a willingness to accept responsibility for influencing the future.

Kenneth and Miriam Clark have selected a provocative title for their masterful discussion. *Choosing to Lead* should trigger reflection on the extraordinary dimensions of their subject. In their two previous works, *Measures of Leadership* (1990), produced after a conference on the methods and styles of leadership, and *Impact of Leadership* (1992), derived from another Center-sponsored conference focusing on the aims and outcomes of leadership, the Clarks outlined a conceptual framework and then included numerous items of original research by a variety of prominent scholars. *Choosing to Lead* provides in one volume a coherent overview of the field, set in historical and operational context that will be relevant and appealing to a wide audience.

One of the realities of our time is the revolution in awareness regarding the inadequacies of contemporary institutions and organizations. Challenges to our economy are translated into the microworld of problems with individual and team productivity. A deeper probe reveals that trust and commitment are at the heart of cooperative productivity. We know of no source other than what we call "leadership" to generate and sustain work environments that gracefully provide the tonic for trust and commitment. "Quality" initiatives, now undergoing some needed scrutiny within American industry, will be successful past an initial spurt of enthusiasm only when they are recognized as requiring a modification of "leader" behaviors that are all too often irrelevant or dysfunctional.

There will never be a sleek, simple cookbook for leadership success. This awesome, sometimes perplexing, always fascinating subject defies tidy boundaries and mechanistic formulae. Arguments persist regarding the existence of "leadership," its applicability in different settings, its generic or environmental sources, and its relationship to "management" and "ethics." Each of these issues is addressed in this text, and with rare clarity and authenticity. Historical perspectives, sophisticated constructs, and practical examples are woven into a readable tour de force.

In a world undergoing dramatic change in the most basic institutions and practices, distributed power coupled with informed responsibility will be seen eventually as *the* solution to challenges in the political, social, and commercial worlds. For such realignment of responsibilities to take place successfully, there must be competent leaders by the millions across the globe. One book cannot, of course, handle the task. Still, *Choosing to Lead* has the potential to make a real difference. The Center for Creative Leadership is proud to have supported the herculean efforts of Kenneth and Miriam Clark in the creation of this book.

Walter F. Ulmer, Jr.
President
Center for Creative Leadership
July 1993

Preface

We started out to write a textbook on leadership. We felt it would be helpful to review the important studies about leadership and provide the opportunity for the uninitiated to draw their own conclusions about study findings. Although we may very well have written a textbook, we felt the need to send a further message. As we studied, we found that the best research in leadership posed a persistent question: Why doesn't everyone act like a leader? We read many reports of people in positions where leadership was expected who did not behave like leaders. Many acted like autocrats, bureaucrats, or aristocrats and failed to have positive effects on their organizations. Many people refuse to accept invitations to fill important positions. Why is it that people of considerable talent so often choose *not* to be leaders?

The title *Choosing to Lead* reflects our conclusion that to lead, in the best sense of the word, people must fervently want to lead and also understand how to lead. People cannot be assigned to be leaders; it is not enough to be assigned a position, given a challenge to take charge, asked to be the tough one in tough times, or want to straighten around a particular situation. Rather, leaders must make a choice; they must commit themselves to lead. *This commitment is more than a contract to fill a position.* It involves the heart and mind of the one who commits and the hearts and minds of those who willingly are influenced by the leader.

Some people choose not to lead and will not accept leadership responsibility; they see the role as too burdensome and unpopular, involving too much responsibility. "Someone else is bound to do it" is a common reaction. Others accept positions where leadership is expected but do not lead. They apparently take charge, impose their will on others, make decisions based on established rules and procedures, enjoy the perquisites and status, and usually depart the organization without leaving a trace.

Most writings about leadership assume that people want to learn how to be better leaders and that additional knowledge will improve practice. We have been forced to conclude that most people who could lead and have powerful effects in fact are satisfied with the way they operate and do not want to change. Therefore, any writing about leadership needs to show the important consequences of changed behavior and the specific changes that produce specific results. People need to know how to behave effectively as leaders and must be willing to change their own behaviors to produce desired effects.

In every case, leadership occurs only when one chooses to lead. To make that choice means that the leader mobilizes the talents and energies of the total group to address a problem, complete a task, or achieve a mission. The leader facilitates. The leader clarifies. The leader inspires. The leader resolves conflicts. The followers of such a leader comment that they exert more effort for the leader, that the leader clarifies the importance of each person's role and is concerned that each person will develop and grow as a result of the experience, and that the organization will improve and prosper.

Leaders come from all walks of life and emerge at all ages. Choosing to lead, to get something done that needs doing, can be part of the life of a school child on the playground or in the classroom, of college students, of residents in a neighborhood with common problems, of adults in community activities, of employees in the workplace, or of residents of a home for retired people. We learned that credentials are not required to make the leap. Some choose to lead early in life, some late.

Large numbers of people choose not to lead but to "boss"; they view their group members as inferior, undisciplined, untrainable, and as requiring "management." We surmise that there may be as much tyranny today as the world has ever seen. However, it is widely condoned as the necessary tyranny of the foreman getting the job done, the enforcement of rules by the bureaucrat preventing disorder, the control of thugs by the police protecting the populace, or the right of "big people" dominating "little people." Our comics and cartoonists find this form of tyranny a dependable source for plying their trade.

We foresee many benefits from increasing the number of people who choose to lead and do our best in this book to provide the knowledge to help make this choice. We believe we show that it pays to lead rather than command, because commands produce only the behaviors demanded, not those that would be most effective. It also pays to lead rather than to contract for services. An honest day's work for an honest day's pay does not induce the worker to help the employer solve problems or to do things better.

Of course, we asked many questions: What is leadership and how is it defined? Can leadership be studied? How? What capabilities are necessary for leaders of complex organizations to be effective? Can potential outstanding leaders be identified early? What do effective leaders do? Do they all behave the same? How are effective leaders perceived by their followers? Does effective leadership make a difference to the organization? Do principles of leadership established in the developed western countries apply as well to the rest of the world? Can leadership behaviors be learned? How does a society without a "leadership class" assure a steady stream of candidates for leadership positions? Which stages in education and development are most likely to produce willing and effective leaders? What prior experiences are most pertinent for increasing the wisdom of leaders? What behaviors, attitudes, and understandings must be developed among followers if leaders are to have a good chance of success? How do we define success for a leader? Must our expectation of leaders change as conditions change? Will we need new types of leaders and followers as our society becomes more diverse? Answers to many of these questions appear regularly in the public media and in professional journals. Some answers ride the fad of the moment and are not valuable because issues are oversimplified. Some answers based on scientific study are impressive but are hard to translate into action. Part of the problem is that some studies seem at first glance to be too technical or provide no clear path to application. Popular literature often provides answers that skyrocket into attention only to fizzle out as their merits prove illusory.

Since the beginning of civilization, humans have been trying out ideas to see if they work. When the idea could be implemented, the innovator often became a leader who attracted a number of followers. Others would copy the idea to discover if they, too, might gain power or status or improve the lot of their people. The trouble was, and continues to be, that an idea or principle will not work every time. Painful trial and error was the way of the past used to test the generalizability of a principle. Today, because of improved research design, we can estimate the limits of generalizations based on results of testing ideas in natural settings.

Geographical boundaries did not confine our investigation. We report studies conducted around the world using methodological improvements that have appeared mainly in the last fifty years. Because this book studies leadership, not all of behavioral science, we skirt the literature related to behavioral principles applied to groups except in those instances where such studies illuminate how leadership and followership operate in groups with actual objectives in the "real" world.

We draw from progress made in the professional study of leadership by investigators who have labored for many years. Prime attention is given to studies that test a proposition by discovering whether its application makes a difference. We emphasize proof: principles that have been proven in some way. We recognize that proof means different things to different people. We do not deal in depth with standards of evidence nor with discussions of how knowledge is acquired and confirmed. These we leave for philosophers of science. What we do, instead, is provide supporting evidence obtained by practical tests for each of the conclusions we present, and we refer to key references at appropriate places. The reader should be able to see whether or not the outcome shown is worth the change in leader behaviors that produces it.

The book is intended to be "user friendly." Chapter sequence is likely to be appropriate for a classroom course in leadership or as a supplement to a short training program. Chapters 1 through 4 define leadership and describe the ways in which leadership might be exercised. Chapters 5 and 6 provide illustrations of research methods used to demonstrate the impact of improved leadership.

Chapters 7 and 8 describe a leadership development program at a well-known training center by describing the tests and materials completed by participants before arrival and then by sampling the program itself. Chapter 9 considers the many programs in education and training of leaders and managers—a $40 billion business in the western world today. Chapter 10 reviews how experience develops and modifies the behavior of leaders. Chapter 11 examines the uses of survey methods to assess the mood of group members and inform leaders of the effectiveness of their communication programs. Chapter 12 reviews studies of the use of power and position and the outcomes of such use.

Chapter 13 presents a part of the enormous literature on leadership and cultural differences with an emphasis on national, regional, and international differences that affect those who have to adapt to an unfamiliar culture. Chapter 14 highlights how reported studies can assist leaders to improve their efficacy in dealing with followers and organizations to meet their objectives. Chapter 15 is a summary of the propositions that have been stated and supported throughout the book.

We acknowledge gratefully the support of many in the preparation of this volume. We are in debt to those whose studies are the pillars of the field of leadership and to their sponsors in business, the military, and academe. For this book, we pay special tribute to the Smith Richardson Foundation, which supports the efforts of the Center for Creative Leadership, and to Walter F. Ulmer, Jr., the current president of the Center. His enthusiasm for the project helped us sustain our commitment. We extend our thanks to the many readers who wrote critical comments on lengthy manuscript copy and helped us clarify our writing, fine tune the research findings, and contributed to our knowledge of what leadership responsibility is all about. They include Walter F. Ulmer, Jr., William Rosenbach, David Campbell, David Noer, Walter Tornow, Gary Rhodes, Janet Spence, Randall White, Jodi Kassover Taylor, Helen Astin, Zeddie Bowen, Howard Prince, Ingar Skaug, Debbie Birnbaum, and William Green. We are grateful to Ellen Hamman for her invaluable assistance in locating references, entering copy, and providing a semblance of order to a mass of notes.

We are deeply indebted to Judy Rock Allen for her loving and meticulous work as the managing editor of this volume and as the person who saw its production through to completion.

K.E.C.
M.B.C.
July 6, 1993

CHAPTER ONE

Leaders Wanted!

CEO WANTED. NO INSIDERS, PLEASE

NATION'S TOP THREE SCHOOL JOBS OPEN

HEAD OF UNITED WAY RESIGNS UNDER FIRE

NEW LEADERS FOR THE NINETIES

IBM NAMES GERSTNER TO RESTORE PROFITABILITY

The height of interest in leadership is amply attested by the number of articles appearing regularly in newspapers and magazines. Many of them suggest that the dominant agenda in business today pertains more to the executive suite than to the shop floor. Other headlines suggest that problems of leadership arise not only in business but also in government, religious groups, and charitable organizations. They telegraph messages that are not in harmony and do not sound a common theme:

DEMOCRACY, THEOLOGY COLLIDE IN CATHOLIC CHURCH

THE TOUGHEST BOSSES IN AMERICA

TAKING CHARGE IN WASHINGTON

CITY, COUNTY OFFICIALS SHOULD TAKE THE LEAD

GE IS NO PLACE FOR AUTOCRATS, WELCH DECREES

NO MORE NICE GUY AT P&G—NOT BY A LONG SHOT

TOUGH TIMES, TOUGH BOSSES

Restoring Loyalty to the Workplace

We know problems of leadership also exist in small organizations and at different levels of organizations, and we wonder whether there are consistent principles about leader behaviors that apply universally. People at the top of an organization usually report on the health of the organization. They also reflect on their success as leaders, putting the best possible face on their record. More and more such judgments are questioned. Parents challenge the school board and the superintendent. Large stockholders urge boards of directors to change the top leadership of major corporations. Voters pay greater attention to the performance of those they elect to positions of leadership. Workers demand more equitable pay relative to the salary and benefits of the executives. Even as diverse a group as local workers for the United Way ensured that their complaints about high pay and perquisites of their national leader were heeded.

No longer can a leader hold himself or herself aloof from the group and announce decisions as though from on high. Increasingly customers, members, neighbors, constituents, employees, and stockholders have become sources of information and influence who can provide vivid descriptions of the top leaders of their organizations; many will do so readily. Investigative reporters, often looking for hidden conflicts, provide details of leadership behavior that do not always match the organization's image.

Thus it is important to adjust the lens through which we view leaders so as to include the context within which they operate and the expectations of those who judge their performance. We must consider the differing purposes that drive the organizations and institutions of a society, the culture from which leaders and followers are drawn, and the group climate they establish to achieve their goals. When are organizational factors critical components of success and when are they irrelevant? We must know more before we adopt practices that worked well in a single setting.

Educational Leadership

Educational institutions are described as different from business organizations: Schools and colleges have no obvious equivalent to profitability and, although fiscal stability is still required, the distribution of power and authority is quite dissimilar. Faculty, students, parents of students, alumni, business staffs, board members, and top administrators of a college, university, or school system all share in complicated and ambiguous ways the decision making that sets policy. Sometimes political pressures intrude into the process.

NATION'S TOP THREE SCHOOL JOBS OPEN

Philadelphia Schools Superintendent Constance Clayton has run the country's sixth-largest school system for a decade, no small accomplishment in an era when urban superintendents are ejected after an average of two years on the job.

Her tenure is testament not only to her managerial skills but also increasingly to her political wits. When the district approved a condom-distribution plan two years ago, it was the school board that proposed the idea, not the superintendent.

Ms. Clayton's political deftness in letting the board absorb the subsequent heat for an unpopular decision is a quality seemingly missing from her contemporaries in other urban districts. And that has often led to their downfall.

It happened again last week, when the New York City Board of Education voted, 4–3, not to renew the contract of Schools Chancellor Joseph A. Fernandez, whose academic innovations won praise but whose political battles with the board and the community over issues from condom distribution to a curriculum that included discussion of homosexual families eventually unseated him.

Fernandez is not alone. Six of the nation's 20 largest school systems are searching for new superintendents or have installed acting ones. Among them are Los Angeles and Chicago, the nations second- and third-largest, and Minneapolis, New Orleans, Oklahoma City and Columbus, Ohio.

Although not everyone agrees that Fernandez mishandled the politics of his job, there is agreement that managing a large urban school system requires more and sharper skills than it once did, from the ability to initiate change in cumbersome bureaucracies to managing finances in tight fiscal times. And growing numbers of educators insist that political astuteness, a quality not taught in education administration courses, has become a major underpinning to an urban superintendent's success, regardless of other qualifications.

In Chicago, where Ted Kimbrough resigned last month, an ambitious decentralization plan that gave communities direct control over their schools, including hiring and dismissing of principals, proved nearly impossible to manage, and as dropout rates and test scores continued to sink, Kimbrough took the heat.

In Los Angeles, Bill Anton resigned last September, saying he felt defeated in part by interference in management decisions by the school board.[1]

When we see urban school superintendents spending most of their time on political or quasi-political tasks, we gain some insight into the reasons for poor student performance in the classrooms. Opportunities for leadership in the teaching and learning programs are narrowed sharply. Studies of school systems—urban, suburban, and rural—suggest that the principal in charge of one school building has much more influence on the quality of teaching and the amount of learning than does the superintendent of the system.

Colleges and universities seek to establish a collegial atmosphere in which many parties share in making policy and decisions. Presidents in such a climate feel obliged to pass the leadership role to others. Even though the faculty insist on a president with an academic background, the president who dares to take the lead in academic reform is seen as meddling in academic affairs, claimed by the faculty as their own turf. Faculty demand higher salaries and expect the president to deliver the money. Students campaign for no increases in tuition or fees but want better facilities and smaller classes. Alumni want faculty and students to pay more attention to tradition and to keep the place the way it was when they were students. Parents expect the institution to deliver a first-class education and to prepare their children for a guaranteed first job and a lifetime career. Trustees, most of whom come from business, want to see fiscal stability, well-maintained buildings and grounds, and no trouble from outrageous faculty or rebellious students. Although these roles may be a bit overstated, the problems faced by leaders of educational institutions in dealing with divergent views of stakeholders are not. Rather, they are comparable to the problems faced by leaders of other organizations. They need the same high quality of management, of adaptation to changes, and of courageous and decisive leadership and are equally affected by forces in the society that call for better quality or different service.

Managerial Leadership

A truly useful description of leadership must extend well beyond theories and move to the observation of how leaders behave when they are "leading." Many investigators are at work developing psychological measures of leaders' behaviors, partly to improve understanding of what leaders do and partly to identify persons whose behaviors have the desired effects in promoting group performance and member satisfaction. Organizations of all varieties support such studies and assist in collecting the necessary data. These studies allow the important aspects of both good leadership behavior and good management to be studied in a natural setting. As might be expected, most of these settings are in business and involve managers as the objects of study.

The leadership literature has many studies that have collected data from business managers. The words, however, are not synonyms: Managers differ from leaders. Managers are more often employed in business. They hold positions that have assigned responsibilities for assuring that certain tasks are completed within a given time limit. They have responsibility for fiscal control and have superiors to whom they report regularly. Managers also exist outside of business and have similar positions. Some managers are leaders because they do more than the minimal demands of their jobs in accomplishing goals. We will address other differences as we proceed.

Henry Mintzberg, Bronfman Professor of Management at McGill University, was among the first to search out firsthand just what managers do on the job. In *The Nature of Managerial Work*,[2] Mintzberg reviewed prior studies and theories about management and found them incomplete because the *content* of the job was not examined. His doctoral dissertation fills the gap, and his findings, which follow, are reported here because they pertain to leader as well as manager behaviors.

Mintzberg's Study of Managerial Work

Five chief executives were studied on the job using *structured observation* to make analysis possible, with enough freedom to allow the development of understanding about little known factors. These five executives were observed and detailed records were kept for one week on each. Each executive's scheduled appointments for thirty days were reviewed, and information was collected about the company and the executive. The profile of executive behaviors emerged looking different from that provided by questionnaire studies.

These executives appeared to be working at an unrelenting pace with no break. The mail (average thirty-six pieces per day), telephone calls (average of five per day—this was over twenty years ago, what is it today?), and meetings (average of eight per day) accounted for almost every minute. Activity was characterized by brevity, variety, and fragmentation.[3]

Managers were continually seeking information. They preferred oral communications to written reports. They welcomed interruption when it added to the flow of information. An average of 48% of their contact time was with subordinates, 7% with superiors, and 44% with outsiders. Each had control over the way time was spent, and each reported that little time was found to attend to longer-range responsibilities. The ability of each to control the pressures for action on a wide variety of fronts varied.

Often their problems could not be addressed without cooperation from persons inside or outside the company over whom they had no direct authority—emphasizing once again the necessity to be able to exercise influence and to persuade. Most of the time the work was inherently hectic and disorderly, most tasks were of short duration, topics changed abruptly, actions were responses to unexpected problems, decisions could be politically tinged, and building relationships with other units was essential. The image of the manager as having a clearly defined job and a clearly developed strategy with ordered priorities did not resemble reality.

The work of other investigators shows there is a bit more planning and orderliness by managers than might be suggested by Mintzberg's work. Leaders and managers report that desired results are attained by attention to key issues, by setting priorities, and by developing relationships. Observation of many individuals in positions of responsibility has identified behaviors that seem to relate directly to increased organizational effectiveness. However, these studies have been criticized because they rely heavily on what observers can "see" in the behaviors of themselves and others.

When Managers are Leaders

Recently a new way of looking at leadership has emerged from the work of James Kouzes and Barry Posner[4] when, as faculty members at the business school at Santa Clara University in California, they became interested in discovering whether managers ever behaved like leaders. Reading analyses of Lincoln, Gandhi, Churchill, Alexander the Great, and Moses did not give them the clues they needed for their classroom study of Silicon Valley managers or community leaders; they decided to start with a new approach.

Everyone, they assumed, had some qualities related to leadership and, once in a while, certain approaches to a problem worked well, with a group responding in an unusual and productive way. Should not such acts be called acts of leadership? Perhaps hunting for examples of leadership on a small scale would provide clues about how persons learn to be more effective in mobilizing a group to great efforts. Kouzes and Posner decided to give it a try, using their classes of full-time managers who were studying part time for an advanced degree.

The Kouzes and Posner Study of Leadership Practices. Students were asked to search their memories, asking, "What was my personal best as a leader?" Kouzes and Posner did not begin by collecting data from those who thought themselves leaders, or from those who considered themselves successful managers. Their basic question revealed that each person has a little of the leader inside that occasionally is exhibited in behavior that produces great results.

Kouzes and Posner were surprised. *Everyone* had an example. *Everyone* had experienced the thrill and excitement that comes when a group turns on, when a group gets caught up in a project or comes alive with enthusiasm to solve a problem, achieve a goal, or make an important breakthrough. *Everyone* wanted to describe the behaviors that had worked, the circumstances that had aided the process, and the various ways in which different people responded to the challenge.

If leadership behaviors occur around us all the time, although sometimes in unexpected settings, the phenomenon should become easier to study because its dimensions can be examined more closely. Kouzes and Posner saw their opportunity and began such an analysis. They hunted for the components of these "best leadership acts." Regularities began to emerge.

They found they could summarize the thousands of reports of best leadership acts as having five essential characteristics that set them apart from usual managerial acts, all of which reflect how the leader transforms the relationship from boss-subordinate to leader-follower. These characteristics are:

1. Challenging the process
2. Inspiring a shared vision
3. Enabling others to act
4. Modeling the way
5. Encouraging the heart

The Leadership Practices Survey was developed, on which managers rated their own behavior and were in turn rated by their subordinates. Individual leaders could be studied to determine their patterns of behaviors, and attention could be given to their weaknesses or omissions. A training program could be devised for leaders based upon these five classes of activities.[5]

Executive Leadership

Top leaders have become more open to interviews and studies as the interest in quality of leadership has increased. The usual corporate biography of a powerful founder, always more laudatory than factual, has given place to independently written appraisals of performance. The major addition to the literature has come in a form in which some fairly general principles emerge. Panels of executives have been queried using a set form of questions. Writers have then been able to summarize the responses to gain insights about the practices of powerful people.

Warren Bennis

Warren Bennis, Distinguished Professor of Business Administration at the University of Southern California, has interviewed and observed people in top positions to gain understanding of how they become leaders and what behaviors they exhibit that make them effective. Summarized in *Leaders: The Strategies for Taking Charge*[6] (with Burt Nanus) are interviews of ninety outstanding leaders who are defined as people with proven track records who construed their roles as leaders, not managers, and who were "vision-oriented."

> The leaders, 60 corporate CEO's and 30 leaders from the public sector, held four strategies, or areas of competency, in common:
> Strategy I: Attention through vision. "Vision grabs. Initially it grabs the leaders, and management of attention enables others also to get on the bandwagon."
> Strategy II: Meaning through communication. "All organizations depend on the existence of shared meanings and interpretations of reality, which facilitate coordinated action."
> Strategy III: Trust through positioning. "We trust people who are predictable, whose positions are known and who keep at it; leaders who are trusted make themselves known, make their positions clear."
> Strategy IV: The deployment of self through positive self-regard. "The management of self is critical. . . . This creative deployment of self makes leading a deeply personal business. . . . To understand and possess positive self-regard does not blind one to the less desirable qualities of human beings; it does, however establish standards for thinking about human possibilities."

Bennis and Nanus provide specific instruction to others about how they can emulate the work of these outstanding leaders.

Bennis is one of many who have studied and described the behaviors of leaders. For Bennis, the chief source of information is the person actively involved in the leadership role. He finds much to be learned by asking about their dreams and their plans for actions to turn dreams into reality. The stories Bennis tells are engaging and informative. Here again, however, we do not see the entire scene nor hear the full story. The leaders and managers themselves cannot be judged the most accurate observers of their own actions; they are not disinterested reporters. They are fully able to "sell" us on their methods, just as they have sold their dreams to the organization and their products to the public. We might ask whether, upon viewing the long-term effects of their work, they might describe their actions differently.

James Bruce

Retired CEOs provided James Bruce, former vice-president for corporate relations of the Eastman Kodak Company, with just such an opportunity. Rather than studying those who were still on the battle line, Bruce, in retirement as a Senior Fellow at the Center for Creative Leadership, interviewed CEOs of many corporations after they retired, asking them to reflect on their strategies for getting things done. Following are some of his conclusions that are described in *The Intuitive Pragmatists*:[7]

A group of thirteen chief executives was selected whose terms in office were hailed as significant. All had headed major Fortune 500 companies (e.g., Monsanto, Armco, Texaco, General Motors, American Can, and the Mead Corporation). Upon succeeding to the top position, each found it necessary to perform acts that asserted their newly acquired authority. They assembled an executive team to provide counsel and feedback, and they sought ways to communicate to all of the stakeholders. They understood the limits of their own authority and developed working relationships with their directors.

Primarily, these CEOs felt the need to move the organization ahead a step, to respond to changing environments, and to assure the future of the organization. They discovered the importance of doing what they said they were going to do. As one CEO said, "There is enough confusion in an organization, enough myth and folklore, without guessing, 'Is what he said really what he meant?'" As leaders, these CEOs identified their two major tasks to be to set the tone of the organization and to decide the direction of the organization.

The need for change and their awareness of the resistance to change determined the strategies of the CEOs. They developed and stated a vision even when it contrasted sharply with current conditions. Some said they found it necessary to "invent a crisis" in order to focus attention on the need for change. Each felt an obligation to prepare the organization for an unforeseeable time with unpredictable problems when they would no longer be on the scene. Many said they had made key decisions that could be described as intuitive when, in the face of uncertainty, logic could not be brought into play. Defending such decisions called on their persuasive abilities and the authority of their positions.

Bruce concluded, "Leadership may start with vision, but the skill of a great leader is to give it the appearance of rationality, which gives people a chance to argue, refine the decision, gain commitment, and get it implemented. Leadership may start with a predilection for a certain course of action; followership starts with the opportunity to argue the logic of that course of action. Both are needed for success."[8]

John Kotter

The need for the leader to orchestrate change is highlighted by John Kotter[9] in his study of the leadership behaviors of chief executive officers.

Interviews of 150 managers from forty firms and responses to a ten-page questionnaire from nearly 1,000 top-level executives were collected. Kotter examined fifteen corporations with reputations for good management to discover whether they actually did create a stronger than average senior management team. Over a three-year period, he studied five corporations involved in organizational change and watched their efforts to attract, develop, and retain leadership talent.

From examination of these data, Kotter concluded that effective leadership in complex organizations has two major components:

1. *Creating an Agenda for Change* starts with a vision of what can and should be that takes into account the legitimate long-term interests of the parties involved and includes a strategy for achieving that vision. Great vision emerges when a powerful mind, loaded with massive amounts of information, is able to see interesting patterns and new possibilities.

2. *Building a Strong Implementation Network* includes supportive relationships with key sources of power strong enough to elicit cooperation, compliance, and teamwork and committed to making the vision a reality.

Kotter reminds us that leaders are not all alike. They may be tall or short, fast or slow, young or old, tough or tender, liberal or conservative, brash or reserved, highly participative or fairly directive. What effective leadership behavior looks like is very much a function of the situation in which it is found. Clearly the need for it is felt most in times of chaos or crises. Effective leaders create a vision and strategy that take into account the legitimate interests of other people and groups in the organization. Putting the plan into action involves much more than announcing it; the need for persuasion, understanding, and support is a critical component. The leader may be at the head of a group that makes decisions, but the effective leader marshals support for implementation of these decisions. The power and prestige of position helps, but it is not enough.

Peters and Waterman

Some things can be learned about leadership by studying organizations directly. Peters and Waterman, in *In Search of Excellence*,[10] drew on their experience at McKinsey and Company, a well-known consulting firm, and on further study of a number of businesses they identified as exceptional. Their message is that traditional methods of managing and leading need to be replaced with new methods and new modes of thought. They provide a provocative perspective on the history and practice of management and leadership and identify eight attributes associated with excellence and innovation:

1. A bias for action
2. Closeness to the customer
3. Autonomy and entrepreneurship
4. Productivity through people
5. Evidence of being hands-on value driven
6. Capacity for sticking to the knitting
7. Simple form, lean staff
8. Simultaneous loose-tight properties

In Search of Excellence sold over five million copies. It appeared at a time when many U.S. firms were having problems with quality; its emphasis on excellence caught the public fancy. But it has been criticized by reviewers who show that some companies cited in the book for their good practices demonstrated poor performance in following years. In these cases, it is impossible to determine if the circumstances that led to organizational decline were within the leader's scope of influence.

Team Leadership

An examination of individuals who lead relatively small groups is another method used to study leadership.

Richard Hackman and Robert Ginnett

Richard J. Hackman, professor of Social and Organizational Psychology at Harvard University, and Robert Ginnett, a retired Air Force officer now on the staff of the Center for Creative Leadership, examined leadership as it emerged and was evidenced in newly formed teams.[11]

Airline crews on commercial flights were studied. Nearly every crew was newly formed and, in most instances, crew members were strangers to each other until the day the crew formed for a series of flights. The leader of these newly formed crews, the pilot or captain, had full authority and was legally in charge of the crew. His word was law. Did the leadership behavior of the captain make a difference? Hackman and Ginnett observed the behaviors of these airline pilots, especially in regard to their leadership responsibilities. They were astonished to find how casually some airline captains treated their leadership responsibilities.

Some captains expressed little concern about what the team did, essentially telling the flight attendants not to bother those on the flight deck, showing no interest in them or their problems, and totally failing to develop a spirit of collaboration. On the other hand, some captains actively engaged team members, asked for their help in having a safe flight, asked for input from them, and reminded them of their duties. Significantly, the capability to perform well in an emergency was demonstrably better when captains demonstrated responsible leadership.

The variation in quality of leadership performance is alarming when cooperative teamwork under good leadership is shown to be a critical component of safety in any emergency. For example, a set of airline accidents when planes crashed needlessly (when the planes were later judged to be clearly flyable) were reproduced in ground simulators. Air crews that worked together as a team under good leadership of the captain were able to deal with emergencies more successfully than those with poor leadership who did not work well as a team.

Sometimes teams and groups can overcome poor leadership or find substitutes for it. When the designated leader does not or cannot perform the duties as leader, followers whose interests are at stake find ways to accept and divide responsibilities, increase the level of team effort as required, and accomplish important objectives. Studying "ideal followers" may produce noteworthy insights into the leadership process.

Leaders Can Change

Leaders, regardless of setting, sometimes find it necessary to change style in order to accommodate to changing circumstances. In 1984, *Fortune* magazine conducted a survey and listed John Welch, Jr., chairman of General Electric, as its premier candidate for "Toughest Boss in America."[12] Welch, then in his fourth year as chairman at GE, received by far the largest number of votes in this category. Comments in response to "How Others See Him" included "Extraordinarily bright," "Penetrating in his questions," and "Determined to get results." Welch had carved out quite a reputation for abrasiveness since going to work for GE in 1960. According to former employees, "Welch conducts meetings so aggressively that people tremble. . . . Working for him is like a war. A lot of people get shot up; the survivors go on to the next battle."

Responses to "How He Sees Himself" included "I have to be perceived as demanding. There are six companies going after every order out there. . . . There is an atmosphere of rigor at GE but not fear. . . . The role for the mediocre is clearly short-lived."

Eight years later, in an article in the *Wall Street Journal*, Hyatt and Naj reported the same John Welch as saying that GE could no longer tolerate autocratic, tyrannical managers.[13] They quoted Welch as writing in the GE Annual Report for 1991: "In an environment where we must have every good idea from every man and woman in the organization, we cannot afford management styles that suppress and intimidate," and reported that Welch had become something of a management guru as GE's profits had grown during his tenure. John Welch might affirm that he had not changed and that his methods were not well described in either report. He did in fact write in 1992 that GE ". . . cannot afford management styles that suppress and intimidate" subordinates. But if Welch had not changed, these differing descriptions presented data collectors with greatly inconsistent leader behaviors.

Presidential Leadership in the United States

The leader who attracts the most attention in any nation is its president, king, prime minister, or chief. Regardless of title, such people are believed to wield enormous power; their behavior is presumed to have effects on the quality of life of all citizens of that nation. The U.S. presidency as an object of study attracts many students, critics, and commentators. The constitutional provision of power with limits upon its exercise makes this position unique. Students of leadership who study the U.S. presidency, although dealing with a special case, produce many points relevant to the better understanding of leadership.

James MacGregor Burns

Many U.S. presidents have been studied in great detail by their biographers. Franklin Delano Roosevelt's prime biographer is James MacGregor Burns, Professor Emeritus of Political Science at Williams College and Senior Scholar at the Jepson School of Leadership Studies at the University of Richmond. Burns describes as miraculous the work of the founding fathers of the United States of America in launching the young democracy. In his book on leadership,[14] Burns compares two forms of leadership: transactional, in which there is a trade of work for rewards or favors, and transforming, in which the leader articulates a compelling vision and engages followers in its pursuit.

Today, according to Burns,[15] the American constitutional system has become almost an anti-leadership system. The checks and balances aimed to restrain power now foster conflicts that lead to endless negotiation about carrying on the business of government. Only in times of crises do citizens of the U.S. come closer to enjoying admirable presidential leadership. For the most part, great tensions arise because of the conflict between preserving the rights of the people and securing effectiveness in the governmental system. A pertinent example was Ross Perot's dramatic entry and reentry into the 1992 presidential race and his establishment of a "gadfly" group following the election. He proclaimed on nationwide television, "Government is a mess. Politics is a mess."

James MacGregor Burns cites an April 1992 poll of American people, who were asked: "Does the political system need rebuilding or just minor change?" Fifteen percent responded "Minor Change," 57% responded "Fundamental Change," and 27% responded "Needs Complete Rebuilding." When that many people call for major change, it tells something about loss of confidence in the system.

Richard Neustadt

Richard Neustadt is a foremost student of the American presidency. His book, *Presidential Power and the Modern Presidents*,[16] provides a rich resource for examining the behaviors of U.S. presidents, building from these behaviors some principles about leadership of people holding highly visible positions.

Neustadt reminds us that all presidents get ratings on their performance. Some are classified as weak or as strong. All are rated on their leadership abilities. Almost sadistically, these ratings are made and published from the day the person takes office and are constantly revised for years. Many of these judgments are based on images sometimes far removed from reality. Neustadt's book is an effort to base judgments of presidential leadership on factual information by examining the ways in which presidential behaviors enhance presidential influence.

Neustadt suggests two ways to study "presidential power." One way is to focus on tactics: how to get a bill through Congress, how to settle strikes, how to quiet Cabinet feuds, or how to stop a Suez Canal crisis. The second way is to step back from tactics and deal with influence in more strategic terms: what is its nature and what are its sources? What does *this* man do to improve the prospect that he will have influence when he needs it? The question then becomes one of examining if what the president does in today's struggles boosts his chances for mastery in any instance tomorrow. Neustadt selects the second of these two ways to investigate the strategy of presidential influence. Thus a large part of his discussion deals with behavior in relation to power.

Neustadt finds in the behaviors of past presidents ample basis for making a number of generalizations about leadership. The first is that the ability to persuade is critical and often is based on calculated exchanges: the president's acquiescence carries a price. As Neustadt explains:

> The separateness of institutions in the sharing of authority prescribes the terms on which a President persuades. When one man shares authority with another but does not gain or lose his job upon the other's whim, his willingness to act upon the urging of the other turns on whether he sees the action is right for him. The essence of a President's persuasive task is to convince such men that what the White House wants of them is what they ought to do for their own sake and on their authority.

Even within the Executive Branch the president often finds his powers severely limited. Federal agencies owe their existence least of all to one another and only in some part to the president. Each agency has its own history and basis for existence and each has its own laws to administer; each deals with a different set of subcommittees in Congress. Each agency has its own clients, friends, and enemies; each has among its employees specialized careerists with their own agendas. The Constitution gives the president appointive power. Statutes give him budgetary control and some personal control. Although all agency administrators report to him, they are also responsible to Congress, to their clients, to their staffs, and to themselves. Neustadt finds the same situation outside the Executive Branch except that loyalty to the president may often matter *less*. Congressmen can do nothing for themselves or their constituents save as they are elected, term by term, in districts and through party structures differing from those on which a president depends. The essence of a president's persuasive task, with Congress and everyone else, is to induce them to believe that what he wants of them is in line with their own appraisals of their own responsibilities acting within their own interests, not his.

Neustadt thus places persuasion at the core of presidential leadership. "Persuasion deals in the coin of self-interest with men who have some freedom to reject what they find counterfeit." The president's own actions in the past form the basis for any future bargaining. A president must make his current choices so as to guard his own prospects for effective influence. He can draw power from those whose cooperation he needs by capitalizing upon their needs for status and authority.

Neustadt poses the problem facing many presidents: How does the president make the most he can of his own reputation? His general reputation will be shaped by patterns in the things he says and does. Decisions are at the center of his reputation. A president is also helped by information. He needs the data that advisors can provide and needs to know the little things they fail to mention. But a president cannot rest content with being informed. He needs to have access to key choices. Critical choices may not reach him; others may preempt them or they may reach him so late that his personal perspective has no bearing on the options. In theory, any president informed enough and sensitive enough could reach for just the choices he wants. In practice, he rarely has the time. However sharp his senses, time constraints imprison him.

A president's use of time and his allocation of his personal attention are preempted in many ways: the speech he has agreed to make, the fixed appointment he cannot put off, the paper no one else can sign, the rest and exercise his doctors order. These doings may be far removed from academic images of White House concentration on high-policy grand strategy. A president's priorities are set not by importance but by necessity: Deadlines rule his personal agenda. Most days, just the deadlines are enough to drain his energy.

The human qualities a president brings with him to the job have three main components: a sense of purpose, a feel for power, and a source of confidence. Neustadt argues that the first two are conditioned by the third and that self-confidence is fashioned from experience and temperament. The concluding lessons he draws from his detailed study of presidents include: Beware the insecure! The presidency is not for amateurs. The presidency calls for experienced politicians; those who perform well in the position are those of extraordinary temperament.

We must ask whether detailed descriptions of presidential leadership can apply to other settings in our own and other societies. The context of the U.S. presidency, with the power the position carries and with the traditions of democracy espoused by the citizenry, makes the need for exercising influence and articulating a vision less obvious. We can find in other contexts examples of powerful leadership when no resources are available and ways of exerting influence based upon total faith of the group in the vision of the leader. However, the degree to which we can carry over our observations of one individual to another and generalize from one setting to another is a perplexing question that will remain as we continue our study of leadership.

Thomas E. Cronin

Thomas E. Cronin, the McHugh Professor of Institutions and Leadership at Colorado College, has also examined the careers of U.S. presidents, looking at their characteristics and the reactions of their constituents. He reports that public opinion surveys show that presidents are more popular in their first year of office than later in their term.[17] Over time, however, approval ratings usually drop, with a number of zigs and zags caused by specific events, conditions, or crises. Presidents lose popularity during midterm elections when the opposition party attacks the White House as part of its campaign. Domestic crises cause presidential popularity to fall, whereas international crises cause it to rise as the nation "rallies round" the president. Presidential approval ratings usually rise late in the first term, perhaps because the president is then being compared with likely opponents.

Cronin reports a typical set of survey results indicating the qualities of an ideal president. The question asked was, "There are all kinds of problems a president has to deal with and all kinds of qualities a president can have. I'd like you to think about an ideal president. In your opinion, what are the most important things about that person?"[18] Responses included the following qualities:

Honesty	35%
Compassion	18
Intelligence	17
Toughness/decisiveness	11
Decision-making ability	9
Leadership	8
Ability to communicate	8
Political skills to deal with Congress	2

Other studies confirm the prime position of honesty in the list of qualities desired in a U.S. president.

Keith Simonton

Dean Keith Simonton, professor of Psychology at the University of California at Davis, studies history in a quantitative psychological fashion. Less easily satisfied than most with generalizations derived from the documentation of past events, Simonton searches for records that can be analyzed using modern economic, sociological, and psychological methods. His analysis is based on the comparison of the following five categories of presidential personalities.[19] The dimensions in the categories overlap, and some presidential personalities may portray more than one dimension.

1. Interpersonal: good-natured; pleasant; easy going. Emphasizes teamwork; encourages independent judgments by aides.

2. Charismatic: outgoing; natural; witty; not shy; not withdrawn. Enjoys ceremony; refines own public image.
3. Deliberative: organized; insightful; polished; methodical; intelligent; sophisticated. Understands implications of decisions; keeps self well-informed; reads background papers.
4. Creative: investive; artistic. Initiates new legislative programs; is innovative.
5. Neurotic: evasive. Places political success over effective policy.

Simonton finds that Interpersonal and Charismatic presidents seem to be more people-oriented while Deliberative and Creative presidents seem to be problem solvers and more task-oriented. Presidents classified as Interpersonal and as Deliberative set more cautious goals and confine their activities rather narrowly. Charismatic presidents try to exert their will; Creative presidents develop visions and legislative programs. The Creative president, unlike the Charismatic, is more likely to get himself re-elected; Deliberative presidents get the fewest of their bills passed by Congress. Interpersonal presidents have better relations with Congress and veto the fewest bills.

Leaders of nations attract attention because of their power and influence and are often the generators of enormous changes in society. We cannot ignore them as we study the nature of leadership although we often wish that they would espouse values and display actions that would make them leadership models.

Getting the Job Done

Groups achieve their objectives in many different ways. Therefore, we need to examine leadership not only in its "pure" form but also in the ways in which it appears in everyday activities. Consider the news story in the *Wall Street Journal* of a person sent in to "turn around" a moribund unit—a frequent assignment given to those who are moving up fast in an organization and are prime candidates for executive leadership positions.

TO ONE XEROX MAN, SELLING PHOTOCOPIERS IS A GAMBLERS GAME

Frank Pacetta, Emulating His Hero Vince Lombardi, Inspires Love and Fear

Cold Calls, Love and Fear

INDEPENDENCE, Ohio—When Xerox Corp.'s district sales manager left here four years ago, the office was in such disarray that some employees wondered if anyone would take the job.

Turnover was high, and the district's performance in the Cleveland area was ranked near the bottom at Xerox. Major accounts were a shambles, lower-priced Japanese copiers were making inroads, and Xerox customers were defecting.

"They had a tactic of selling by confusion," says Nancy Vetrone, president of Origiani Copy Centers Inc. in Cleveland, which leases Xerox machines.

"When Xerox came out with its 'Leadership Through Quality' literature, she says, "we read it and laughed."

They aren't laughing now. Xerox found a new district manager, a can-do whiz kid named Frank Pacetta, who had joined the company out of college as a copier salesman and quickly rose through the ranks. On his first day as district manager here, Mr. Pacetta, who was then only 33 years old, stood before the entire staff and vowed that the Cleveland district would finish the year No. 1 in the region, which included 11 other districts. It had finished last the previous year. "We thought he was on drugs or something," says Bruno Biassiotta, an account manager.

But Mr. Pacetta, a maverick manager who's willing to take risks and defy supervisors, proved to be right. In his first year the district soared to No. 1 in the region and No. 4 among Xerox's 65 districts, as measured by how far the districts exceeded goals set by headquarters. (No. 1 in the nation that year was midtown Manhattan.) Since then, operating profits in the district have jumped 43%, and corporate headquarters has rewarded it with increased freedom to set the terms of the deals.

Mr. Pacetta's experience shows how one hard-charging personality can quickly revive a moribund sales office. Managing by a system of perks and penalties, Mr. Pacetta plied his staff with sales incentives and pep talks while swiftly weeding out employees who couldn't meet his pumped-up sales targets. "Patience is for someone without a budget," he says.

Mr. Pacetta, now 37, takes his management cues from his hero, Vince Lombardi. Like the legendary football coach, Mr. Pacetta is Italian, was born in New York City and attended a Jesuit college. Like Mr. Lombardi, Mr. Pacetta is a taskmaster who evokes both love and fear in his troops. "I'll recognize you lavishly," he says of his management style, "but I expect you to pay the rent. And if you don't, you'll pay the consequences."[20]

In addition, the *Wall Street Journal* article listed Pacetta's Ten Top Tips, his guidance to success for members of the team:

- Prepare customer proposals on weekends and evenings.
- Never say no to a customer; everything is negotiable.
- Make customers feel good about you, not just your product, by sending cards for birthdays and promotions and taking them to lunch, ball games and other outings.
- Meet customer requirements, even if it means fighting your own bureaucracy.
- Do things for your customers you don't get paid for, like solving billing problems.
- Know your competitor's product better than your competitor does.
- Be early for meetings.
- Dress and groom yourself sharply so "you look like a superior product."
- When it's time to go home, make one more phone call.
- If you stay in the shower a long time in the morning because you don't look forward to work, find another job.

This article illustrates a number of points and raises some questions about defining leader behavior.

1. A leader can have enormous effects.
2. When not the CEO, the leader must have support from above.
3. In many circumstances, the leader must be willing to take risks.

4. Goals must be stated clearly, so that all understand.
5. Goals that are assigned must be high but attainable.
6. Having a hero to emulate is helpful.
7. The desirability of an assignment is often difficult to assess.
8. Even a strong leader cannot influence everyone: Some of the team must be replaced.
9. The leader may add an emotional component.
10. To succeed, do leaders need to involve followers in decisions?
11. When leaders fail in their efforts to inspire, what is a proper course of action?

The story about Mr. Pacetta is compelling. While some aspects of his behavior seem to be managerial, others seem to exhibit leadership qualities. Yet most would agree that Pacetta held a leadership position. However, certain issues pertaining to leadership were not addressed in the article. Will Mr. Pacetta's style continue to work when the office is stable and still prospering? What happens to organizational loyalty when many people are fired? Will the new team continue their extra efforts? Will they find satisfaction in their work? Will they enjoy working for Mr. Pacetta? Because leaders must solve not only short-term problems, they also must lay the groundwork for achieving long-term goals. Although Mr. Pacetta was clearly on the right track for what he had to face immediately, what changes in style should he consider for the future?

Some studies of leadership have been criticized for portraying what leaders *seem* to do rather than what they *really* do. By attending only to general principles, the specifics of the behaviors of individual leaders are lost. Some approaches provide an intellectual orderliness to thinking and theorizing about leadership but fail to capture the variety and the impact obtained by observing how organizations function and how leaders achieve their successes. Studies in functioning organizations offer few clues about the qualities of those people best able to exercise leadership in a given set of circumstances, but they do demonstrate the behaviors that have desired effects. Research studies must be supplemented by case studies, interviews of successful leaders, and examination of organizational outcomes to provide advice to those who must make decisions, organize teams, increase productivity, turn an organization around, or select a successor to the top position.

Leaders *are* needed. They are needed in large numbers. To call for better leaders seems obvious. To find the person who will have all the qualities desired requires us to know much more about the processes of selection and the capabilities and limitations of training methods. Even then, changes in circumstances may make the leader's task impossible. Or, worse, supporters will lose faith either in the leader, or in the system, or even in the worth of the goals being sought. We must learn more about how organizations function as we seek those who are willing to be our leaders.

Studies of leadership are not simple. Trying to identify that part of the success of an organization that is due to its leadership is not easy, but it is not impossible. Even more difficult is prescribing a pattern of leadership behavior that will work in a given situation. Picking a new leader combines these two uncertain domains as committees or voters try to identify one person to lead an organization that needs help. We can make some progress if we remember that we must learn a lot more about leaders, much more about supporters or followers, and a great deal about the contexts in which leaders and their followers interact.

CHAPTER TWO

Definitions and Dimensions of Leadership

Often we wish that a great leader would come along, take a strong position, and with vision and determination solve our many problems. We blame the absence of solutions on the leaders we have and wish we had more confidence in their abilities. We want to make judicious choices and wish that we knew more about leaders and leadership to guide our search for the ideal leader. Rarely do we blame ourselves for the failures of our leaders, although followers are as central to the accomplishment of group objectives as are leaders. We cannot discover the secrets of leadership without unraveling the mysteries of loyal followership. Leadership pertains to the interrelationships of leaders and followers in various settings as they seek to solve problems and accomplish their goals.

Because people with great power have done terrible things, we must examine constantly how they gained such controls and structure our institutions to prevent outcomes we abhor. Although we tend to see leaders as different somehow from those who exercise power, leaders need power to accomplish honorable objectives as well as to constrain the actions of the inflexible, the greedy, and the inhumane. Therefore it is essential to comprehend fully the interrelationship between power and leadership.

In our search to understand the intricacies of leadership, reading popular books and articles about leadership provides little help and can be confusing. We are left with many questions. Is it better to be tough or to be understanding? Is it better to act decisively or to deliberate to find the best action? Can one delegate important tasks or should the leader do all the important jobs? Can a leader have friends and still be a good leader? Is a leader occasionally required to be mean? Is it satisfying to be a leader?

As they go about their daily activities, the behaviors of actual leaders and their followers can be studied in an orderly way. Both the short-term and the ultimate effects they have on their groups, organizations, and institutions can be assessed. We can identify leaders and followers whose beneficial relations and behaviors lead to successful attainment of group goals. Actions of leaders and actions of nonleaders can be contrasted, and findings can be tested for similarities across different settings. Training programs can be implemented; follow-up tests can measure attendees' abilities to improve their interactions with others and thus become better leaders.

Introductory Principles

Hundreds of studies have been completed and published. Our review of many of these studies provides strong support for the following propositions:

1. Leadership can be studied. The study of leadership has been inappropriately called elusive by many. However, it is elusive only to those who have not examined the evidence of how and when leadership is effective. Reputable

students of leadership have developed methods to measure how leaders behave when they are at their best and then have tested the effects of such behaviors. It is this portion of the large and diverse research literature that we draw upon.

2. Leadership behaviors that work in one setting usually work in other settings. Research findings in business settings apply to schools and community organizations. Successful leadership in not-for-profit organizations looks very much like successful leadership in business.

3. Studying followers or members of groups and organizations, asking them about leader behaviors as they see them, and comparing the effectiveness of various perceived leader behaviors with group or organizational outcomes are essential components of the study of leadership.

4. Calling one's self a leader does not make it so. A person in an important position who is designated a leader may or may not lead. Often those who oversee others in the completion of specific tasks are not leaders, nor are those who gain compliance by coercion or by threats. Our focus is on people identified by their followers as leaders and on groups that accomplish more than expected. By combining these two sets of evidence we will find some individuals who approximate the ideal, and we will study their behaviors closely.

5. Leadership can be recognized when it emerges. Observers, especially followers and subordinates, can report the behavior of leaders with enough accuracy to identify credibly their behaviors and qualities. Leadership behaviors can be identified without evidence of effectiveness because the descriptions from others, especially team members, are convincing and usually consistent.

6. Leaders themselves are poor judges of their own leadership qualities. Thus, interviews of leaders do not tell us everything we need to know about identification, although interviews are helpful in finding out what leaders think they are doing.

7. The study of leadership includes the leaders, the followers, and the context within which acts of leadership occur. Leader behavior and follower reactions are part of a leadership event that has consequences only within a group setting, whether organized or not.

8. Leaders of today seem to represent leaders of all time in their capacity to envisage the future, to struggle and persist, to recall their initial determination, to refine and redefine their objectives, to face each setback with courage and humor, to learn from failure, and ultimately to attain cherished goals. Among today's leaders we may expect the same behaviors that made a difference in the past and that are likely to make a difference in the future.

9. A substantial number of people in positions of responsibility, who thereby have power and authority, exhibit leadership behaviors. Thus, for purposes of study, leaders are often defined as those who produce desired effects identifiable only after the leader has acted. Some studies sharpen the definition of leadership by comparing effective leaders with less effective leaders.

10. Leadership may be profitably studied using many methods. We can learn a great deal from historians, philosophers, and astute observers of the social scene. Improved research methods rely on a broad spectrum of interviews, analysis of survey data, questionnaires given to subordinates, assessments collected by superiors, inventories completed by presumed leaders, and studies of organizational effectiveness. Knowledge and understanding expand rapidly when data are collected across organizations, nations, and cultures. When larger samples are studied and research designs become more complex, the opportunity to generalize findings increases.

Leadership Defined

The terms leader and leadership have numerous definitions, which are applied in many ways. However, the following is our definition that is used either implicitly or explicitly throughout this book: **Leadership is an activity or set of activities, observable to others, that occurs in a group, organization, or institution involving a leader and followers who willingly subscribe to common purposes and work together to achieve them.**

Leadership is an observable activity. It is not mysterious. It can be described, and its effects can be traced back to the activity. Leadership involves willing collaboration as part of the relationship between leaders and followers. The leader persuades; the leader does not coerce. The leader articulates a vision for the group, illuminates a path to the goals, builds confidence in the group's ability to achieve them, and earns trust by evidence of integrity, commitment, courage, and a demonstrated willingness to take personal risks for the group.

How critical is the element of willingness in the identification of a leader? If we agree that President Abraham Lincoln was a great national leader, do we have to call him something other than a leader because some people in the country did not vote for him and felt coerced into following his leadership? If a person takes a job out of need to earn substantial money but works for a superior whose leadership behavior causes the employee to become involved and enthusiastic, must we avoid using the term leader because money constitutes an element of coercion? Our answer is NO. We define leadership in terms of leader and follower behavior and not by the setting in which these behaviors occur.

A critical distinction, however, is between the person who has legitimate authority as a leader and the person who does not have authority yet acts like a leader. Although their leadership behavior surfaces from different sources, both persons may be called leaders and studied as leaders if their behaviors produce the desired follower responses; such leader behaviors and resulting follower performances are the basis for an acceptable definition of leadership.

Leadership involves followers, for the term refers to activities that include both. Leadership incorporates in its definition the notion that one person has a special effect on the accomplishments of a group. The definition need not include, however, a requirement for face-to-face relations between leader and follower.

It appears that a person working in a solitary setting does not demonstrate acts of leadership. However, a person whose intellectual activities are original, profound, and produce enormously exciting effects on others is also a leader, even though leadership is exercised only through writing or discovery. Thus Aristotle, Newton, Marx, and Darwin are recognized leaders of thought in our society. The definition of leadership is not limited to completion of concrete tasks in the surround of an eager team; it can exist in the realm of ideas, concepts, beliefs, and values. Ultimately, many of these various aspects of leadership, which are discussed in this book, are greatly important and persistently provocative.

Holding high position does not make one a leader. Presidents of nations, whether appointed or elected, are not automatically leaders. They may be leaders at some times, but they certainly do not act like leaders all the time. Sometimes they act, appropriately, like administrators or politicians. Sometimes they enforce the law or take actions mandated by conditions that require them to act in particular ways. However, on many occasions the main role of a president, especially in a democracy like the United States, is to engender support for a particular idea or course of action directed toward specific objectives. On these occasions, the president is engaged in acts of leadership, is usually highly persuasive, and certainly can be defined as a leader. The same general principles apply to chief executive officers and presidents of companies, directors of enterprises and agencies, community leaders, governmental and quasi-governmental officials, chairs of cultural and social organizations, coaches, and clergy.

A given position does not thereby define a person as a leader other than in title. However, careful selection processes can identify above average numbers of people with leadership capabilities. Although many individuals want the responsibilities of leadership, frequently people elected or appointed to positions of leadership abuse their power and authority. Case studies provide innumerable illustrations of individuals who are intolerable as bosses and tragic as leaders.

Other Definitions of Leadership

Students of leadership have provided numerous variations—some minor, some major—on the definition of leadership. John Gardner's recent definition of leadership is one often quoted: "Leadership is the process of persuasion or example by which an individual (or leadership team) induces a group to pursue objectives held by the leader or shared by the leader and his or her followers."[1]

James MacGregor Burns presents the following definition in his classic book *Leadership*: "Leadership is the reciprocal process of mobilizing, by persons with certain motives and values, various economic, political, and other resources, in a context of competition and conflict, in order to realize goals independently or mutually held by both leaders and followers. . . . Leaders can also shape and alter and elevate the motives and values and goals of followers through the vital *teaching* role of leadership. This is *transforming* leadership."[2]

The ideal leader identified by Burns is called "transformational" by Bernard Bass of the State University of New York at Binghamton. The transformational leader is described as more charismatic and inspiring and as providing individualized consideration and intellectual stimulation, a definition that emphasizes the behaviors of leaders. Bass contrasts transformational leaders with "transactional" leaders, those who "accomplish well the tasks at hand while satisfying the self-interests of those working with the leader to do so."[3] Bass equates transactional leaders with management and transformational leaders with leadership.

Many writers use the words management and leadership interchangeably. Some writers use the word "management" to refer to lower levels within a hierarchical organization and the word "executive" to refer to top levels. In this usage, leadership might be exhibited at any level. The interchange of these terms is part of the reason people think of leadership as an elusive concept. Executives are not necessarily leaders; leaders may emerge in any level of an organization or absent of any organization. In contrast, management refers to any system of structure and control that leads to the timely accomplishment of specific tasks within defined resource limits. The chief advantage of leadership behavior over management practices is the positive effect on group processes and performance. In the definition we propose, leadership refers to the highest use of human capabilities in the pursuit of goals. However, most great leaders exhibit excellent management skills and superior managers exhibit leadership qualities.

Abraham Zalesnik, the Konosuke Matsushita Professor of Leadership at the Harvard University Graduate School of Business, is critical of his colleagues in business schools across America for their attention to management issues when the real challenge is to address the shortage of inspiring leaders without regard to gender.

> Whether his or her energies are directed toward goals, resources, organization structures, or people, a manager is a problem solver. The manager asks himself, "What problems have to be solved, and what are the best ways to achieve results so that people will continue to contribute to this organization?"
>
> Managers tend to adopt impersonal, if not passive, attitudes toward goals. Managerial goals arise out of necessities rather than desires, and therefore are deeply embedded in the history and culture of the organization.
>
> Leaders tend to be twice-born personalities, people who feel separate from their environment, including other people. They may work in organizations, but they never belong to them. Their sense of who they are does not depend upon membership, work roles, or other social indicators of identity. What seems to follow from this idea about separateness is some theoretical basis for explaining why certain people seek out opportunities for change. The methods to bring about change may be technological, political, or ideological, but the object is the same; to profoundly alter human, economic, and political relationships.[4]

John P. Kotter, professor of Organizational Behavior and Human Resources at the Harvard University Graduate School of Business, joins Burns, Bass, and Zalesnik in a definition of leadership that distinguishes it from management.

> Management is basically a process, the function of which is to produce consistent results on important dimensions. . . . Leadership, by contrast, is a process whose function is change. Usually, leadership involves creating a vision of the future and a strategy for achieving that vision. It involves communicating that direction to all the relevant parties so that they understand and believe it. It also involves providing an environment that will inspire and motivate people to overcome any obstacles that may arise along the way. In this way, leadership produces change; effective leadership produces useful, adaptive change for an organization.[5]

Ronald A. Heifetz, of the John F. Kennedy School of Government at Harvard University, defines leadership as "an activity, *not* as a set of personality characteristics. . . . The activity of leadership I define as the mobilization of the resources of a people or of an organization to make progress on the difficult problems it faces."[6]

Gary Yukl, of the State University of New York at Albany, examined numerous definitions of leadership and conducted extensive studies of leader behaviors. His definition of leadership emphasizes the influence a leader exerts: "Leadership involves influencing task objectives and strategies, influencing commitment and compliance in task behavior to achieve these objectives, influencing group maintenance and identification, and influencing the culture of an organization."[7]

Joseph C. Rost, professor in the School of Education at the University of San Diego, offers the following definition: "Leadership is an influence relationship among leaders and followers who intend real changes that reflect their mutual purposes."[8]

Incorporated in some definitions of leadership is the existence of a problem and the availability of resources to deal with the problem. Jacobs and Jaques, for example, propose the following definition of leadership: "Leadership is a process of giving purpose [meaningful direction] to collective effort, and causing willing effort to be expended to achieve purpose."[9] They add that leadership must be viewed as a process that occurs only in situations where there is choice; it is the opportunity for discretion that makes leadership possible.

David Campbell, Smith Richardson Senior Fellow of the Center for Creative Leadership, incorporates into his definition of leadership the concept of a task to be accomplished and the availability of resources to accomplish it. He uses this definition to develop measures of leadership in the Campbell Development Surveys (CDS).

Walter F. Ulmer, Jr., the president of the Center for Creative Leadership in Greensboro, North Carolina, proposes the following definition: "Leadership is an activity—an influence process—in which an individual gains the trust and commitment of others and without reliance on formal position or authority moves the group to the accomplishment of one or more tasks."[10] Under this definition, status as a leader is not bestowed by promotion or appointment, or because one is powerful or influential. Trust and commitment cannot be bought but must be earned. The exercise of power and authority is not encompassed within this definition.

Summary of Definitions

The similarities and overlap of leadership definitions are conspicuous. Differences in definitions often reflect the theoretical or research orientation of the writer. However, in almost every definition the process of leadership in organizations involves leaders, followers, members, subordinates, or constituents as they interact, create visions, become inspired, find meaning in their work and lives, and gain in trust and respect. As conditions change, leaders have an obligation to initiate actions that ensure adaptation to new circumstances. Leadership is critical in organizations of all types and sizes, whether formal or informal, public, private, or independent. Benefits accrue to the organization with the exercise of ideal leadership.

Leadership is not the private domain of individuals who are highly visible in society. Many acts of superb leadership occur with small groups of followers or in obscure settings and can involve people who exercise little power and have few resources. Leadership acts are not always performed by only one leader; members of a group often take command and work collaboratively to produce astonishing effects.

We must always keep in mind that *leaders are human*. They are men and women with strengths, weaknesses, and special traits. They are people who accept extra responsibilities in the workplace or in the community. They may seek out a position of advantage for either complex personal reasons or simply to help a group achieve important objectives. Many sacrifice personal advantage because they have a compulsion to get things moving. Great leaders inspire their followers to believe, to expend more effort, and to accomplish great things that otherwise would not get done. No one merits the title of leader whose group or organization has accomplished little.

Followers, members, subordinates, and constituents are also human. They have hopes, aspirations, doubts, and fears and need reassurance, support, instruction, and praise. They perform best when given respect and opportunities to do their best. The leader who has no respect for his or her followers is not a leader. Followers invest much more of themselves when they see reason to trust their leader.

Leaders often pay a high price for their contributions. Only when we ask questions of those who must shoulder great leadership responsibilities do we begin to understand the human costs of leadership. Abraham Lincoln is reported to have said:

> If I were to try to read, much less answer, all the attacks made on me, this shop [the White House] might as well be closed for any other business. I do the very best I know how—the very best I can, and mean to keep doing so until the end. If the end brings me out wrong, ten angels swearing I was right would make no difference.[11]

Leaders in Recent History

Historians record the accomplishments of great leaders as well as their virtues and faults. Yet their descriptions can be flawed because they quote from unreliable sources, because the reports of actions that brought fame or dishonor have been embellished or tarnished in their retelling, or because of the long-term consequences of these actions. Behaviors are often described in terms of the actor's place in history. Tiny incidents grow into legends and are turned into truths. The great leaders of history have been set apart by those who glorify them or by those who seek to dishonor them. Although their accomplishments have been recorded, documentation of the behaviors that made them effective is tailored to fit the outcome or is merely inferred or even invented.

Therefore, historical study provides an interesting but imperfect guide for leaders to emulate because of confounding factors. For example, most early societies were male dominated, with those led by women characterized as curiosities rather than as models. Earlier times condoned slavery and abuse of minorities. Because the context in which leadership is exercised has considerable influence on its nature, commonly held stereotypes about the talents of women and the qualities of members of nondominant groups in any culture are not to be trusted. Such distortions have produced grave injustices. Talent is scarce; it must be discovered and developed in every segment of society and in every time. The nurturance of talent must not be guided by false premises concerning its distribution.

From Management to Leadership: A Historical Review

Early management studies provide few cues about effective leadership. Most management-worker relations were contractual, sometimes with the work being involuntary. In the early days of the Industrial Revolution, cottage industries and labor guilds fostered personal relationships between the master and the apprentice. The development of "scientific management" increased the distance between workers and their superiors as the superiors took charge of the design of each job. The classic studies of Taylor and Gilbreth showed ways to increase production by each worker but did so by usurping all decisions about each step of the job. Although production increased, worker motivation and satisfaction did not. To eliminate the need for rest periods and promote almost continuous work throughout the day, the workman's shovel was reduced in size. Workers' attitudes toward management, however, continued to degrade because of the unpopular "speed-up." Worker reaction to scientific management surely accelerated the development of labor unions and the campaign for more enlightened human resource management.

Management studies prior to World War II reflect the division between those who held to traditional beliefs—a day's pay for a day's work—and those who emphasized the increased participation in decision making of members of the work force. Contrasts emerged between democratic employee-centered management on the one hand and authoritarian production-centered management on the other. Training programs taught the former and regarded authoritarian management as unproductive and out of tune with the times. Social-psychological studies emphasized the positive effects of democratic and participatory processes on the development of individuals, and methods were proposed to apply these results in the classroom and in the workplace.

World War II put enormous pressure on the productive capabilities of the industrial establishment of the United States. Driven by the need to reduce defects in ammunition, new statistical methods for quality control were invented. New methods of testing and classifying personnel were devised as millions of civilians were trained in military specialties. The war was won by new technologies. After the war, the most popular career choice of ambitious civilians was in a research-related field. The U.S. government, having experienced an acute shortage of persons with great leadership capabilities, invested in research programs to aid in the understanding of this phenomenon. A major federal contract for one such study was awarded to the Ohio State University.

The Ohio State University Leadership Studies

The pioneering studies of leadership were instituted in 1945 by Carroll L. Shartle, director of the Bureau of Business Research of the College of Commerce of the Ohio State University. Shartle had observed the importance of leaders and leadership during his government service both before and during World War II. He recognized the advantages of a new approach to the study of leadership and sought federal funds to support a major project.

Earlier studies of psychological traits of leaders had not been particularly fruitful. Even the use of newly devised measures of intelligence and personality did not yield a list of common traits applicable to all leaders; no profile emerged of qualities characteristic of effective leaders. Instead, Shartle and his team started with descriptions of leader behaviors. They developed a long list of statements descriptive of different components of supervisory or leader behavior.[12] These items were formed into a questionnaire and grouped into subscales. The questionnaire was administered to a sample population of Air Force crews who described their aircraft commander; a statistical study based on the resulting data was completed to determine the major dimensions of leader behavior.

The major dimensions of leadership behavior that emerged from this analysis after some scrutiny were designated as *Consideration* and *Initiation of Structure*. Consideration is defined as behaviors that evidence concern for the members of the group. The considerate leader emphasizes good two-way communication among members and between members of the group and the leader. Good work is recognized. Self-esteem is nurtured. Good ideas are accepted. Mutual trust is developed. Participation is encouraged. Actions are explained. The orientation is toward the people doing the work—a people orientation. The second dimension, Initiation of Structure, is defined as behaviors that organize the group, define relationships, and specify the task and how it is to be done. The leader emphasizes the need to meet deadlines and maintain quality, defines limits of responsibility, and clarifies roles. The orientation is toward the work to be done—a task orientation.

More data were collected; further studies that used the same methods but different samples of respondents confirmed these two dimensions. The item content in the questionnaire was refined and formalized in the Leader Behavior Description Questionnaire (LBDQ). Instructions in the questionnaire were made more specific: Describe as accurately as you can the behavior of your supervisor or leader by thinking about how frequently the leader behaves this way, and marking *always*, *often*, *occasionally*, *seldom*, or *never*. A typical item is, "He lets group members know what is expected of them."

The identification of the two dimensions of Consideration and Initiation of Structure changed the direction of the study of leadership to deemphasize *traits* and to emphasize *behavior* of supervisors, managers, or leaders. A large literature grew in the U.S. and Canada; data were collected in business and educational settings, the military, health facilities, and nonprofit organizations. Investigators in other countries became acquainted with the work, repeated the analyses, and found two dimensions quite similar to Consideration and Initiation of Structure. Some called the two *relationship-orientation* and *task-orientation*.

> I believe no review of leadership work would be complete without some description of the early days at the Personnel Research Board, where The Ohio State University Leadership Studies were formed under the direction of Dr. Carroll Shartle (1956). The key people there in the late 1940s, 1950–1951 period were Ralph Stogdill, John Hemphill, Donald Campbell, Alvin Coons, Melvin Seaman, and several others. I was initially an assistant to Ralph Stogdill on his Office of Naval Research Naval leadership project and subsequently received a grant from the International Harvester Company to study industrial leadership and management training. The Rockefeller Foundation had provided the original funds for the overall program and later funds came from the Office of Naval Research, industry, agricultural co-ops, and a large Air Force contract directed by John Hemphill.
>
> I can recall the excitement and stimulation of that group at the time and the feeling of being in on an exciting new venture, breaking new ground. It might be well to point out the prevailing thought about leadership at the time The Ohio State Leadership Studies were funded. At that time, leadership was thought of as a personality trait, or at least a combination of personality traits, that some people "had" and others did not. To pick leaders, the trick was to find people who had these traits well developed. The catch was that it was difficult to get hold of what the traits were. The early reviews of Ralph Stogdill (1948) and some others made it apparent from a wide variety of studies that traits describing leaders in one situation were not the same as those which describe leaders in others; that little agreement could be reached as to which personality traits were, in fact, leadership traits.[13]

The influence of the Ohio State Studies is still strong. The Leadership Opinion Questionnaire and the Supervisory Behavior Description Questionnaire are directly derived from the original studies and are in wide use.[14] Many training programs in management and leadership are based on these two dimensions. These programs stress the need for leaders to assign tasks clearly and to assist followers in learning to do their work well, meet deadlines, and maintain quality. But they also accentuate the importance of communicating with followers, building their self-esteem and confidence in their ability to accomplish important things, and resolving conflicts.

The Ohio State researchers replaced with two dimensions a prior one-dimensional division of management practice with *participative* or *democratic* at one end and *authoritarian* at the other. When two dimensions emerged from the factor analyses of the Ohio State group, the outcome was given great weight. A leader could be high or low on people orientation and also be either high or low on task orientation.

The way in which these dimensions emerged has had a major effect on their interpretation. The scales were developed using ratings by people asked to identify differences *among* leaders, not differences *between* leaders and followers. Consequently, these findings have been applied in an effort to discover whether a given leader was mainly task oriented or mainly relationship or people oriented. Research studies conducted in the U.S. have tried to determine if one dimension is as important as the other. However, strong evidence suggests that best results occur when *both* types of behaviors are exhibited.

Building on a Two-Dimensional Model

The strong influence of the Ohio State University Studies on later work occurred not only in the U.S., Canada, and western Europe, but worldwide. In 1953, Jyuji Misumi, a graduate student in Japan, learned of the work of Kurt Lewin, then at the Massachusetts Institute of Technology in the U.S., and of the Ohio State University Studies. Misumi recounts the beginnings of leadership research there:

> Soon after World War II ended Professor Kanae Sakuma of Kyushu University received a letter from Professor Kurt Lewin, then the Director of the Research Center for Group Dynamics at the Massachusetts Institute of Technology. I was a graduate student at the time, but I still vividly remember Professor Sakuma sharing the communication with me. In his letter, Professor Lewin made reference to Ron Lippitt and Ralph White's comparative study of democratic, autocratic, and laissez-faire leadership styles, and furthermore, proposed a joint research effort on the subject to be conducted in Japan. This letter undoubtedly served as the motivating force behind my subsequent devotion to the study of leadership.
>
> When we began our study of leadership, Japanese cities and towns were still wild stretches of burnt ruins as a result of the war. The occupation forces soon moved into Japan, however, and as a result of the occupation policy, the general headquarters of the Supreme Commander for the Allied Powers carried out a series of programs at universities at major Japanese cities under the title of The Institute for Educational Leaders (IFEL). It was through these IFEL programs that I became familiar with the procedures and results of Lippitt and White's research. As a student who participated in the program, I had some doubts as to whether or not the results obtained in the experiments conducted in the United States could be duplicated in Japan. Thus, I decided to undertake a followup study in Fukuoka. This is how I began my study of leadership. Recognizing the fact that Japanese children of that time had not been accustomed to democratic leadership, I did not anticipate obtaining any result indicating democratic style leadership to be as effective as it is in the United States. To our surprise, however, we found that the major part of our findings were very similar to the findings of the United States' study. While we allow for socio-historical and cultural differences in human social behavior, we cannot help but recognize the general and universal nature of group dynamics.
>
> Our study of leadership began as a study of group dynamics. When the IFEL program was complete in 1949, the Japanese Group Dynamics Association was formed at Kyushu University. Our first study on leadership was conducted over a period of several years using fifth and sixth grade school children as subjects. However, as teachers' union activities intensified in the late '50s, we found it increasingly difficult to conduct surveys in the elementary and junior high schools. As a result, we found it necessary to phase out the surveys in the school and seizing

upon an unexpected opportunity, we shifted our efforts to a leadership study at a coal mine. At this coal mine and later at such diverse institutions as steel mills, shipyards, chemical factories, banks, and railroad and bus companies, we conducted surveys designed to evaluate leadership behavior, diagnostic work, and counseling and training sessions with first-line supervisors, middle management, and project managers. We first classified each supervisor into one of four categories based upon leadership scores obtained through ratings given by subordinates. We then examined the validity of the resultant categorizations in relationship to such variables as group performance, accident rate, team work, communication, mental hygiene, and workplace meeting scores, as well as subordinate satisfaction with work, wages, promotion and sense of belonging to company and labor unions. As a result, we found that regardless of the industry or type of job, rankings of the four categories based on relative leadership effectiveness nearly always produced the same order.

We would like to make it clear ... that our studies have been inspired by leadership studies conducted not only in Japan, but in other countries as well, particularly the United States.[15]

Misumi employed methods similar to those used in the U.S., leading him to two dimensions, *Performance* and *Maintenance*, that are quite like those of the Ohio State University Studies. There were, however, significant differences. Misumi defined them as follows:

1. *P Leadership Behavior (Performance)*. Leadership behavior that prompts and motivates group goal achievement Misumi called P Leadership. Any group has some set of goals and engages in a process to achieve those goals. P Leadership Behavior is oriented toward goal achievement and problem solving.

2. *M Leadership Behavior (Maintenance)*. Once a group or hierarchical organization has been formed it tends to preserve or maintain itself. M Leadership Behavior is oriented toward promoting and reinforcing the tendency toward self-preservation. Maintenance organization behavior is directed toward dispelling excessive tensions that arise in interpersonal relations within a group or organization, promoting the resolution of conflict and strife, giving encouragement and support, providing an opportunity for minority opinions to be expressed, inspiring personal need fulfillment, and promoting acceptance of interdependence among group members.

Misumi's PM Leadership Theory does not deal with P and M separately. Either the P or the M function may be emphasized, but every leadership behavior contains some degree of both P and M at the same time.

Misumi credits the Ohio State work as setting the model for his own work. While both the Ohio State project and the PM Leadership Project engaged in extensive validation of their measures, the emphasis in the Ohio State Studies was on improving and validating the questionnaire. The PM Leadership Project moved to discover the relative validity of each of the four leadership types in producing desired effects and to learn the conditions under which each pattern would be preferred.

In Japan, a combined emphasis on both performance and maintenance has been proved to be generally constructive. In United States research, the relation to performance has not been uniformly confirmed for either dimension; consideration is found to relate consistently with follower satisfaction. This difference in results may reflect a greater emphasis in Japan on groups, the greater formality and social distance in Japanese institutions, or the differences in methods of testing results between the two groups of investigators. Western design of the work setting has been imposed mainly from the top, using outside consultants for planning. Japanese organizations are often described as giving more control of the work design to those who conduct the work, through quality circles.

Misumi has emphasized group dynamics in his explanations of the need for PM Leadership. Joining a group sets limits on one's independence—the price paid for the desired outcomes of joining. Any group must plan to handle problems that arise as a result. When such frustrations erupt, a group may disintegrate. Strong desires to belong to the group aid in combating frustration. The M function aims to prevent disintegration by strengthening the tendency toward integration.

Three studies involving a shipyard, a steel mill, and a set of banks were conducted to test the idea of the PM theory. Supervisors were divided into groups in accordance with their behaviors as rated by subordinates. Those that performed with strong performance and maintenance behaviors (PM behavior) scored highest on a variety of variables. The criterion variables were teamwork, job satisfaction, sense of belonging to a company, sense of belonging to a labor union, and group meeting quality. The Japanese studies reported by Misumi consistently show that best results are obtained when both P and M measures are high; that is, when leaders and managers place strong emphasis both on supporting high task performance and on providing a group whose members work well together, avoiding conflict. The Ohio State Studies did not provide the same consistent results.

Two Dimensions Are Not Enough

Many leadership research programs have sought to identify more than two basic leadership dimensions as a more complete way of describing various leadership styles. Bowers and Seashore developed measures of the following four dimensions aimed at predicting organizational effectiveness:

> *Support.* Behavior that enhances someone else's feeling of personal worth and importance.
> *Interaction facilitation.* Behavior that encourages members of the group to develop close, mutually satisfying relationships.
> *Goal emphasis.* Behavior that stimulates an enthusiasm for meeting the group's goal or achieving excellent performance.
> *Work facilitation.* Behavior that helps achieve goal attainment by such actions as scheduling, coordinating, and planning, and by providing such resources as tools, materials, and technical knowledge.[16]

These dimensions were tested as predictors of satisfaction and performance in forty agencies of a leading life insurance company. When agents emphasized goals among themselves, business volume increased; when they supported each other in such matters as paperwork, there was greater job satisfaction. Bowers and Seashore concluded that the role of the leader was less critical than the patterns for the agency as a whole.

Later studies have established the role of the leader as a key to determining the pattern of operations, setting goals with subordinates, and establishing the climate in which work occurs. However, factors other than leader behaviors are involved in leadership. In the absence of effective leadership, the corporate climate, working rules, and the structure of the organization can provide substitutes for leadership that enable subordinates or followers to establish their own leadership structures.

Gary Yukl, professor of Management at the State University of New York at Albany, indicates that the degree of participative leadership is a dimension conceptually distinct from consideration and initiating structure.[17] Yukl asserts that survival of the institution as well as the ability to change in order to assure survival is high on the list of obligations of a leader. Other researchers attend to the development or utilization of talent as a responsibility of leadership. Leaders must judge the value of new technologies and provide resources, support, and training in their use. Recently Yukl, Wall, and Lepsinger presented a measure with many dimensions that identify the practices and behaviors of leaders as well as managers. The Managerial Practices Survey (MPS) lists the following scales developed by psychometric analysis and tested for usefulness in various settings:

1. Informing
2. Consulting and Delegating
3. Planning and Organizing
4. Problem Solving
5. Clarifying Roles and Objectives
6. Monitoring Operations and Environment
7. Motivating
8. Recognizing and Rewarding
9. Supporting and Mentoring
10. Managing Conflict and Team Building
11. Networking[18]

Yukl's scales of the MPS were subjected to detailed analyses to determine the correctness of scale names, to assure reliability of scale scores, and to test the independence of each scale.

Leader Behavior in Different Situations

Leaders accomplish important things in different ways. An individual's leadership style may be task oriented, or people oriented, or a combination of both. Finding that leaders can act in such different ways and still have well-performing teams has led some students of leadership to develop models or "contingency theories." For example, unskilled and inexperienced workers need to have close attention given to their every act in performing the task so that the best ways of accomplishing the task can be learned; workers with considerable experience and high levels of skill, on the other hand, need freedom to make their own decisions about how best to organize their work. The behavior of the leader cannot be the same with both groups. Worth noting are the following brief samplings of several contingency theories.

Cognitive Resource Theory

Fred Fiedler, professor of Psychology at the University of Washington, and his students have conducted research since the early 1950s on how individual leaders behave and which situations influence the effectiveness of their performance. Fiedler has found that leaders performed best when the leader's style or motivational pattern was appropriate to the degree of control and influence that the leadership situation provided. Knowledge of one's own leadership style is critical, as is knowledge of the amount of control the leader is given. Fiedler advises leaders to learn to avoid situations that clash with one's own style.

Fiedler developed the Least Preferred Co-Worker Scale (LPC) to indicate the degree to which an individual is motivated primarily to accomplish assigned tasks or to develop and maintain close relationships with others in the work group. Fiedler assumes that each individual is motivated to do both but prioritizes them differently.

Persons with low scores on the LPC scale are considered task motivated. A low score occurs when a person identifies ineffective co-workers as obstacles to getting the job done and views them as unfriendly, uncooperative, and hostile. Those with high scores on the LPC scale are considered relationship motivated. A high score on the LPC occurs when responses of the person taking the test indicate that relationships with others are so important, compared to the task, that negative reactions to a co-worker who performs poorly can be separated from appreciation of that person as an individual.

Fiedler's Cognitive Resource Theory predicts the leader's directive behavior from the LPC score and the situation. In the absence of stress, the leader focuses his or her cognitive resources on the group task. If the leader is under stress or is nondirective, the leader's experience and the abilities of the group members will contribute to task performance.

Situational Leadership

Hersey and Blanchard[19] built a model to guide leader behavior so as to meet the needs of subordinates. The model assumes that no one style is "best," that leadership behavior should be appropriate for the circumstances. Effective leader behavior is contingent on the amount of task orientation, personal encouragement, support, and recognition that followers require and on the level of "development" apparent in the followers' behavior. Thus, a newly formed group with a specific task needs a high degree of structure and recognition, with praise and recognition tied to improved performance. However, the leader of a well-developed group that possesses requisite knowledge and skills and is well motivated does well to delegate responsibility.

The Hersey and Blanchard model is the prototype of a long series of "situational" models of leadership that tell the manager how to deal with a given set of problems as conditions vary. Most of these models are prescriptive and provide a useful tool for the novice manager. Although research studies provide little evidence to support the assumptions on which these models are built, each theory has a rationale that seems to match real situations.

Theory X and the Managerial Grid

Some of the earlier models of manager behavior quite influential in their time are mentioned less frequently today. Douglas MacGregor[20] categorized leaders and managers into two classes. The first, the *Theory X* type, believes that people prefer to be told exactly what to do and that people are motivated only by money, benefits, or threats of punishment. This type of leader and manager emphasizes structure and control and considers subordinates to be immature and in need of constant direction. The second, the *Theory Y* type, views people as able to enjoy work and be self-directive, responsible, and creative. These managers and leaders give freedom and resources to their subordinates or followers that enable them to maximize their abilities and continue to find joy in their work.

In 1964, Blake and Mouton[21] generated a matrix with two dimensions:

Concern for Production and *Concern for People.* In their matrix, behaviors are rated on a scale from 1 to 9. A manager described as a 9,9 is considered the ideal, one who satisfactorily accomplishes the work with a committed team of people whose relationships are based on trust and respect. A 9,1 manager gets the work done with minimal attention to the human elements, while a 1,9 manager provides a friendly and comfortable organizational atmosphere and work tempo with little concern for production. The 1,1 manager exerts minimum effort to get the work done and minimum effort to support the group.

In summary, leadership is a critical component of organized activities. Although some aspects of the phenomenon seem mysterious, leadership is a subject that can be studied. We define it as an activity or set of activities, observable to others, that occurs in a group, organization, or institution involving a leader and followers who willingly subscribe to common purposes and work together to achieve them. A leader is a person who earns the trust of followers and thereby increases their commitment to achieve the common purposes of the group.

CHAPTER THREE

Charismatic and Transformational Leadership

Some leaders of nations, some campaigners for action, and some religious leaders demonstrate an unusual capacity to move their followers to implement the ideas and visions they espouse. Their behaviors are compelling and their personalities attract others to believe in them and to follow their lead. This type of leadership differs from types of leadership previously discussed. What these leaders have in common is an ability to arouse passion or strong emotion and gain a profound commitment from followers. A dedicated follower of one who is portrayed as a *charismatic* leader may be described as a loyal employee, a patriot, a true believer, a disciple, a groupie, a devotee, a fan, or a worshiper.

Another class of leader behaviors identified in recent years produces exceptional effects in the attitudes and commitment of followers with a subsequent increase in group performance. The leaders who evidence these behaviors are called transforming or *transformational* leaders. These leader behaviors also go beyond the behaviors described in prior chapters. We need to understand these forms of leadership, for they call into action beliefs and values held deeply by different segments of society.

Charismatic Leadership

Charisma is not a new concept. Charismatic leaders are those who by force of personality have a great influence on others. Such individuals have been objects of study and fascination throughout the history of mankind. Charisma, a theological term referring to favors vouchsafed by God, such as a gift of grace, has been a major source of wonderment; why do people respond so fully to those who display it? Max Weber[1] discussed the phenomenon and its effects on institutions. Writings of Robert House and others[2] have described how the charismatic leader inspires confidence by expressing high self-confidence and strong convictions, spelling out an appealing vision, defining ideological goals to build follower commitment, and by setting high expectations for performance and showing confidence in the ability of followers to achieve them. Charismatic leaders set examples by their own behavior and engage in acts that increase their followers' motivation.

Charismatic leadership is presumed to increase the self-esteem of followers as they embrace the vision and mission articulated by the leader and accept as their own the leader's values and goals. As commitment strengthens, followers become willing to subordinate their own self-interests for the sake of the cause, be it nation, family, tribe, club, group, or organization. Charismatic leadership appeals to values other than self-interest. Followers work for the overall good as explained by the leader and no longer say, "If you will do this for me, I will do this for you." The conviction that one is a member of an important cause is motivating; group goals then supersede individual goals. The charismatic leader takes advantage of these human qualities by setting goals that transcend the normal, thus giving greater impetus to activities. The group and its goals become exceedingly important.

Extraordinary outcomes occur only when faith is deep; the leader must not only be persuasive but must be viewed as having some special place in the destiny of the group or of a larger entity. Although their deeds were not always noble, charismatic leaders have played major roles throughout history. The tragedies bred by Hitler, Stalin, and Saddam Hussein make people understandably wary. Nevertheless, by inspiring followers and setting goals, charismatic leaders who do not succumb to the temptations of glory can yield many benefits. However, when incompetence is obscured and value systems distorted, charisma becomes dangerous; when the leader is motivated by hate, revenge, or fear, catastrophes may result. To be a charismatic leader requires followers to attribute charisma to the leader, which occurs in response to the behaviors of and results achieved by the leader. Leaders must persuade followers that the job to be done has meaning for them, must articulate a vision of the future that followers believe and accept, and must model behaviors they wish to evoke in their followers. The process promotes devotion to and trust in the leader, emotional involvement in the mission, motivation to perform beyond expectations, confidence in one's own ability to perform, and faith in the outcome.

To create such effects requires a dominant, self-confident personality with strong convictions and a need for power. Persuasive abilities are required. A strong ideological position is often helpful. Such descriptions, which call to mind the many candidates for political office in democratic societies, clearly apply to the U.S. presidency. Outcomes of many elections have been greatly influenced by behaviors that can be described as charismatic. In fact, U.S. presidents who fit these descriptions are rated by historians as more effective in office.[3]

Measures of presidential charisma have been developed by analyzing presidential biographies.[4] Presidents with high charisma have much closer rapport with members of their cabinet, who in turn have more positive feelings about their role, accede more readily to presidential wishes and orders, and agree with more presidential policies.

Charismatic behavior of the American president has been shown to be strongly and positively related to both social and economic presidential performance.[5] During a crisis, the relationship between presidential charisma and presidential performance increases.

Efforts have been made to understand what drives individual U.S. presidents to act as they do in particular circumstances. Most of the variability in their behaviors can be accounted for by assessing presidential power motives and charisma, controlling for the time in which they served and the number of crises they encountered. Analysis suggests a greater orderliness and predictability in presidential actions and performance than most students of the American presidency would have predicted.

House and Spangler, in a lighthearted letter to the *New York Times*, added a note to the literature of the 1992 presidential campaign with the observation that they saw no direct correlation between presidents who have mistresses and objective measures of presidential effectiveness. They did, however, speculate that presidents who are tall and charismatic are also more likely to have mistresses. They wrote, "Perhaps having a mistress goes with the territory covered by effective Presidents."[6]

Charismatic leaders increase the intrinsic value of effort and thus make work more appealing. As a "can-do" attitude becomes associated with increased performance, the intrinsic value of goals increases as well. The leader who emphasizes faith in a better future thus diminishes the role of personal and material rewards. The follower's commitment increases. The leader continues to provide a model of the behavior expected from all. Then ceremony, symbols, ritualistic procedures, and tradition sustain the emotional commitment of the group to higher goals.

Warnings About Charisma

Robert Hogan, McFarlin Professor of Psychology at the University of Tulsa, and his associates have sounded a warning about the charismatic leader.[7] Their message is clear: The charismatic personality often so enchants observers that fundamental flaws in character and personality are obscured, permitting ignoble goals to be ignored. Therein lies what Hogan calls the dark side of charisma. Evidence that flawed leadership abounds is provided by studies cited by Hogan, which show that between 60% and 75% of workers report that the worst part of their jobs is dealing with their supervisor. "Boss stress" is widespread. Although much of this stress is due to managerial incompetence, a large and unhealthy portion is due to the personality defects or flaws of charismatic leaders. Hogan cites three of the most common:

1. *The High Likeability Floater.* Exceedingly pleasant, congenial and charming, these leaders fail to perform. At some time this becomes obvious to those who must work with them and depend on them. Any negative action becomes difficult to explain, for this person has no enemies and a host of friends.

2. *Hommes de Ressentiment.* Beneath a surface appearance of charm and social skills lies a deep strain of hostility and resentment, and a desire for revenge. These persons feel betrayed. They poison group interactions, for their agenda is based on their own feelings of suspicion and distrust. They are often described as passive-aggressive; that is, they always seem agreeable, but somehow manage to subvert any actions separate from their own priorities.

3. *Narcissists.* Narcissism is a personality disorder that has been recognized in history, literature, and modern study by psychiatrists and psychologists. It is defined to include exhibitionism, feelings of entitlement, expectations of special privilege, feelings of omnipotence in controlling others, and intolerance of criticism. It is common for those persons who are dominant and assertive, and thus seeking leadership positions, to have in addition a broad streak of narcissism. The most dangerous part of the behaviors of such persons is their exploitation of others, associated with the feeling that they have the right to do so. Many charismatic personalities may also be described as narcissists.

Manfred F. R. Kets de Vries[8] holds the Raoul de Vitry d'Avauncourt Chair of Human Resource Management at the European Institute of Business Administration in Fontainebleau, France. He has written extensively on leaders and their behaviors, rational and irrational. Why, he asks, do some people fall short *after* they reach the top? One key factor is the change in their network of friends and advisers as social distance increases with promotions. Socializing cannot be the same, for friendliness to a subordinate is interpreted as favoritism. Reactions to the new isolation require new modes of gratification, which some leaders find but others do not.

Leaders who do not adapt may change the very modes of behavior that led to their promotion. They may become more authoritarian as increased subservience makes them believe in their own infallibility. Kets de Vries suggests that the responsibility to improve interchanges is shared by both leaders and their subordinates: Listening to each other and respecting each other's points of view are critical. A frank interchange between leaders and followers is key to preventing regressive behavior in leaders; this requires a relationship of equity, consistency, and trust.

Transformational Leadership

The distinction between charismatic leaders and transformational leaders is not clearcut. The transformational leader as one who excites, arouses, and inspires was proposed in 1978 by James MacGregor Burns in his classic book *Leadership*.[9] His support for the concept came from historical review and was clarified by numerous case studies. Burns's definition of the transformational leader hinges on the leader's appeal to the loftier ideals of followers rather than to their selfish interests. Thus, ideals such as peace, justice, fairness, liberty, equal opportunity, and the general welfare are central to the appeals made by transformational leaders. Burns views transformational leadership as an influence process that involves not only followers but also peers, superiors, or members of other groups.

Since its introduction by Burns, many studies of the concept of the transformational leader have incorporated it into psychological measures to test it in practice. Although transformational leadership as a concept places less emphasis on the personal qualities of the leader and more on a set of specific behaviors of the leader and followers, the descriptions of the behaviors are quite similar to those of charismatic leaders. However, transformational leaders inspire greater involvement in work and assure more self-fulfillment by increasing the intellectual and emotional involvement of followers. A vision is articulated; the reasons for decisions are explained; goals are set and sold to the group so that they are accepted; the transformational leader works to engender trust and respect.

Bernard Bass, Distinguished Professor of Management and director of the Center for Leadership Studies at the State University of New York at Binghamton, has conducted with his research team extensive studies of transformational leadership. His Multifactor Leadership Questionnaire (MLQ),[10] developed to identify individuals who exhibit transformational as well as other more traditional leadership behaviors, is completed by subordinates who describe how their superiors act when they are "leading." Bass's findings show that subordinate ratings provide the single most effective tool to identify outstanding leadership qualities. Examples of items in the questionnaire completed by subordinates that clarify the attributes of the transformational leader include: "I am ready to trust him/her to overcome any obstacle," "Gives personal attention to me when necessary," "Shows me how to think about problems in new ways," and "Provides vision of what lies ahead."

Yammarino and Bass measured and assessed transformational leadership using a sample of Naval officers, graduates of the U.S. Naval Academy on active duty in the fleet. Using the Naval Academy records of the young officers, they were able to differentiate between those whose basic leadership styles were transformational and those whose were not and could identify the behaviors of transformational leaders from the reports of their subordinates. Teams led by those officers identified as transformational leaders proved to be superior in fleet competition and in ratings by their superiors. What do they do that is different?

1. They are more inspiring and charismatic in the eyes of their subordinates. When leaders broaden and elevate the interests of their subordinates and when there exists a general understanding and acceptance of the goals of the group, members begin to work more, expend more energy, and move beyond self-interest to the larger interests of the group.

2. They provide more individualized consideration. Attention to the individual needs for growth and development inspires loyalty to the organization and meets the needs of group members for coaching, mentoring, and support.

3. They provide more intellectual stimulation. Within each group there are opportunities to link the work done to larger goals, to explain why certain policies are in effect, and to listen to questions about the basis for certain procedures. Reducing the feeling of alienation is critical in many groups.

Sashkin and Burke developed a Leader Behavior Questionnaire (LBQ)[11] to assess leader behaviors and to collect evidence on the existence of transformational leadership in educational as well as business settings. Most samples for study were drawn from school systems, with attention to student performance. The item content of the LBQ was drawn from a review of the literature to provide a comprehensive measure of transformational leadership by measuring behaviors, personal characteristics, and the impact of the leader on the organization's culture.

The LBQ, which is more comprehensive than most other measures of leadership, consists of fifty items, with five items forming each of ten scales. Different forms are provided for self-ratings and for other-ratings. Following are the scales, and a sample item from each:

1. Focused Leadership: I have a clear set of priorities.
2. Communication Leadership: I sometimes make points in strikingly clear and even unusual ways.
3. Trust Leadership: I am extremely dependable.
4. Respectful Leadership: I show that I care about other people.
5. Risk Leadership: I find ways to get everyone fully committed to new ideas and projects.
6. Bottom-Line Leadership: I can see clear effects resulting from my action.
7. Empower Leadership: I think that the real value of power is in being able to accomplish things that benefit both the organization and its members.
8. Long-Term Leadership: I think about how the plans and programs I've developed in my own unit might be expanded to benefit the entire organization.
9. Organizational Leadership: I try to express and support a set of basic values about how people should work together in this organization to solve common problems and reach shared goals.
10. Cultural Leadership: I strive to take actions to reach goals rather than contributing to keeping things the way they are.

Used in numerous studies, the LBQ has identified differences between principals of high schools with high- and low-performing students, as well as between managers whose subordinates had high and low perceptions of quality of work life. It has been used with business and public leaders in the United States and in Australia. Outcomes of the studies indicate that transformational or visionary leaders obtain more positive organizational outcomes as compared with nonvisionary leaders; their organizations are characterized by more effective adaptation, goal attainment, and teamwork and by stronger shared values and beliefs.

Deal and Peterson[12] compiled case studies to illustrate the influence of school principals on the school culture. Their work, similar in many ways to that of Sashkin and his colleagues, also focused on leadership in educational institutions. Deal and Peterson identified six major themes shared by transformational school principals:

1. They develop a sense of what the school could become; that is, a vision.
2. They recruit and select staff whose values fit with those of the principal.
3. They resolve conflicts, disputes, and problems in ways that shape values.
4. They communicate values and beliefs in daily routines and behaviors.
5. They identify and articulate stories that communicate shared values.
6. They nurture the traditions, ceremonies, rituals, and symbols that communicate and reinforce the school culture the leader is constructing. [13]

In 1992, Mansour Javidan, professor and chairman in the Policy and Environment Area of the Faculty of Management at the University of Calgary in Canada, presented findings of a survey of over 500 managers in middle, upper-middle, and senior management ranks who assessed their own immediate superiors. Based on the findings from his work, which support those of Bass and others, Javidan makes several suggestions to top leaders:

1. Make sure subordinates understand what is expected of them. Provide a sense of direction by communicating a vision of what the organization stands for and where it is headed. Explain the role of subordinates in accomplishing the organization's goals and, through open discussion, help clarify the issues.
2. Help subordinates develop a sense of self-worth and self-confidence through training, development, encouragement, mentoring, and public recognition.
3. Provide intellectual stimulation to subordinates by encouraging independence and self-reliance.[14]

Javidan's findings also suggest that executives are expected to be more than just transformational leaders: They must be successful ambassadors for their units and must have a global view of their function and a recognition of its fit in the overall organization. Effective executives are responsible for establishing high performance standards and assuring results and must be regarded as tenacious and able to pursue their dreams with determination and high energy. Their commitment must be obvious to all.

Leadership for Change

The studies we have presented provide a description of leadership behaviors. However, it is also useful to examine situations in the real world when the qualities desired of leaders in times of change, innovation, restructuring, mission reexamination, market share, and global competition are center stage topics.[15] System-wide organizational change is a critical determinant of an organization's ability to adapt and survive in a rapidly changing environment. Leadership must orchestrate such changes. Special leadership qualities are critical in effecting such major changes, descriptions of which sound like those of a charismatic or transformational leader: *Envisioning*—articulates a compelling vision, sets high expectations, and models consistent behaviors; *Energizing*—demonstrates personal excitement, expresses personal excitement, and seeks, finds, and uses success; *Enabling*—expresses personal support, empathizes, and evidences confidence in people.

Leaders who behave in these ways can serve as catalysts to change by providing a focal point for the hopes and aspirations of group members; they can be role models and can develop personal relations with others in the organization. On the other hand, these behaviors may produce undesirable outcomes. When unrealistic expectations are generated and disagreements with the leader are suppressed, trouble looms. When the leader appears under pressure or disenfranchises the next levels of management, the organization is faltering. It is usually too late then to remember that such underlying management behaviors as Structuring, Controlling, and Rewarding must be interwoven into the fabric of leadership along with the charismatic behaviors of Envisioning, Energizing, and Enabling.

Accounts of top executives suggest that leaders vary in their value to organizations as change is considered and undertaken. In addition, the nature of the organization, as well as the contemplated change, influences the decision-making process and the time and effort required to succeed. We provide two illustrations.

Resignation Spurs American Express Shares

Robinson's Plan Sets off 6% Rise: Voluntary Nature of Decision is Disputed

Shares of **American Express** Co. rose 6% yesterday on news that the longtime chairman of the company would resign, as investors signaled their eagerness for a quick resolution to the company's succession plan.

The announcement that James D. Robinson III would step down sparked American Express shares to rise $1.375 to $24.75 in late trading on the New York Stock Exchange yesterday. It was the most active stock with more than eight million shares trading hands, and the trading raised the market value of American Express by $667 million.

Meanwhile, even as Mr. Robinson maintained that his decision was voluntary, a person close to the company's board [reported that members had] pushed for a change in leadership.[16]

Staying Power
Motorola Illustrates How an Aged Giant Can Remain Vibrant

Endless Self-Criticism Keeps Walkie-Talkie Creator Thriving in the Pager Era

Bosses Who Invite Dissent

The Motorola executive was impressed. A small Oregon company was demonstrating a revolutionary type of video screen that Motorola Inc. badly wanted to produce. This was an ideal chance, concluded the Motorola executive, Charles Shanley, but he'd have to move fast; some Japanese executives were gathered around the same demonstration.

In 22 days, Motorola's chief executive, George Fisher, met with officers of the Oregon firm, In Focus Systems Inc. Three months later, the two companies announced a joint venture to manufacture the screens in the U.S., and a month after that they launched it. The plant will cost as much as $70 million to reach full production.

Motorola . . . provides a map for other companies, both large and small, showing the road back to manufacturing supremacy and market-share dominance. . . . When he founded the company in 1928, Paul Galvin, a salesman and saloon-owner's son, knew that new technology would soon render his first product, called the "battery eliminator" irrelevant, so he used its short-lived sales to get into a new and longer-lasting business, car radios. From that successful move, his company segued into two-way radios, inventing the walkie-talkie, and into television, selling the first solid-state TV sets under the Quasar name.

In 1949, the senior Galvin and his son, Robert, decided to divert many of the company's resources into a nascent business that his chief engineers correctly believed would change the face of communications. It was integrated circuits, or semiconductors. Twenty-five years later, the junior Galvin made an equally pivotal move. Sensing the coming Japanese hegemony in consumer electronics, he sold Quasar to Matsushita Electrical Industrial Co. of Japan, to focus solely on microchips and wireless devices. . . .

This prescience didn't happen by accident. Anticipation is a religion at Motorola, codified in the culture in a number of ways and designed to keep critical information flowing quickly to the top. . . . Most important, Motorola makes a cult of dissent and open verbal combat. Each employee is entitled to file a "minority report" if he feels his ideas aren't being supported. The reports are read by bosses of the teams' bosses. Unlike at other firms that have such devices, retribution at Motorola is considered "macho" or craven. Engineers say they are encouraged to dispute their superiors and one another at open meetings . . . the cult of conflict quickly identifies and fixes mistakes, unmasks and kills weak or illogical efforts, keeps top managers fully informed and sometimes unearths enormous opportunities. An example of the latter is Motorola's bellwether computer microprocessor, the 68000 series, which emerged from a minority report and dispute, according to Robert Galvin, 70, who now is chairman of Motorola's executive committee.[17]

The Alverno College Experience

To accomplish change effectively and smoothly is the central objective of leaders not only in the business world, but also in education, government, and not-for-profit institutions. Persistence, patience, and ability to articulate and re-articulate a vision are required, a process illustrated in the following examination of an unusual developmental program in a liberal arts college. We can credit its president, Sister Joel Read, with exhibiting transformational leadership.

Beginning in 1973, Alverno College totally restructured its educational program. Five years of intensive planning and a history of eighty-five years as a traditional independent, four-year liberal arts college for women preceded this massive change. The college, located in Milwaukee, Wisconsin, serves women of all ages, races, and financial means. The five-year planning effort, which required extraordinary cooperation and self-evaluation throughout the institution, was guided by a clearly articulated vision generated by the president and embodied in a college mission statement.

The precipitating events for change began in 1968 with the inauguration of a new lay board of trustees and a new president. In the 1960s, students everywhere were raising questions about the relevance of traditional educational practices and the viability of women's colleges. However, Alverno College had a longstanding and stated dedication to teaching and curricular improvement, and its new president affirmed its mission to educate women. She led faculty in each discipline to deliberate on questions worth probing in both general education and major programs of study. She challenged them with: What kinds of questions are being asked by professionals in your field that relate to the validity of your discipline in a total college program? What is your department's position on these? How are you dealing with these problems in your general education courses and in the work for a major in your field? and What are you teaching that is so important that students cannot afford to pass up courses in your department?

Ferment grew as faculty met regularly within departments and then began to meet biweekly as a group to listen to and discuss each other's conclusions. Commonalities were found. By the third year, an expanded list of "competences" that had been developed was given to an academic task force to shape into an actual curriculum. Although encouraged by their increasing ability to discuss educational issues in interdisciplinary settings, the three-year process was long, difficult, and often uncertain. During these deliberations the faculty was supported visibly and constantly by the president. The academic community debated, experimented, revised, and eventually reached agreement on an ability-based curriculum that would be augmented by a program of performance assessment.

As the date for implementation approached, the faculty asked the president to postpone installation of the curriculum for a year or two. Although the faculty believed they had learned a great deal, they felt they needed more time to get the curriculum "just right." In spite of faculty reluctance to begin, the president opted for implementation as planned. She stated that there were no educational experts in this area, that the faculty had to rely on their own professional experience as educators, and that the curricular design was the best the faculty could do at the time. The next step was to work with the new program and learn its strengths and weaknesses with an agreement to continually revise and refine the educational program based upon faculty practice and theory.

This decision point—to begin program implementation—is illustrative of many decisions made during this initial period and in the twenty years since. Dealing with conflicts, ambiguities, and frustrations associated with the process of change has become a regular feature of the college's collaborative style. Faculty and administrators deal with these potential barriers to change by learning to distinguish between the substantive and the peripheral, by being able to take a breather to get a new perspective, and especially by recalling for one another that the design is under the faculty's direction and can be revised in a timely fashion when mistakes are made.

What distinguishes Alverno today from virtually all other American colleges and attracts attention from educators around the world is its "ability-based" curriculum. A student body of over 2,500 women is expected to acquire the knowledge traditionally associated with a baccalaureate degree *and* also to master eight complex abilities needed to apply that knowledge effectively throughout their lives. The abilities are Analysis, Problem Solving, Communication, Social Interaction, Valuing in Decision Making, Effective Citizenship, Global Perspectives, and Aesthetic Response.

Alverno College has established eight competence departments parallel to the departments that represent the various disciplines. Faculty from all disciplines make up the membership of the competence departments, serving on a voluntary basis in addition to working within their individual disciplines. Every semester each competence department reviews the syllabuses, the teaching and assessment materials, and the results of student performances in its area. They assist their colleagues with consultations, team teaching, workshops, and other means of in-service support. They discuss problems, discoveries, and questions that have arisen in teaching and assessing each student's ability.

Faculty in all twenty-four liberal arts and professional areas have reshaped all of their courses to foster student development of eight abilities. Faculty have also developed systematic programs of performance-based assessment to measure student demonstration of these abilities at progressively higher levels of sophistication as they move through their college careers.

Leadership at All Levels

Charismatic or transformational leadership seeks to put meaning into even the most menial task in an effort to help every follower understand that seemingly little things are important and have an effect on the total organizational plan. But sometimes the task to inspire and motivate requires extraordinary effort, as illustrated by the following account by the chairman and chief executive officer of Wendy's International:

Wendy's Successful "Mop Bucket Attitude"

After feasting on success for more than 15 years, Wendy's Old Fashioned Hamburgers restaurants developed heartburn in the mid-1980's. Costs soared, sales dropped, and formerly enthusiastic analysts waxed gloomy about Wendy's prospects, convinced our company had lost focus.

I came as president in 1986 and found we had indeed lost our focus—on people. We had such a fear in our hearts about numbers, about the power of computer printouts and going by the book, we'd managed to lose sight of our customers and employees both.

There's a special purgatory for service businesses that forget their business starts with people. What happened to us was typical: Managers weren't getting the respect they needed and were passing their frustrations along to the crew. The crew, feeling unappreciated, made the customer feel the same. And the customers voted with their feet—as customers are wont to do.

As sales fell, store labor was cut and sales dropped even further. Morale took a nosedive, quality became spotty, and consistency in operations was nonexistent. It was time, clearly, to heave the charts and the printouts and to concentrate once more on the basics. Beginning with the most basic tenet of all: Mop Bucket Attitude, or M.B.A.

Mop Bucket Attitude says that all the business sophistication in the world pales before the "wisdom" of a clean floor. Fancy price-cost tabulations or quarterly earnings have no meaning to the customer, but quality food, variety and atmosphere do. Those had traditionally been our strengths, and they hadn't lost one bit of value; we just weren't playing to them any more. With our priorities now firmly in hand, we turned to our employees.

Ours is an industry once defined by high employee turnover. It was viewed as normal if not inevitable. We questioned that view, and decided the best way to become the customer's restaurant of choice was to become the employer of choice. Our plan on this front was two-pronged: to work harder to develop the potential of the people we already had, and to move aggressively to attract and retain the best people we could find.

We began by raising employee training to uniformly high standards, seeing that everyone, from the newest kid on fries all the way up to the manager, received the same basic training. (Previously, anyone with two weeks on the job might train the last person in the door.) Then we worked to make the "manager" truly a status position, giving the manager more control and latitude in day-to-day decisions.

Still, we knew young people of ambition might forsake us the first chance they got for "real" jobs with benefits to match. So we improved basic compensation, offered a package of top-flight benefits and a cash bonus paid out each quarter. We created an employee stock option plan called "We-Share" to give our employees a larger stake in the company. And, reflecting the special concerns of our founder, Dave Thomas, we included paid leave and reimbursed medical and legal costs for company employees who adopt children.

It worked. Our turnover rate for general managers fell to 20% in 1991 from 39% in 1989, while turnover among co- or assistant managers dropped to 37% from 60%—among the lowest in the business. With a stable—and able—work force, sales began to pick up as well. To win back repeat business, though, we would have to concentrate not just on this transaction but the next.

We know it's easy to increase store traffic and sales short term. You flood the market with coupons, let fly a few specials, maybe go for a splashy new ad campaign. But if you get customers in the door and disappoint them, it's a disaster. Not only must you offer customers quality, value, and a pleasant experience: You must offer it consistently.

With the aim of increasing consistency throughout the 3,800 Wendy's restaurants world-wide, we launched "Sparkle" in 1989—a program that is part incentive, part strategy for elevating and measuring quality, service and cleanliness on a daily basis. We refocused our managers and crews to look at their restaurants from the customer's point of view.

We also looked at our menu lineup and added more products to the premium side of the business, an acknowledged area of strength. At the same time, we reached out to our cost conscious customers with a Super Value menu of nine items priced at 99 cents—not just on Wednesdays or for a "limited time only," but every day of the year.

The customers who'd deserted us began to come back. I won't say it was a flood; more of a trickle at first. When we started these programs in 1987, we made just five cents a share. In 1991, by contrast, we reported earnings of 52 cents a share. Amid flat sales in the rest of the industry and a recession that wouldn't go away, Wendy's realized a 31% increase in earnings last year for a profit of $51 million—its best year since 1985.

I wish I could say there was some kind of magic wand behind all of this. In fact, the "magic wand" approach was the first thing to go. The main reason we have sustained 12 consecutive quarters of sales gains over the prior year—and look to continue it into the next 12 and beyond—is because we returned to the solid unmagical principles of management that put us on the map in the first place.

These are principles that focus on people—and never go out of fashion.[18]

When combined with tools which assess effectiveness, the review of case studies like Wendy's, interviews, questionnaires, and observational methods not only enhance the understanding of the nature of leadership but also provide guidance to individuals who have leadership responsibilities.

It is usually assumed that transformational or charismatic leaders emerge only at the top of an organization. However, many of those who produce unusual effects and are viewed as charismatic and transforming are found in lower levels of organizations and small groups since the provision of individualized consideration to each follower is easier to deliver face-to-face. In contrast, other qualities, such as articulating a vision or setting a new direction, require an environment in which influence and discretion can be exercised and in which individuals can contribute their own solutions to common problems. In organizations with centralized controls, this is difficult for people not at the top.

Leaders can change the climate of an organization to foster leadership at all levels. The choice for the organization is theirs: whether to implement programs that identify and develop charismatic and transformational leaders or whether to penalize the innovative and challenging effects of such people. If organizations provide subtle or obvious cues that leadership behaviors at lower levels of the organization are neither welcomed nor rewarded, we can expect few charismatic or transformational leaders to emerge from the ranks to be among those being considered for top positions.

CHAPTER FOUR

The Leader Sets the Tone

Organizations faced with the need to replace top leadership look for someone who will move to take charge quickly and address major problems. Yet even the most successful leaders describe their first weeks in a top position as the most difficult period. Enthusiastic and ready to move, they found how hard it was to establish their authority, to communicate their views on organizational issues, to launch a campaign to turn things around, to improve the quality of products or services, to summon willingness to tackle hard problems, or to stimulate interest in reexamining goals or restructuring the organization. Those who sought to reaffirm or reformulate the values of the group faced a truly formidable task that required abundant self-confidence, communication skills, and talent in influencing others.

The Challenge to Newly Appointed Leaders

The moment of accession is an ideal time to announce with clarity a firm stand on issues, particularly those that are sources of disagreement and dissension within the organization. How, where, and to whom to say, "Here is where I stand, here is where we need to go" may hold the key to their later success. People who have held powerful positions often report at the end of their service, "My aim was to move the organization a step forward. I could have done it more effectively, but I didn't quite get my message across in the beginning."

Followers or subordinates hail the new leader's advent with excitement, apprehension, and expectation, for they view him or her as one who can produce unlimited beneficial changes. The recorded stories and the mythology of heroes support this fantasy. Historical occurrences are generally credited to the ruler in power at the time. The name of an incumbent president is incorporated into the name of the period, as in "The Kennedy Administration." Presidents, kings, and emperors are seen as totally in charge and responsible for most events. Locally, when we seek to influence a community organization, we ask to speak to its president. When we have a complaint, we want to know if the president or person in charge is aware of the problem. Ultimately, we expect the leader to speak for a group, defend its actions, and establish it goals; it is the leader who is credited with accomplishments and blamed for shortcomings.

Previously disaffected followers who feel a pressing need for change see a new leader as a potential supporter of their aspirations. They attend carefully to every pronouncement and take seriously any remark that bolsters their hopes and ambitions. Accession to a position of leadership provides the opportunity for a leader to address issues of fairness and justice, to mobilize the talents of everyone in the organization, and to call for support of restated objectives.

Thus, the newly appointed leader must be ready to sell the program and gain trust. Plans must be carefully laid, for there are always persons in a group who resist change. They like things the way they are and see change as a threat to their own security or status. Some distrust change because their hopes have been dashed by prior changes. Some see a hidden plot behind every change. There will

44

be many who will wait to see if the new leader delivers on promises and if the new plan works.

In the corporate world, appointment of a new chief executive increases the value of the organization even before the new leader announces or launches a program. New leaders signify a new prospect, especially for those disenchanted with the status quo. Change at the top is associated with a reexamination of the course of the organization and increased attention to its objectives. Even the necessity to select a successor sets in motion procedures that can be helpful to an organization.

College and university presidents exercise leadership in ways quite different from top executives in business. Business leaders challenge the process to respond to the marketplace. College presidents articulate a vision that ties closely to traditions of the institution. Not all new presidents of colleges and universities address the need for change in their institutions; to do so requires that they confront trustees, faculty, students, and alumni in unsettling discussions that reveal the conflicts in objectives among varied constituencies. They know the limits of their influence, and many avoid conflict by sustaining the sacred distinctiveness of their traditions or the myth that their institution is a faithful copy, even if it is smaller and poorer, of Harvard, Princeton, Swarthmore, or Notre Dame.

Community organizations often change top leadership annually. Long-term incumbencies are rare. Such organizations continually have problems in preparing adequate numbers of persons to accede to leadership positions. The quality of leadership often varies enormously from year to year. In the absence of stable leadership, organizations must have diligent boards of directors to ensure that needed changes occur. By employing paid directors, some boards achieve needed continuity of planning and the facility for change; when the paid directorate becomes moribund, the organization is frequently not organized appropriately to accomplish a renewal without suffering dissent among supporters.

Organizations differ, but they have features in common. Every organization has individuals who desire greater attention to their innovative ideas, who seek greater empowerment. These activists are resisted by others who want things to remain the same. Some want to see more attention paid to the environment; others think this unnecessary. Some want the chance to try a new promotional plan to increase membership in the organization or to increase sales for a new product. Others want the power of their immediate boss reduced and more attention paid to worker complaints. Some want particular individuals in important positions dislodged. And still others are offended by their organization's failure to recruit more women and minorities and want to hear a new policy enunciated.

When the organization has a history of white male dominance, especially in its highest levels of management, a statement of new policy directives that recognizes talent among women and minorities will not be enough. Those who have heard promises but seen no resolution of the problem will be impressed only if specific actions taken by the new leader lead to changes in the system. Training programs, challenging assignments, and promotional opportunities must support new policies that promise equal opportunity. Such actions can be expected to provoke opposition, especially from those who have been favored in the past.

Members sometimes become disenchanted with the organization; they bemoan the loss of spirit and purpose it used to have and relish the possibility of enlivenment and renewal. The appeal of a new voice means a new sense of direction that is rejuvenating. Such members may recommit themselves to the organization's objectives as they read and listen to the words of a new leader. Especially in religious and service groups, the appearance of a new leader at regular intervals may increase loyalty to the organization and increase the efforts of the participants. Sometimes this phenomenon is exhibited dramatically with new national leaders.

The studies we examined assign to the leader a host of key responsibilities. They include organizing and completing tasks, persistent evaluating of processes, expanding and adjusting the vision, responding to altered circumstances and technological advances, resolving conflicts, and maintaining a cohesive and harmonious group of followers. In addition to these responsibilities, a leader must also balance commitment to the organization and its mission with his or her own set of values and self-interests. The success of these activities depends to a substantial degree on getting a good start.

Personal Values and Leadership

A leader can marshal many sources of ideas and energy by announcing a personal set of values that may encourage those who share the values and inspire those who are uncommitted. Such statements assign priorities to actions that followers perceive as a promise by the leader to give attention to certain especially worthy options. Values determine the choices people make or, at least, values are ascribed to the choices made by them. If values are not spelled out or acted upon by the leader, followers will assume they need not remain committed to them.

Leaders who announce that they can neither affect nor determine the behavior of their followers are denying the major responsibility of leadership. Such denial empowers their followers to engage in unethical or even criminal acts in which the leader, by default, participates. The influence of the leadership role, however exercised, cannot be overestimated. Actions of leaders, or their inaction, can have powerful and often unintended consequences that legitimize similar actions or inactions by their followers. The thin line between committing a misdeed and standing by while it happens can be blurred and have serious consequences, especially when followers are mesmerized by the leader and dedicated to the group's purpose.

Therefore all leaders must take great care about what they say and must assure themselves that their followers have heard and understood them. Followers or subordinates listen closely to what leaders say and remember their leader's less publicized thoughts and ideas, asides, innuendoes, and humorous remarks. Followers look to leaders as role models, as special people who know which actions will further group purposes. Many followers believe that leaders are omnipotent and may even act in accord with some carefully crafted design. The emotional commitment of followers to remain loyal may linger well after their reason tells them that such feelings are unwise.

The Effect of Value Differences

Individuals vary widely in the values they hold. Wealth is the prime objective in life for some, while others seek the esteem of their peers or give highest priority to the happiness of their children. Some seek to be the very best in a special pursuit, while others surround themselves with friends. A few seek privacy or isolation. Thus, every organization experiences conflicts in values and in the priorities assigned to tasks. It is important to take into account the problems that arise because of these differences and ask how they can be reconciled.

Loden and Rosener[1] cite culture clash as a conflict that occurs when the values and behaviors of the dominant group are questioned by others. It is not easy for an organization to accommodate the values and experiences of all its members. However, an organization can establish common ground and true integration so that diversity of cultures is an asset, not an abstract concept to be challenged, misinterpreted, or viewed as a threat. Diversity among leaders and followers in any organization produces tangible benefits for all, but it is an outcome achieved only with overt and enthusiastic support from the leadership of the organization.

Loden and Rosener caution that "cultural differentiation" can be an unnecessary beginning in a move toward greater "jointness" because it emphasizes group differences and can lead to still more stereotyping. They report that when institutions set up work teams with diverse membership and empower them to solve problems jointly, the value assigned to diversity by group members increases.

Elliott Jaques writes, "The organization must value the individual, promote his or her development, and must generate mutual trust and confidence, shared values and commitment, and support democratic free enterprise and its opportunities."[2] He sees these general values becoming an integral part of all aspects of the functioning of an organization and becoming obvious to all through communication, participation, and a clear articulation of accountability and authority. True values are portrayed in the actions of superiors toward subordinates and in the ways schools educate students for various careers and giant corporations make decisions. Max De Pree, chairman of the board of Herman Miller, Inc., writes:

> Leaders are responsible for such things as a sense of quality in the institution, for whether or not the institution is open to influence and change. Effective leaders encourage contrary opinions, an important source of vitality. . . . In a civilized institution or corporation, we see good manners, respect for persons, an understanding of "good goods," and an appreciation of the way in which we serve each other. Civility has to do with identifying values as opposed to following fashions.[3]

We provide the following examples, the first fictitious, the second an actual experience:

> Henry Winner, the leader of a sales group for a major business firm, addressed the issue of values in his first encounter as sales manager with his salespersons. He made it clear that "a sale" was the thing. He imposed a discipline on them that led some of them to resign. They understood him to say that making another call was more important than getting home to one's family for dinner at the expected time. He wanted them to know that from then on, meeting his arbitrary goal—his sales office becoming Number 1 in the firm—was going to be more important than providing a job for nonperforming salespersons. Not a word was said about retraining. Close adherence to company rules could be less important than making a sale. Mr. Winner, by his tone and aggressive behavior as he voiced his pronouncements, made his values crystal clear to the group he headed. In succeeding months, he demonstrated the sincerity of his stated objectives by holding fast to those values. Some heads rolled. He had "set the tone" on the first

day, and it soon became obvious that to make it in his division, the acceptable behavioral pattern was one of compliance and concession.

Mr. Winner was obviously facing a serious situation requiring him to put spirit into his sales force. But did he have to act to set a tone that would bring them all to heel in order to accomplish his objectives? Are there better ways to address a poor performing group? What must be done to get the group's attention? Any answers given to these questions reveal the values of the person responding, reflect the experiences one has had, and represent an individual's understanding of the climate of the organization. To introduce change effectively requires sensitive feelings about the kind of response a given mode of action will receive.

How extensive and intense is the effect of a leader's statements about the standards of the organization on the day-to-day decisions of employees? Using the business simulation *Looking Glass, Inc.*,[4] Karen Gaertner[5] looked for answers to these questions in a study in which business school students were asked to make decisions on a selected set of purchases. The first set of students received policy memos indicating that decisions should take into account what is best for everyone in the company and everyone should comply with laws and adhere to professional standards. The second set of students received memos on the same topic, but the policy emphasized doing anything necessary to further the company's interest, regardless of consequences; it suggested that ethically suspect behaviors might be tolerated or even, if results were good, rewarded.

The first set of participants, those directed to consider the interests of all the persons in the company and follow the law and proper practices, were the *only* ones who took these factors into account. Those participants directed to consider only business results made all of their decisions based solely on the business benefit, having interpreted the policies as permission to deny the use of any other criteria in making decisions. Differences in stated company policy made a difference in the ethical quality of decisions made by the participants.

Gaertner reports that classroom discussions after the simulation reveal an underlying problem in the thinking of the students. They referred to ethical criteria as "soft" and not business-like and could not see merit in attending to the legitimate needs of others; they said there was no room in business for emotional criteria. The MBA program in which these students were enrolled rested on an economic model that assumes that rational behavior is motivated by individual self-interest. The students knew the model, were comfortable with it, and believed in it. However, ethical reasoning asks that the needs of others be considered, a criterion that made these students uncomfortable. The effect of the difference in the two policy memos was therefore contaminated by the infusion of another value system.

Organizational Values

Should organizations set standards for the conduct of their employees or members? Does a publicly held corporation have any responsibility other than to its owners, the shareholders? Everyone acknowledges the need to obey laws, but many have the view that moral values do not apply to organizations. Most persons find a problem in using words to differentiate morals from ethics.

Jack N. Behrman defines morals as individually held and ethics as societal:

> **Moral** values are seen as absolute for the one holding them and often as universal;
> **Ethical** values are those which are social in origin and culture-bound. **Pragmatic**

values are specific to the situation—what works is deemed good. Moral values, being absolute, are not affected by the situation, they are what informs our conscience and make us feel guilty, even when we are violating no law or social ethic. **Absolute** values tend to have religious or philosophical foundations. Ethical values are **relative**, relating to different cultures and within them to different situations. Pragmatic values are strictly ad hoc or temporary, justifying any workable solution.

The same set of "acceptable acts" could be reached by any one of the value sets. Thus, honesty and truthfulness could be seen as absolute, or derived from the value of having an open democracy, or as a pragmatic necessity in an effective student-teacher, doctor-patient, lawyer-client, or buyer-seller relation.[6]

Behrman clarifies these distinctions by asserting that absolute values lead to concepts of "good and evil." Ethical values lead to concepts of "good and bad." Pragmatic values lead to concepts of "right and wrong." Universal values—wisdom, courage, reverence, love, compassion, kindness, gratitude—are deemed inherent in human nature, distinguishing human beings from "lower" forms of life. Because universal values are considered inherent does not mean we practice them but does mean we know them and know we should practice them.

Is it the obligation of a system or organization to establish a value system for its constituents? Should it, for example, provide the greatest good for the greatest number? Should businesses both maximize profits and strive for the good of their employees? Many say that business does not try to maximize profits; it merely talks that way. To maximize profits, every decision is based solely on profits. But there are simply too many complex tradeoffs against profit for business to rely entirely on maximization. Does an inflexible no-returns policy on goods improve or degrade profits? Does a contribution to the local United Way add to profits? Are we speaking quarterly profits, or profits ten years from now? How can we maximize profits and still modernize a plant? How do we justify attendance at costly executive seminars when it is difficult to prove that costs incurred will help maximize profits for the company?

Individual values are reflected in the way people live, the work they do, the goals they set, the games they enjoy, and the ways they relate to their associates, friends, and families. Although people may have difficulty expressing their beliefs to others, a discussion of values need not use the vocabulary of philosophers and clerics. Rather, it is important to reflect on one's own decisions, note how they reveal one's priorities, understand the values they express, and act accordingly. Values of the leader intrude into decision making in every organization. Frequently, leaders must address moral dilemmas when personal values impinge on rational decision making. The following event at Pillsbury Co. described by Rebecca Roloff clearly indicates the importance of the values of its responsible officers.

Rebecca Roloff, Director of Marketing for Vegetables and Side Dishes, Pillsbury Company, described her experiences in decision making to a conference on Leadership Education in 1987. The Pillsbury Company discovered that a pesticide residue remained on food products long after it had its intended effect. What stance should the company take?

A task force convened by the corporation decided that it would release all the information it had about the problem, and work to get that pesticide out of use as rapidly as possible. That was accomplished in two years—three years sooner than anyone had thought possible. Roloff commented on the relevance of her experience as chairman of this task force for persons in leadership roles. She said: A leader has four responsibilities to keep in mind.

First. The right ethical decision will ultimately be the right long-term strategic decision.

Second. Very little difference can ultimately exist between your own personal philosophy of what is right and wrong and the organizational philosophy of what is right and wrong.

Third. The individual person—you, me—is responsible for doing what's right and wrong.

Fourth. You cannot call a meeting on what is the right, ethical decision and try to separate the ethical decision from the other decisions that are ongoing. The decisions which will be made are going to be the result of the value system which is ingrained in the company. A company acting unethically short-term via hundreds of little decisions cannot call a meeting of a group of experts and say, "Now we are going to act ethically on a big decision."[7]

Should the actions of organizations be influenced by the personal values of its leaders? Management at Pillsbury thought so. Although their decision did not take into account any bottom-line consequences, they must have believed there would be long-term beneficial consequences of their open and constructive approach to the problem. However, the example cited earlier of the sales manager illustrated the opposite approach: Mr. Winner made his decisions about turning around his sales office based only on the bottom line.

To prevent an erosion of principled behavior over time, an institution needs to subscribe to statements of values. Albert Bandura,[8] a noted professor of Psychology at Stanford University, says that individuals initially may perform questionable acts only when the acts can be tolerated with little self-censure. After repetitions of the acts, the discomfort and self-reproof of the individual diminishes and the level of reprehensibility of the behaviors progressively increases. Eventually, acts originally regarded as abhorrent are performed with little distress. This same process occurs when inhumane behavior is construed as serving a moral purpose. When people subjected to maltreatment are viewed as lesser beings, those who inflict pain and death do not censure themselves. This psychological mechanism operates in everyday situations in which decent people, for their own profit, routinely perform activities with injurious human effects. Self-exonerations or excuses are needed to neutralize self-sanctions and to preserve self-esteem. Leaders have a responsibility to ensure that their organizations do not unwittingly provide a rationale for unprincipled behavior among their members and can do so most directly by providing a clear statement of organizational values. The same pathology exhibited by individuals can be exhibited by organizations when, with public-spirited vindication or in response to the call of a "higher morality," they cause harmful effects to individuals, the larger society, or the environment.

Although many companies express concern about the welfare of their employees, their decisions may consider only the bottom line. They are accused of a lack of integrity. Badaracco and Ellsworth, with extensive experience in case-method teaching, addressed the issue of integrity in leadership through analysis of extensive discussions with seven senior executives respected for their outstanding achievements. The researchers observed that "In real organizations, the most difficult, anxiety-provoking and dilemma-ridden problems rise to the top. Resolving dilemmas involves a person's philosophy of management, a philosophy everyone has, whether formalized or not. These philosophies are based on fundamental assumptions about human nature, about people in organizations, about the work of managers, and the kinds of activities that lead to outstanding results."9

Badaracco and Ellsworth define integrity as consistency between what a manager believes, how a manager acts, and the manager's aspirations for his or her organization. But this definition of integrity is not enough, because an incompetent or corrupt manager can be perfectly consistent. Integrity must be based on those beliefs, actions, and aspirations that are more likely than others to lead to outstanding results. Since most problems that are faced by leaders are inescapably messy, Badaracco and Ellsworth argue for the development of guidelines for action to assure consistency. They call these guidelines "prejudices" to action that are necessary to make integrity come alive and be powerful and effective. The word is chosen to suggest a deliberate "set" to behave in a particular way—and to suggest that this prejudice is fully internalized by each individual.

An Amoral Philosophy of Success

For many leaders there are no moral dilemmas. They believe that each person in the organization is a role incumbent with a particular assignment for whom the organization, as such, has no moral obligation. Thus each organizational decision is judged not on moral grounds but on the degree to which it furthers the objectives of the group. Extraneous issues are ignored in the pursuit of single-minded goals. So employees in the tobacco industry believe in and participate in launching advertising campaigns for cigarettes to increase market share, even when the campaign targets young people or people of developing countries; a college makes unrealistic promises to outstanding faculty or students it wishes to recruit; a political party sets a platform that cannot be actualized, promising benefits to constituents that cannot be fulfilled. Some writers compare organizational behavior to chess: "It is all a game, the rules are known, do anything to win."

Business schools have been accused of teaching such singlemindedness to their students, hammering home the message that business corporations are formed to make profits for the stockholders; all decisions should be made so as to maximize profits, and we will teach you the formulas so that you can make decisions about alternative investments in terms of this ultimate goal. Accordingly, organizational morality is easily defined. Improper behavior, also easily defined, is any behavior that is not oriented to stockholder benefit.

Christopher Hodgkinson campaigns against philosophical claims that morality is absent in organizations and organizational decisions. While he agrees that an administrator might act only as an agent pursuing, by whatever means, the objectives of an organization, he calls attention to the capability of the administrator to alter the moral climate and moral destiny of his organization. The administrator may choose whether "to become his organization's faceless creature instead of its creator."

> The difficulty in the present context of argument has to do with bodies corporate. That one cannot hang a common seal has already been stated. And it is clear that corporate acts cannot always be reduced to the acts of individuals. If I own ten shares in General Motors I am not responsible if it violates the anti-trust rules, or does those things which are not good for the nation. And if it goes bankrupt I am not financially responsible beyond the rules of legal limited liability, even if the greatest economic hardships are a consequence. On the other hand, accountability

of a sort can be impressed upon the individual actors who are *agents* of a corporate body through such legal devices as fines, imprisonment, and loss of licence. Law has the sanctions of naked power. The force of legal responsibility is real enough, especially since the corporate agents are usually administrators, but it is distinctive from moral responsibility.

Formal responsibility can be considered as a subset of legal responsibility. It refers to the accountabilities sanctioned by the game rules of an organization. Acts are constrained by a potent system of rewards and punishments, including salaries, promotion, demotion and termination. The monitoring functions of administration and management are part of this responsibility system. And, just as law seeks a ground in societal values, so the system of formal responsibility seeks its ground in the organizational values and policy. Again, the organizational parallel to corporate bodies would be found in those group acts (group decisions) stemming from group processes and structures (committees, boards, and ad hoc groups) established formally within the organization. So if a committee of peers decides by secret vote, or unrecorded consensus, that a colleague should be dismissed, against *whom* can the injured party point his finger? The popularity of committee action is understandable. It can be a way of responsibly avoiding responsibility. But the responsibility then avoided would be moral responsibility.

This last, moral responsibility, can reduce to the individual only. It is uniquely phenomenological. It is the responsibility of a person to himself for his adherence to his entire range of values but especially to those Type I values with which he is authentically engaged. It is the ultimate sense of responsibility.[10]

Hodgkinson states the case for assigning to each member of an organization accountability for morally responsible behavior. His argument is hard to ignore and should not be denied. An organization embodies individual values when it encourages people to behave in ways consistent with their personal values. An entire social order can embody a value to the extent that it provides conditions that nurture social interrelationships embodying that value.

Our belief system evolves in response to our early experiences, interactions, and education as well as to the culture in which we live. Role models, by their example, illustrate what is beneficial or detrimental. Challenges from peers help shape our behavior patterns. Values are not magical entities derived by uttering a few nonsense syllables. Instead, our values develop relative to our life experiences, most of which are fraught with ambiguity.

Some people impress us almost instantaneously because their value systems appear meritorious and worthy of emulation. We recognize at once that they seem to respect the value of human life and dignity, are committed to lofty goals, and seem to live worthwhile lives. Following is a sensitive account of one such individual by Mark Patinkin, a columnist with the *Providence Journal*.

Helping People to Live, Prosper Where They Are

I last saw him five years ago, in the most difficult, uncomfortable country I'd ever been to—Sudan. His name is Jim Geenen and he worked there for Childreach, a Rhode Island-based agency that helps the world's needy.

I recall Sudan clearly; the phones didn't work, the traffic never moved and the scenery was parched.

"You must be glad to be out of there," I said to Geenen.

"Actually," he said, "I miss it a lot."

"Why?"

"I think it's because its not done," he said. "Things that are done are boring. Things that aren't done are challenging."

He didn't fit the picture of the kind of American I expected to find in the hunger business. He looked more like a college jock than a missionary type. He told me his two dreams were, one, to make the desert bloom and, two, to find a cold beer. He achieved the first but not the second; Sudan's Islamic laws forbid alcohol.

He was back in the States last week visiting headquarters, and I went to see him. Back in Africa, Americans like him were referred to as Third World Groupies. Only most burn out by their late 20's. You get to a point in life where you want hot showers, malls and cable. I figured Geenen, now 45 with three kids, would be there by now. He isn't. He's still at it, these days in a part of the Philippines called Baguio where the phones also don't work.

"Why didn't you at least request Manila?" I said.

Because, he said, the challenge in the developing world—"Third World" is now politically incorrect—is to help people build lives where they are, to keep them from crowding already over-crowded cities.

His goals are similar to what they were in Sudan—making crops grow in bad soil. In Baguio, the soil's been half-killed by too many people cutting too many trees and pouring too much chemical fertilizer into it. Geenen's working to introduce more natural fertilizers, and other local industries, too—like a new crop that can be used in place of trees to make paper.

He has a staff of 56 who work with 13,000 families. He stresses that he doesn't do dole-outs. That's a quick way to make people dependent. I told him I'd always pictured do-gooders like him to be inclined toward dole-outs. Not exactly. I asked what he'd do if one of the people there said he didn't want to work in return for help from Childreach. "Adios, amigo," said Geenen.

So what does he think of our own welfare system?

"I think it's a disgrace," he said. "It robs people of their pride." American welfare, he said, can learn from the way groups like his own do development.

I asked if he's ever tempted to focus his efforts at home? We have needy here, too.

"The world's one neighborhood," Geenen said. "And Americans are considered leaders. We have an obligation to share what we have."

I pointed out that some might say America has to cut back foreign aid during these hard times at home. That's when Geenen made a point I've been thinking about ever since.

"The only way we can keep our prosperity," he said, "is to share what we have."

Why?

Because a world full of have-nots, he said, will increasingly turn on the haves, first trying to get through our borders by foot and boat, perhaps later more violently. "We'll become an armed camp," he said, unless we find a way to help people prosper where they are.

That is his mission. He deserves our applause.[11]

How can so many people find great satisfaction in life while so many others find little to live for? There seems to be a secret that is worth discovering in the lives of leaders and their followers. As we pursue the study of leadership, we must pay attention to the role of values in the life of each individual and to the tremendous influence leaders have on the development and refinement of the value systems of their followers and on their organizations. Even if we could find no other effect of great leadership, this influence is reason enough for us to invest in better programs of leadership development.

CHAPTER FIVE

Statistics and Formulas in Leadership Selection

Choosing to lead, accepting the responsibilities of leadership, and electing to relate effectively to followers are options available to all people at any age and at any level. How do we identify those who will perform well as leaders? Every organization would like to know. Every person aspiring to high position would like to know. Methods for finding such talent are not obvious; if they were, we would have known the answer long ago. "What do you want to be when you grow up?" yields little relevant information, for the answers have little relation to decisions made later in life. College graduates have minimal knowledge about their own leadership qualities. Although hindsight provides the opportunity to identify childhood signs of greatness in proven leaders, hindsight does not offer the benefits of a "control group" for comparison; many individuals who have seemingly similar experiences never become prominent. The early identification of talent is complicated and requires sophisticated testing with comprehensive, well-planned studies. Conclusions drawn from observing single cases are shaky at best.

Every organization has units that work better than others. Sometimes "work better" is defined in terms of member enthusiasm, performance, profitability, accident rates, turnover, or internal conflict. All sorts of advice is given about how to bring the poorer units up to the standards of the better units. We propose in this chapter the use of orderly methods that not only give an independent assessment of the quality of the unit, but also suggest specific ways to improve the poor performers.

Information on a large sample of individuals that is collected systematically and combined objectively provides a better basis for prediction than observer judgments, even when the judgments are made by people who know a great deal about a candidate. Evidence to support this proposition has been accumulating for thirty years and often includes a comparison of the predictive judgment of a highly trained professional with a formula derived from large studies that combine diverse items of information about the individual.

The Value of Statistical Methods and Formulas

Paul E. Meehl, Regent Professor of Psychology and Psychiatry at the University of Minnesota, began studies over thirty years ago to compare decisions based on *statistical combinations of data* with decisions based on the *best clinical judgment* of professionals.[1] Over fifty studies have made such comparisons. We must pay heed to the findings. In over thirty years of study, every judgment about people reviewed by Meehl showed that a formula based on objective data would yield a better prediction than the very best judgment of the most qualified and experienced observers. Clearly, if a prediction formula is available, it should be used. Meehl demonstrates beyond a doubt that the use of tests, assessments, and items of information, properly combined, provide a better basis for prediction than does the judgment of an executive-search professional, a management team, the leader whose successor is being sought, or in fact, anyone else.

Thus, there is good reason to collect systematic data to determine the measures that carry the most weight in the prediction formula. Multiple regression analysis is the procedure that detects which items of information should enter the formula and the weight each item contributes. The professional literature on the systematic measurement of human characteristics, which includes many studies that relate to leadership and effective functioning of organizations, provides the basis for studying how to identify leaders and how to measure their impact. Contributors to this literature rarely publish their works in the mass media; their reports appear in journals in psychology, management, and closely related fields. Often their reports are too technical for easy comprehension even by those who might be interested in applying the findings. These investigators specialize in measurement of aptitudes, abilities, personality, opinions and attitudes, and performance levels. Some of them specialize in the identification, development, and utilization of leaders, executives, managers, and team leaders as well as their followers, supporters, or constituents.

New knowledge is produced as orderly methods are used to frame questions, record answers, and then develop hypotheses that are tested by rigorous research methods. Almost all major advances in psychological knowledge have come not from great cognitive leaps or the development of better theories but from the gradual accumulation of more and more tested findings about human behavior.

When well-planned studies are reviewed, the track record for applied psychology is very good. The following examples required years of work, great dedication, and a substantial expenditure of dollars. Although the first example is not related to leader selection, it exemplifies the method.

Choosing Aviation Cadets for Flight Training

During World War II the Army Air Force needed to train large numbers of pilots. The training program was rigorous and dangerous. Large numbers were failing out of an expensive program; when the failure occurred in flight, lives were lost and scarce planes were wrecked. A team of psychologists under the direction of John C. Flanagan studied the records of successes and failures in order to analyze the causes for failure. Flanagan then devised a battery of tests to screen applicants for admission to this training program. The combined test results were used to divide candidates into nine groups. The survival rates for each group are shown in Figure 1,[2] which indicates that low scores on the test battery predict a greater than 50% chance of failure while high scores predict a very good bet for success in training. Although these tests were administered to all aviation cadet applicants, they were initially not used in the selection process because the efficacy of such a screening battery was doubted by many. However, once the Air Force used the screening battery, its success was greater than expected and contributed substantially to the ability of the Air Force to put enough trained pilots into combat.

These data are unusual and impressive. Although previously the prediction of success in training had been well demonstrated, tests had not been used in the domain of flight training and had rarely been used with such clear evidence of accurate prediction involving large numbers. Note, however, that what was predicted was survival through a rigorous flight training program, not success in a leadership position. Although the two domains are quite different, the method of prediction from a formula is the same.

Success in training—the criterion—is first determined by allowing all

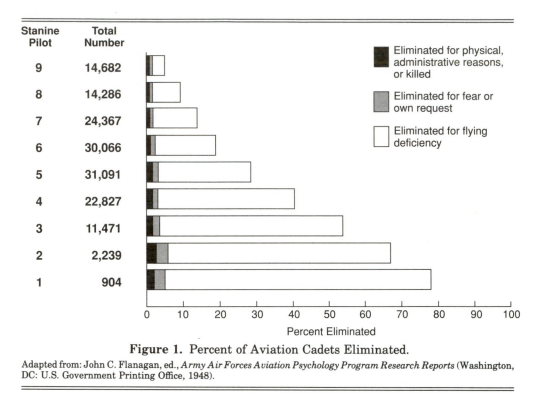

Figure 1. Percent of Aviation Cadets Eliminated.

Adapted from: John C. Flanagan, ed., *Army Air Forces Aviation Psychology Program Research Reports* (Washington, DC: U.S. Government Printing Office, 1948).

candidates to try to complete the course. Their success is predicted based on a single score derived from a combination of scores on different predictors—tests and questionnaires that quantify data about aptitudes, knowledge, preferences, personality, and prior experiences. Predictor scores for each candidate are weighted and combined. The degree of relationship between this combined score and the criterion is expressed as a correlation coefficient. The correlation between the combined predictor scores and the criterion in the Aviation Cadet study was +.70. This is a high correlation, as is clearly indicated by the data presented in Figure 1.[3]

Predicting Promotion and Executive Success

The first step in a systematic study to predict leadership effectiveness is the same as the first step in the Aviation Cadet study: to examine the causes of success and failure among leaders and determine if it is possible to develop measures for a set of predictors. In the Aviation Cadet study, this was relatively easy, for crashes, near-crashes, and failure to follow a prescribed course meant failure. This is more difficult in a study of leadership, for we must first agree on measures that define leadership success and failure. The first step in this process is to review any earlier studies that might suggest ways to begin. The following three classic studies in business, aimed to predict promotions high into the organization, illustrate the method and provide the starting point that enables us later to change the criterion to leadership potential.

The Exxon Study

Can we predict with good success which newly employed managers will end up in the top ranks of an organization? C. Paul Sparks led a team of psychologists

Rank on Test

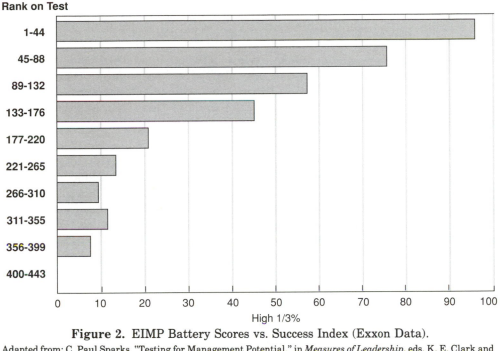

High 1/3%

Figure 2. EIMP Battery Scores vs. Success Index (Exxon Data).

Adapted from: C. Paul Sparks, "Testing for Management Potential," in *Measures of Leadership*, eds. K. E. Clark and M. B. Clark (West Orange, NJ: Leadership Library of America, 1990) 106.

in a study at what is now the Exxon Corporation to develop a system that would test for executive-level potential.[4] Sparks administered tests and collected data on a sample of 443 managers and then followed their records through twenty-five years with the company. His research team divided the group into the top third, the middle third and the bottom third based on their success as defined by top company executives.

Following are the tests included in the battery initially administered to the 443 managers:

1. *Miller Analogies Test*, a very difficult measure of verbal reasoning.

2. *RBH Non-Verbal Reasoning Test*, a measure of abstract reasoning.

3. *Guilford-Zimmerman Temperament Survey*, a 300-item standardized measure of ten personality or temperament dimensions considered "experimental" for item-analysis purposes at that time.

4. *Individual Background Survey*, a multiple-choice inventory of life experiences constructed specifically for the project.

5. *Management Judgment Test*, a set of verbally described situations that called for a choice of action or a decision from among several alternatives.

6. *Self-Performance Report*, a rating form to be completed by the job incumbent.

7. *Survey of Management Attitudes*, a set of questions on occupational, social, and educational attitudes developed specifically for the project.

8. *Picture Technique*, a set of eight pictures flashed on a screen for ten seconds and removed. Examinees then wrote a brief narrative describing what was going on in each picture that was scored to reflect motives deemed important in the writer's life.

9. *Personal History Record*, a record of the number and type of assignments accumulated throughout the examinee's career. The record was reviewed with the incumbent and each assignment was classified as line/staff, overseas/domestic, functional/general, and so forth.

10. *Interview*, a one-on-one interview between incumbent and researcher focused on career planning before employment with the company, critical periods for advancement, identification of the most important achievement, and designation of the person who contributed the most to incumbent's advancement. Interview data were recorded on two checklists.

Figure 2 portrays the findings. Of those who twenty-five years earlier had scored among the top 10% of the 443 managers on the Exxon battery of predictors, 42 (95%) of the 44 achieved status in the top third of the group. None of the 44 in the original bottom 10% appeared in the top third. Note that this gradation of achievement from bottom to top of the test score range is strikingly similar to Flanagan's data on aviation cadets. The relationships in the two studies are equally high, with correlations of .70 between the predictor test and the achievement to be predicted, although the Exxon study predicted promotion, not survival in flight training.

The Sears Study

V. Jon Bentz conducted a study at Sears that, like Sparks's Exxon study, aimed for early identification of individuals who might be developed as senior

---

Table 1. Components of Success at Sears

Mental Alertness is associated with effectiveness in a wide range of studies. The *Quantitative Problem Solving Score* (logical, rational thinking ability) is the best and most frequent predictor. Mental ability appears to be very important for early success, less so as people progress onward. Even so, long-term studies show that *Problem Solving* (as measured 20 years ago) predicts current behavior.

Sociability (ease in social relations) is so frequently associated with such a wide range of criteria that we can say it is prerequisite to executive effectiveness. With its presence, other things become possible.

Social Leadership (the natural tendency to move into a leadership role when part of a group) is fundamental to success at Sears.

Political Values (the personal importance of being important—a status orientation) plays a major role in the leadership behavior of effective Sears executives.

Persuasive Interests (the desire to sell and engage in promotional activities) is a strong and consistent predictor of executive effectiveness. Sears is a merchandising organization and selling is central to its function. In Sears an executive must sell whether the persuasion be associated with ideas, programs, or merchandise.

Self-Confidence (self-assurance and confidence in the initiation of action) is consistently associated with success. The effective executive harbors few self-doubts. This score "colors" and affects much executive behavior such as assurance in social relations or assurance in decision making. Like Sociability, Self-Confidence may well be prerequisite to executive effectiveness.

When Sociability, Social Leadership, Self-Confidence, Political Values, and Persuasive Interests are combined we interpret the combination as the *Competitive Personality*, capable of exerting competitive social leadership.[6]

---

officers in the company. His work, which also occupied most of his working years, enabled him to gather long-term data on the development, effectiveness, and success of his sample of potential executives. Bentz discovered not only that individual success was predictable, but also identified the components of success for Sears as an organization. From information on many aspects of performance, Bentz sorted the criterion into the interrelated factors that defined success, an analysis that yielded the results displayed in Table 1.[5]

Recognizing that all executives do not perform equally well in all of their tasks, variability within each individual was the target of Bentz's analysis. His battery of tests most successfully predicted effective leadership, these items being mainly judgments of informed observers, and least successfully predicted the quality of actions displayed by each subject in his study. Consistent predictors of effectiveness were found.

The AT&T Study

In the Management Progress Study,[7] Ann Howard and Douglas Bray present research findings of a longitudinal study sponsored by AT&T that followed the careers of managers who began work in six telephone companies in the middle 1950s. The 422 white male participants were all considered sufficiently promising to reach levels of middle manager or higher. College graduates made up 65% of the 422; the remainder were not college graduates when hired.

Data on each participant were collected in an initial three-day assessment program during which a variety of tests, exercises, and observations were administered and recorded. Assessments were repeated after eight years and after twenty years. After each assessment session, a panel composed of assessment specialists and senior managers in the firm made judgments about the potential for promotion of each participant. In addition, interviews with participants and their superiors were conducted in intervening years.

Predictions of managerial success at AT&T involved the development of the following seven dimension factors: Administrative Skills, Interpersonal Skills, Intellectual Ability, Advancement Motivation, Work Involvement, Stability of Performance, and Independence.

The data presented by Howard and Bray reveal the development and change in persons aspiring to leadership positions as a result of experience and maturity. Their work also tests the usefulness of assessment methods to identify characteristics that would earmark an individual for promotion or increased responsibility. Figure 3 summarizes the central finding of their work: College men who were rated as good bets by their assessors—"Will Be Promoted"—outnumber those not so predicted by two-to-one in being promoted to fourth level or higher in the company; the odds for noncollege men being promoted to third level or higher were nearly three-to-one when they were rated "Will Be Promoted." As the data show, most promotions at AT&T went to college men.

The initial selection of promising managers was obviously done well: 77% of the college men selected for participation achieved level-three or higher positions during their careers. Being a college graduate at entry was also a great advantage, as only 32% of noncollege men reached the level-three status or higher.

The results are significant, for they reflect the value of assessment processes not only for predicting the success of individuals but also for auditing the personnel practices of an organization. At AT&T, tasks required cognitive

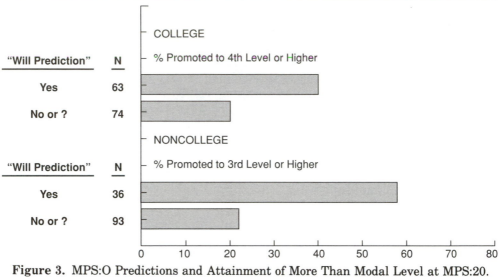

Figure 3. MPS:O Predictions and Attainment of More Than Modal Level at MPS:20.

Adapted from: Ann Howard and Douglas W. Bray, "Predictions of Managerial Success Over Long Periods of Time: Lessons From the Management Progress Study," in *Measures of Leadership*, eds. K. E. Clark and M. B. Clark (West Orange, NJ: Leadership Library of America, 1990) 116. Reprinted by permission of the authors.

capabilities as well as verbal and numerical competence. Do career paths of the college versus the noncollege men in the study reflect this need, or does the perception of the need for these competencies lead to a bias against noncollege candidates? Would present-day business needs of AT&T lead to similar actions on promotion, or have times changed? Can we generalize these results to organizations with different purposes and different distributions of talent among their members?

Qualities of Corporate Leaders

The studies at Exxon, Sears, and AT&T provide ample evidence of the predictability of potential for promotion. In all three studies, the investigators started with ideas about behaviors and qualities required for advancement. They then checked these ideas with individuals well informed about the processes for promotion within their company and reviewed studies in the published literature. They hunted for or developed methods to measure variables used to identify young candidates for promotion, which included:

1. *Intellectual Ability*. Exxon used the Miller Analogies Test and the RBH Non-Verbal Reasoning Test. Sears used the American Council on Education Psychological Examination with linguistic and quantitative scores. AT&T used a college-level scholastic aptitude test.

2. *Personality*. Exxon used a published personality test and a projective test using pictures to which the candidate attached a story. Sears used a published personality test, the Allport-Vernon-Lindzey Scale of Values, and the Kuder Preference Inventory, a measure of vocational interests. AT&T used several personality tests and a picture projective test.

3. *Personal History*. Exxon collected information on background and asked for a self-performance report and a personal history record. Sears collected data

on performance in various assignments as part of an overall qualifications questionnaire. AT&T held annual interviews with participants and interviews every three years with bosses and also administered biographical questionnaires.

Each prediction study adapted its procedures to the nature of the organization and the nature of the tasks to be performed. Each also took into account the climate of the organization, especially with regard to providing information and processes that would match the expectations of those who would be making decisions about individuals. In other words, the development of the prediction process took into account the nature of the criterion to be predicted. What is most unusual is that neither Exxon nor AT&T used any of the predictor measures in making decisions about advancement, thus permitting an uncontaminated estimate of the merit of adopting the prediction system.

Promotion cannot be taken as a good measure of leadership. For one thing, promotions are made by a candidate's superiors who, as a group, know less than others in the organization about the leadership qualities of their subordinates. (As we will show later, they are also poor judges of their own leadership abilities.) Nor does promotion guarantee the ability to lead a campaign for change, which often results in failure and being dubbed a "troublemaker."

Theoretically, promotion comes to those who do a good job and show the capability to handle a more complex assignment. Mental abilities are required, for large amounts of information must be stored, processed, and used for decision making. Components of the job task enlarge as responsibilities increase. The nature of the firm dictates which personality characteristics enhance promotability. At Sears, people talked about the competitive personality, described as sociable, a social leader, persuasive, self-confident, and politically sensible. At Exxon, management attitudes were important. At AT&T, motivation for advancement in management proved critical. In all three companies, attention was directed to evidence that candidates had learned a lot not just about their own assignment, but about the business as a whole.

Measuring and Studying Leadership

The utilization of psychological methods such as those described in the preceding studies has demonstrated real and important differences among people, and the findings are applicable in many practical settings. In order to select more able students, more productive workers, and more effective supervisors and managers, studies have been conducted in a wide range of settings. The need to identify the unusual person—the gifted, the creative, the charismatic, the deviant, the depressed, and the disturbed—has led to better methods for understanding and responding to needs of individuals. Techniques that identify leaders have developed more slowly; the stumbling block has been developing a criterion for leadership that is generally acceptable.

Predictor measures abound, for there is no absence of ideas, concepts, theories, hypotheses, principles, and reported truths about leadership and how it works in manifold settings. Because at first leadership and personality were assumed to be closely related, many organizations relied on personality tests for selection. However, later studies have suggested better measures to use, none of which is simple. Even the most basic study involves the completion of numerous technical steps (see Table 2).

Table 2. Steps in a Prediction Study of Leadership

Step 1. Review the published literature on leadership to identify the important components of leadership behavior. Because this search will produce an enormous list of studies, pick only those where evidence exists that the components are critical to producing excellence in performance of a group, team, or organization. Add in items from personal experience if any essential ingredients seem to be missing.

Step 2. Translate the items obtained into a common form—declarative sentences, questions, short descriptive phrases, adjectives, adverbs—phrased for answer by the individual under study and by close associates, subordinates or followers, or superiors.

Step 3. Pretest your list with judgments about relevance and importance from knowledgeable people. Eliminate or rephrase items as appropriate.

Step 4. Set up response categories for items so that the respondent can answer an item about a given person or situation as "Very Well," "Rather Well," and "Not at All." A five-step scale may be used: "Strongly Agree," "Agree," "Undecided," "Disagree," and "Strongly Disagree."

Step 5. Ask willing associates to use your infant questionnaire to describe a person who should rate high on leadership abilities and a person who should rate low on leadership abilities. Ask them if they were able to give a full description using your items.

Step 6. Find the items that are marked quite differently for those rated high and low on leadership.

Step 7. Complete the technical steps that check the psychometric qualities of your instrument to make sure it measures what it is supposed to measure (validity) and provides consistent and stable scores (reliability).[8]

Step 8. Find several large organizations with an interest in improving leadership to pay for collection of data with your questionnaire. These organizations must be willing to provide accurate information on the achievements of those who complete your questionnaire.

Step 9. Identify a population of people in these organizations who are expected to exercise leadership roles. Either use all of them in your study or a random sample drawn from the group. Obtain from the sponsoring organizations information about their current level of performance in leadership roles.

Step 10. Ask all participants in the study to complete your questionnaire and to provide information on age, gender, education, work experience, and leadership experiences.

Step 11. Determine by current best methods which responses relate to performance data. You may want to follow the career of each person for a decade or more in order to determine how each of your subjects prospered and showed effectiveness in leadership.

Step 12. Combine the discriminating items into groups to achieve internal consistency by using psychometric methods to produce scales whose items belong together.[9]

Step 13. Observe differences in scale scores among those who perform well as leaders and those who perform poorly.

Step 14. Test the magnitude of the difference statistically and form conclusions about the meaning of your findings.

Step 15. Write a complete report detailing what you have done, how your findings relate to those of others, and how your results may prove useful.

Step 16. Arrange for wide dissemination of your report.

The work of Sashkin and Burke, as well as the work of Wilson, O'Hare, and Shipper, illustrates this type of study. Marshall Sashkin, senior associate, Educational Networks Division of the United States Department of Education, collaborated with W. Warren Burke, professor of Psychology and Education at the Teachers College, Columbia University, on the development of the Leader Behavior Questionnaire (LBQ).[10] The LBQ, which has fifty items and ten scales, had emerged from several earlier versions that included items that discriminated between leaders and managers (see Table 3).

Table 3. Scales of the Leader Behavior Questionnaire[11]

Scale One: Focused Leadership
"I pay attention to what others say when we are talking."
"I have a clear set of priorities."

Scale Two: Communication Leadership
"I make points in strikingly clear and even unusual ways."
"I sometimes don't notice how others feel." (negative)

Scale Three: Trust Leadership
"I am extremely dependable."
"I often find it desirable to change or alter my position." (negative)

Scale Four: Respectful Leadership
"I recognize others' strengths and contributions."
"I show that I really care about other people."

Scale Five: Risk Leadership
"I worry a lot about the possibility of failing." (negative)
"I find ways to get everyone fully committed to new ideas and projects."

Scale Six: Bottom-Line Leadership
"I can see clear effects resulting from my action."
"I have found that no one person can make very much of a difference in how this organization operates."

Scale Seven: Empowered Leadership
"I think that the real value of power is in being able to accomplish things that benefit both the organization and its members."
"I believe that some of the most significant aspects of my position are the little 'perks' that demonstrate my importance to the organization and its members." (negative)

Scale Eight: Long-Term Leadership
"I focus on clear short-term goals rather than being concerned with longer-range aims." (negative)
"I think about how the plans and programs I've developed in my own unit might be expanded to help the entire organization."

Scale Nine: Organizational Leadership
"I have not generally been able to help the organization attain its goals." (negative)
"I try to express and support a set of basic values about how people should work together in this organization to solve common problems and reach shared goals."

Scale Ten: Cultural Leadership
"I strive to take actions to reach goals rather than contributing to keeping things the way they are."
"I help others understand that there is often little we can do to control important factors in the environment." (negative)

The usefulness of the LBQ was demonstrated by K. D. Major, who identified thirty high-performing high schools and thirty low-performing high schools in

Southern California.[12] To assess performance, schools were classified using a set of quantitative criteria, including student achievement scores, after equating the high performance and low performance sets of schools on such factors as minority student population and socioeconomic status. Major administered the LBQ to the principals of the 60 schools and found a strong and significant difference, with principals of the high-performing schools scoring significantly higher than principals of the low-performing schools. The schools whose principals described themselves as behaving like a leader are the same schools where assessment indicated that students learn more and dropouts are fewer.

Major's study of high school principals, which demonstrates a close relationship between LBQ questions and school outcomes, illustrates an important step along the way to understanding and promoting higher quality leadership. The behavior of high school principals does makes a difference in their effectiveness, and low-performing schools might improve by investing in well-planned training programs to develop crucial qualities in their principals. However, a lingering question remains: Do people such as school principals who begin acting like leaders instead of managers have a correct image of their own behavior? The preceding study suggests they do, but a great deal of contrary evidence suggests that many people in positions of authority do not view their own behavior in the same light as it is viewed by others.

Answers to this question have been sought in many different settings. The behaviors of subordinates have been rated by superiors, the behaviors of superiors have been rated by subordinates, and everyone has rated their own behaviors. The descriptions differ, sometimes greatly. Further, ratings by others are more predictive of good performance than are one's own ratings, and the ratings of superiors by subordinates are the best predictors of good performance as leaders. The view of one's own behavior may be quite different from the view of others, a principle demonstrated many times in succeeding chapters.

Clark L. Wilson, Donal O'Hare, and Frank Shipper conducted a study in the Veterans Administration Center in Phoenix, Arizona.[13] To evaluate productivity, the VA used a measure of Weighted Equivalent Work Units (WEWUs), each a standard number of personnel hours it should take to perform a specific task or work unit. Using repeated measures over time, standards were established to evaluate future performance.

As part of the study, a Survey of Administrative Practices was completed by the direct reports (subordinates) of sixty-four managers for whom WEWUs were calculated. Responses of subordinates to this scale accounted for a significant portion of the variance among managers' performances, whereas neither supervisor ratings nor self-ratings accounted for any significant variance. Key to the work of Wilson, O'Hare, and Shipper was the development of measuring instruments that made possible the collection of rating data from one's subordinates. These ratings proved to be the most important measures of manager behavior and related more closely than any other measures to manager effectiveness. Some of these managers went on to complete a training program aimed at increasing their effectiveness; the productivity of the groups reporting to these managers increased almost 8%, an increase that still persisted a year after the end of training.

The use of item responses in which others describe the behaviors of leaders they know is a component of the Ohio State University Studies. This technique can differentiate behaviors of those leaders who produce desired effects from those who do not. The principle is simple: *You* may not know whether or not you might be a great leader, but those who report to you, are members of your team, or work to elect you know if you are and will be a good or great leader.

In the preceding studies, research teams developed methods and applied them in real-life organizational settings. They demonstrated that before actually being entrusted with leadership responsibility, good performers can be distinguished from poor performers. Because innumerable decisions must be made about selection of managers, CEOs, or presidents, and about promotions from one level to the next, this is good news indeed.

Measuring the Magnitude of Effects

Knowing which behaviors have the optimal effects is important to anyone who wants to change practices in order to benefit the organization. Using a predictor battery for this purpose requires a high degree of relationship to the criterion. Correlation coefficients are linear measures of the relationship between two variables. They permit comparison of the merits of various tests for selecting leaders by telling us the relative strength of the relationship between two variables. For those who must decide upon selection procedures in hiring or promotion, the highest possible correlations are desired. Sometimes correlations between predictors and the criterion that are high enough to make real differences often seem small. But these can be important, especially when large numbers of observations are being summarized. One must take care not to dismiss a good procedure without careful examination.

Correlations of .30, or gains of .44 standard deviations, are large enough to make substantial differences in a real life setting. Correlations of .70 have great value: Flanagan's ability to predict who would not complete the pilot training course is indicated in his correlation of .70. The Exxon data, equally convincing, can be summarized as a correlation of .70. In Clark Wilson's data, an 8% gain in work output (even a year after training), was enough to provide an annual saving of $2,300,000 in one VA center, even though the relationship, if expressed by a correlation coefficient, would have been rather low. Many studies of effects of improvement in selection or development of leaders show correlations of .30 to .45 or group differences of a third of a standard deviation. Findings of this sort must not be overlooked.

Are Low Correlations Meaningless?

How high must a correlation coefficient be in order to be useful? As a way of understanding the size of effects associated with correlations of various sizes, let us compare the correlations found in our earlier studies with correlations observed in other fields. Professor Robert Rosenthal of Harvard University recently published data drawn from biological and medical fields to illustrate how much smaller relationships among variables can be interpreted as astounding. Table 4[14] presents results from a recent physicians' study of the effects of aspirin in preventing heart attacks. The physicians running the study found the results so striking and the implications so important that they called off the study. Why? Because they felt it would be unethical to withhold aspirin from the placebo group when the evidence of the benefit of aspirin was so apparent. Look at the data that led them to that conclusion, as presented in Table 4. Expressed in terms of correlation coefficients, the same measure of relationship used in this chapter, the relationship between taking aspirin and the occurrence of heart attacks is .03.

Table 4. Effects of Aspirin on Heart Attacks (r = .03)

Measure	Heart Attacks	No Heart Attack	Total
Raw Count			
Aspirin	104	10,933	11,037
Placebo	189	10,845	11,034
Total	293	21,778	22,071
Percentage			
Aspirin	0.94%	99.06%	100
Placebo	1.71	98.29	100
Total	1.33	98.67	100

Another striking example of the significance of a low correlation coefficient is presented in Table 5. There are more alcohol problems among Vietnam veterans in the United States than in the general population. A look at the numbers is pretty convincing. Yet had the relationship been presented as a correlation, r = .07, most would be unimpressed.

Table 5. Vietnam Service and Alcohol Problems (r = .07)

Measure	Alcohol Problem	No Alcohol Problem	Total
Vietnam Veteran	53.5%	46.5%	100%
Non-Vietnam Veteran	46.5	53.5	100%
Total	100%	100%	

When a formula is available, it is easier to portray to the user the strength of the relation between a set of predictors and the criterion. But it is not easy to persuade users to substitute for their own judgments the results of a statistical formula, even when the mass of evidence shows that the formula would be better. For example: The Medical School Aptitude Test plus undergraduate college grades are good predictors of success in medical school. However, admissions committees of medical schools persist in adding their own judgment; this produces a *decrease* in the quality of the entering class. How can this happen? One observed behavior is that they may favor less-qualified students who have repeated organic chemistry for a better grade or have taken extra courses in biology. The admissions committees credit these students with extra motivation and, for some reason, believe they will be more successful doctors. In truth, an excess of these students leave medical school before completing the degree.

Every point at which a search for a qualified candidate occurs requires an adequate pool from which to select. The larger the pool, the better the prospects. Successful businesses recognize this and translate the principle into carefully planned recruiting procedures. Good promotion procedures are also essential in order to increase the number of qualified candidates at each succeeding level.

However, it is essential to recognize that prior findings may not apply in every setting; it is necessary to test for generalizability. We cannot always trust that what worked yesterday will apply today. World conditions are changing at an increasing pace. The need will become greater for leaders flexible enough to adapt. This may very well influence the formulas that will work best in the future.

CHAPTER SIX

Leadership and Organizational Outcomes

Results of objective studies demonstrate that certain leader behaviors have a direct effect on organizational success. They provide information that helps an organization select leaders and establish training programs so as to improve leader behaviors and eliminate poor management practices. The simplest design to verify the impact of excellent leadership is to compare the performance of similar groups and to obtain a measure of the effectiveness of the leader of each group. We should find that excellent leaders have high-performing groups, and mediocre leaders have low-performing groups.

Performance is hard to measure in some groups. But measures of favorable outcomes for a group are always possible. Favorable outcomes for some organizations—churches, service organizations, neighborhood associations, and national interest groups—might be increased membership or success in achieving stated objectives. Business organizations prize increased market share, increased profits, or increased worth of the firm. Military organizations seek success in battle, increased combat readiness, increased troop reenlistments, or higher scores on training exercises. Symphony orchestras measure success by musicians' judgments of musical quality, critical reviews of their concerts, increased recording opportunities, or improved attendance at concerts. Political figures cite re-election to office, the appearance of their names on important legislative acts, or increased contributions to their campaigns as indicators of successful outcomes. In any case, outcome measures relate directly to fundamental organizational objectives.

Strategies for Selecting Good Leaders

Robert Hart is president of Eagle Stores, a retail grocery chain with thirty stores. Some of the stores do very well, some barely break even, and three are in serious trouble. Hart has tried changing managers; he has relocated managers of stores that were prospering to poorer performing stores and some managers of failing stores to other assignments. He finds that new managers make a difference but that some of his better stores do less well when the old manager leaves. Can studies in leadership help him?

Hart has adopted a policy for action based on incomplete knowledge of the causes of good and poor store performance. True, he learned something—that managers make a difference, that good managers are important, and that managers of stores with poor performance do not do well when reassigned. But he has not learned enough about the qualities of each manager; he has not identified the strengths and weaknesses in each and has not improved selection and training methods within his organization.

Robert Hart could improve the performance of his group by relocating or dismissing all managers whose work is below average and hiring replacements in just the way he hired the current group of managers. Half of the new group would be expected to perform above average, and half below. The dismissed managers were all below average, so now three-fourths of the managers would be above the old average. Why doesn't he do that? Probably because such actions introduce turmoil and add to training costs. And the procedure provides no insight into what produces the differences in store performance. If the predictors were better, 70 to 80% of the new hires—not 50%—would perform above the old average.[1]

Hart is interested in finding leaders who will work with a group of employees to help each of them develop and become wholly committed to the organization. How should he proceed? He notes the advantage of increasing the number of applicants and decides to set up training programs for potential managers in each store. Giving special assignments to promising candidates would enable the store manager to collect data on some of the leadership variables already described. When an opening occurs, candidates from all stores are welcome to compete. As choices are made, they are tested against later performance in order to improve the prediction formula.

Will such a system work? We report a real test (Hart was fictional). Shipper and Wilson[2] studied a large southwestern hospital administered by a government agency. They found that 61% of managers did not exhibit appropriate managerial behaviors. They estimated that the average competent manager outproduced the incompetent manager by 24%. The U.S. as a whole, they figured, incurred a cost of incompetence in management in the year 1990 of $676 billion.

Shipper and Wilson identified behaviors that worked and behaviors that were not helpful, providing guidance both for methods of improving the selection of persons for managerial positions and ways of training those selected to make them more effective. They also identified behaviors that are critical even though they do not show effects on profitability, variables such as worker loyalty, motivation and satisfaction, and subordinate attitudes toward superiors. These variables are not trivial; they enhance unit performance. A business that emphasizes only profits will lose customers if it tries to squeeze the last nickel out of every sale. It may also lose customers if employees become more and more disaffected.

Good performance by leaders in organizations that are not-for-profit can be shown to have many important consequences. Unresolved conflicts within an organization can cause turbulence and disorder even when they have no apparent relation to profits or survivability of the organization. Members of churches often split on the nature of beliefs and practices or may overlook the needs of parishioners. Political leaders who concern themselves primarily with actions to assure their re-election must heed not only the furious outcries of the citizenry, but also the long-term effects of their actions on their own and larger constituencies.

A good leadership study demonstrates that different modes of leadership produce different results. Each study adds evidence about how such effects are produced. The criterion variable must be important and tied to real effects. Studies of leadership that do not relate to important criteria are not valuable. As studies progress and build on former findings, they become more complex, using methods of analysis that tease out otherwise hidden relationships.

Focusing on organizational outcomes reduces the need to have a definition of leadership that distinguishes it from all other forms of influence or control. The behaviors that relate to successful outcomes can be noted and taught to others. Some of these may be related to the quality of executive decisions, some to managerial and leadership behaviors, and some to particular aspects of the organizational climate or the nature of members. Research studies will help us decide which influences are the most significant; we can then seek to increase these influences.

Some of the greatest insights into the impact of a particular form of leadership have been derived from the individual perceptions of peers, followers, or subordinates or from study of one particularly effective person or one especially successful leader of an organization. Frequently the more *qualitative* studies provide ideas from which major changes in practice evolve that are adopted in other settings. The more *quantitative* studies test the effectiveness of such practices whenever they are adapted to a wide variety of settings.

Variability in Performance

It is clear that some workers get more done than others, some managers have teams that get more done, and leaders vary in the ways in which they inspire, motivate, and gain the trust of followers. Variability in organizational outcomes of all sorts is also widely recognized. We continue to study leadership because it varies greatly; we try to find ways to improve group performance because it also varies enormously. We need to know how the two phenomena relate to each other. This requires use of standard methods for statistical studies. There is no mystery here—only the need to become familiar with several terms.

In quantitative studies the measure of organizational performance is called the *criterion*; its *variance* is a measure of the variability in the criterion.[3] When the variance in performance is high, greater attention to selection and training procedures in order to eliminate low performance will produce gratifying results. A good program will aim both to increase *average* performance and to reduce the variance in performance.

How much variance in performance is to be expected? In relatively simple tasks—a clerk at a supermarket checkout counter, for example—the best worker accomplishes more than twice what is done by the poorest worker. Persons with more complex tasks—financial analysts, computer specialists, and middle-level managers—vary even more; best workers produce three to five times the output of the poorest workers. The nature of the task affects the variance in worker performance: The more complex the task, the higher the variance. The performance of executives and leaders is harder to quantify for their responsibilities are ill-defined, and sometimes the results of their efforts are not revealed immediately.

Even so, if we could score CEOs on their performance and could display a distribution of their performance scores, we would discover that the impact on organizational performance accounted for by differences in CEO performance is much greater than what is found in the performance of grocery clerks or computer specialists. Only a few CEOs are spectacular performers, able to respond in foresightful ways to major changes in circumstances and able to reorient their organizations as those circumstances change. When poor leadership prevails, plants may close, workers may lose jobs, and the costs may be immeasurable. Newspapers and magazines are full of accounts of those who fail, who do not move quickly enough, or who ignore competing forces or are forced out of their positions. When such wide differences in performance outcomes are observed, actions to improve performance are mandated, especially when the methods and programs for identification and development of leadership qualities are available.

How do we collect evidence that leaders make a difference? Generally, it is necessary for an organization—a business firm, an educational institution, a community organization or a public agency—to note that some of its units perform better than others and then to examine the behaviors of the leader for each unit. When these two variables—unit achievement and leader behaviors— prove to be related, training programs or replacement programs might be instituted. Improved leadership then would be expected to lead to higher levels of performance.

Measures of performance that management considers important are agreed upon (the criterion). They might include measures of quality or quantity of production, profitability of a unit, specific performance measures that are averaged for each unit, or measures of member attitudes and satisfaction. The quality of leadership for each unit (the predictor) can be estimated quite well by asking followers to describe the behaviors of their leader, as in "My superior helps me understand why my work is important," "I have lots of support to help me do my job well," or "My superior listens to my ideas." A questionnaire is used; respondents give a rating, usually "1" to "5," to indicate how often such behavior is displayed. Items are grouped into scales that constitute the predictor measures.

The resulting sets of data are analyzed to discover relationships between the subordinates' descriptions of how the leader acts and the criterion score—the measure of organizational outcome. The degree of relationship is reported either as (a) a difference in average criterion scores for groups of units with supervisors who are highly rated by subordinates and average criterion scores for groups of units with supervisors rated low on leadership by subordinates (exemplified by the teams whose captains were rated high on leadership winning three times as many games as those whose captains were rated low on leadership) or (b) a *correlation coefficient*, which measures the degree of relationship between the criterion measure and the subordinate ratings on leadership (exemplified by team captains' scores on the Leadership Behavior Survey correlating +.45 with the team's number of games won).

Correlation coefficients may range in value from −1.0 (a perfect inverse relationship) to +1.0 (a perfect positive relationship). The size of the correlation coefficient reflects the degree of relationship: When a correlation of at least .30 is observed, the relationship is strong enough to merit action in an applied setting; when it is considerably larger, action is mandated.[4] Correlations in the low .30s we shall call "modest." When they get into the .40s and .50s we shall call them "substantial," and when they exceed .60 we shall call them "high."

Effects of Leader Behaviors on Organizational Outcomes

Hundreds of studies of the relationship between leader behaviors and unit or organizational outcomes have been completed and published. Following is a summary of some of them.

Yukl, Wall, and Lepsinger reported on 262 elementary school teachers who described the leadership qualities of their twenty-four principals using the Yukl Managerial Practices Questionnaire (MPQ).[5] When teachers rated their principals high on *Problem Solving, Clarifying, Monitoring, Motivating*, and *Networking/Interfacing*, the performance of students on standard tests and the school's reputation was significantly higher. This study demonstrates that the principal's leadership behavior is important to the learning process in the school.

One hundred fifty-one employees in twenty-six beauty salons completed the Yukl MPQ on their managers. The variables *Clarifying* and *Motivating* correlated substantially with average monthly profit margin during the year following administration of the questionnaire. Clarifying refers to the manager outlining the duties for each persons, including how tasks are assigned or shared, and defining what is outside each person's responsibility. Motivating refers to those actions that induce the subordinate to exert extra effort and to believe in the importance of the task. This study finds that how the manager relates to the staff in a single salon has an effect on that shop's success in attaining its prime goal—profits—which presumably reflects customer satisfaction.

Two hundred twenty-three insurance salespersons in retail department stores described their twenty-six managers using the Yukl MPQ.[6] Three scales, *Problem Solving*, *Recognizing*, and *Rewarding* correlated substantially with a performance measure of managers based on sales and profits.

Misumi and his associates[7] in Japan estimated leadership qualities using measures of *Performance* (P) and *Maintenance* (M). Scores on these predictor measures correlated substantially with performance measures for units within a variety of organizations including coal mines, shipbuilding yards, banks, local government offices, and bus companies. These findings support the two dimensions of leadership—*Consideration* and *Initiating Structure*—that emerged from the Ohio State University Studies. They support the view that the leader must attend not only to the requirements for getting the tasks done but also to the needs, concerns, and conflicts within the group assigned the tasks.

Bond and Hwang[8] reviewed studies undertaken in Taiwan. Studies in factories, local government offices, and schools uniformly found modest to substantial correlations between behaviors classified as *Consideration* and performance and between *Initiating Structure* and performance.

Yammarino and Bass[9] used subordinate ratings of the performance of Navy officers as a criterion and scores on the Multifactor Officer Questionnaire (completed by subordinates) to identify transformational leadership (the predictor). Correlations between scores on transformational leadership and performance varied from modest to very high among the groups studied. Teams led by officers rated high as leaders in the Naval Academy performed better five years later in fleet performance than did teams led by officers who were rated low on leadership in the Naval Academy.

Javidan[10] surveyed managers at middle and upper levels in a telecommunications company, asking them to describe by their questionnaire responses the behaviors of their immediate superior and to rate that superior on effectiveness. Javidan found very high relationships between certain descriptors and rated effectiveness. His results suggest that superiors who want to be considered effective must make sure that subordinates know what is expected of them and have a sense of direction. The leader must communicate a vision of what the organization stands for and where it is headed. Each person's role should be explained, and issues should be clarified in open discussion. Subordinates must be helped to develop a sense of self-worth and self-confidence and should be encouraged to be independent and self-reliant.

Posner and Kouzes[11] established a performance criterion based on a questionnaire that asked subordinates about the extent to which the manager meets job-related needs of subordinates, builds a committed work force, and gains influence with upper management. Scores on their Leadership Practices Questionnaire, which asks questions about the behaviors of the superior, were used as predictors. The correlation among the criterion measure of performance and the ratings of leadership behavior was very high. The behavior subordinates want to see in their leaders is summarized in these aspects of leadership behaviors:

1) Challenging the process; 2) Inspiring a shared vision; 3) Enabling others to act; 4) Modeling the way; and 5) Encouraging the heart.[12]

Avolio and Howell[13] studied seventy-six senior executives and their 237 immediate subordinates employed in a large Canadian financial institution. They found that leader ratings on transformational leadership were highly related to follower satisfaction and modestly related to unit performance. When leaders and followers were alike on Rotter's Locus of Control scale, satisfaction and performance among followers was significantly higher.[14]

Effects of Leader Behaviors on Subordinate Satisfaction

Tallarigo and Rosebush collected subordinates' descriptions of their supervisor at the Air Force Academy using a Leadership Development Questionnaire. They concluded that leader behaviors have a direct and strong impact on satisfaction with supervision. The behaviors identified by the subordinates that were closely related to satisfaction with supervision are shown in Table 1.

Table 1. Items Best Predicting Satisfaction with Supervision

Acts in a very encouraging manner to me.
Seems to have a solid plan to accomplish tasks.
Tells me he/she is willing to help me.
Appears friendly and approachable.
Holds effective meetings.
I am kept up-to-date on important events and situations.
Leads by providing an example of what is required.[15]

Effects of Psychological Interventions

Guzzo, Jette, and Katzell[16] examined many studies pertaining to the effects of psychologically based interventions on the performance of an organization. They combined these findings in order to measure the strengths of effects, using such "hard" measures as productivity, absenteeism, and grievances with the methods of meta-analysis.[17] Interventions such as team building showed strong effects on productivity but not on withdrawal or disruption (for example, absenteeism or grievances).

Rodgers and Hunter[18] reviewed seventy studies to obtain a better understanding of the value of programs of Management By Objectives (MBO). The key factors in an MBO program are goal setting, participation in decision making, and objective feedback to managers. Goal setting is critical, since it makes clear to the manager what the organizational objectives are and what the role of the manager is in achieving these objectives. Feedback provides information about whether the goals still remain important and, in the case of unmet objectives, indicates that new work methods might be tried to improve effectiveness. Participation in how the decision process is constructed varies by organization. Worker participation in the process improves communication within the organization; subordinates are made aware of top management objectives, and top managers learn about problems that must be resolved in order to achieve the objectives they see as important.

Empirical evidence about the impact of MBO programs was obtained in each of the studies reviewed. Improvement in productivity, increased performance, reductions in costs, and average attendance were used as criteria. The impact of MBO programs was substantial: In 97% of the studies reviewed, positive results were found. Criterion measures improved on the average by 44.6%. Effectiveness was closely related to the degree of involvement and commitment by top management: When commitment was high, there was a 56.5% gain in productivity; when commitment was low, the gain was 6.1%. Clearly, such programs are most effective when top management sustains an interest and a commitment.

These results confirm some widely held beliefs and practices. What general would send an army out in the field without trying to convey to them what outcome they were seeking? What organizational president would start a year of work for volunteers without describing what they were all going to achieve—whether the objectives had been formulated by the whole group or by an established committee. And what organization can ignore the effects of its efforts on achievement of goals?

Whatever is outlined, whatever means are used to convey the message, organizational objectives often remain unclear to those who have to achieve them. How persons will contribute to group attainment is not always apparent. The leader must assume responsibility for assuring that each person sees purpose in each task and can relate that task to the success of the organization. Business, industry, or any organization that pays employees can learn some lessons from organizations that depend on volunteers. After all, volunteers hang on because of a special sort of dedication to the organization and its goals. Although they can just walk away, some do, most don't.

Pritchard and his associates[19] studied work groups in the U.S. Air Force over a two-year period to learn how feedback, goal setting, and incentives affect group productivity. A Productivity Measurement and Enhancement System was developed with the participation of work group members. Group-level feedback increased productivity an average of 50% over baseline; when group goal setting was added, productivity increased to 75% over baseline; adding group incentives increased productivity to 76% over baseline. The increases in productivity were accompanied by other beneficial effects—job satisfaction improved, turnover intentions reduced, and morale was as good or better. Control groups in Air Force units showed no or little increase over the same period.

Latham, Erez, and Locke[20] designed an experiment to determine how crucial it was for subsequent performance to have subordinates participate in setting goals. Latham's earlier work had found that assigning goals was generally as effective as setting them participatively. This study showed that motivational effects of goals set by others are as powerful as those set participatively, both for generating goal commitment and subsequent better performance. This effect occurs only when a definite effort is made not merely to describe the goals, but also to sell the importance of achieving them.

Each of the efforts reported in this section required the active participation of the leadership of the units and of their superiors in order to create the conditions in which favorable results had a chance to occur. Then a team of specialists needed to obtain measures of productivity. Often these measures were not ideal; whenever that is the case, the effectiveness of the changed methods are underestimated. The Pritchard study is one in which the measures of productivity were closer to the ideal, with results showing greater changes than had been reported earlier.

The effects of improved practices are well known among the professionals who study them. The evidence comes from all sectors of the society. As we have shown, they are substantial—75% better is surely a dramatic improvement. They can be achieved in almost every setting. But they are evidenced only when the program is supported from the top of the organization and involves the willing participation of leaders of all of the units or subdivisions involved and of those who have the primary control over the performance of each group—the group members themselves.

Leadership involves selling of the idea that more can be done, that what is being done is worthwhile, and that each individual will benefit if more is done. Leadership also involves gaining the trust of each person that fairness will prevail, that the individual will not be exploited, and that decisions will be made taking into account the interests of all.

Many persons ask how the leader can achieve the well-articulated vision. The studies just reported suggest one direction of activity involving changes in the way things are done so that more feedback is provided and so that individual groups participate in setting their group goals and receive recognition in some form when the job is well done. Those who aspire to leadership need to attend to the studies just described, for they define an effective leadership role.

Does a Change in Leadership Benefit an Organization?

The effects just described can be attained not only at the lowest levels of an organization but at higher levels in complex and hierarchical ones as well. The involvement of top leadership is essential to make a change in an organization; few desirable changes that occur are due to factors other than leadership. How much can the top leader accomplish? A number of studies have dealt with this issue.

Lieberson and O'Connor[21] studied organizations before and after a change in leadership. They examined critical aspects of organizational performance and found consistent improvement after such changes. The magnitude of change has been challenged by other analysts but not the direction and consistency of change. But any analyst must sort out the many factors involved in the changes that may be associated with leadership, such as profitability and productivity. The very fact that significant changes occur whenever leadership changes is noteworthy.

Alan Berkeley Thomas,[22] in a reanalysis and replication of the Lieberson and O'Connor study, found that the mere fact that there was a new chief executive officer in place had a substantial impact on firm performance beyond what could be accounted for by year, company, or industry. Perhaps the fact that a former CEO had not lived up to expectations leads to the positive reaction to a new CEO. But the effect does exist. Thomas reported that over 60% of the variance in profit and sales of U.K. retail stores was associated with changes in the top executive.

In a related study, Day and Lord[23] found that executive leadership can explain as much as 45% of an organization's performance. In a study of nuclear power plants, Osborn and Jackson[24] showed that some styles of executive leadership can increase safety risks.

Effects of Charismatic Leaders

Howell and Frost[25] tested the effects of charismatic leadership in a simulated work setting in which Considerate, Structuring, and Charismatic leader behavior styles were taught and then portrayed by "leaders." The units that had leaders who played the charismatic role outperformed other groups. The finding is significant, for it not only supports many of the other studies on effects of charismatic leaders but also suggests that behaving like a charismatic leader can be taught. In this study, there was also higher task satisfaction and fewer conflicts in the groups with charismatic leaders. Projecting a powerful, confident, and dynamic presence worked best; so did a captivating and engaging voice tone, direct eye contact, and animated facial expressions. Perhaps charisma is not a gift given to a select few but a set of behaviors that can be adopted by many.

Evidence has been presented to support the notion that beneficial effects result from certain behaviors of leaders—effects on organizational objectives being given major attention. Sometimes effects were reported without identifying the behavior that produced them. Relationships were found between classes of behavior and organizational outcomes. Those who behave more in line with a given pattern of leadership produce better results than those who do not. Criteria used are generally accepted measures of organizational or institutional effectiveness.

The outcome measures used to test leader performance in the workplace should attract the attention of those who control organizational resources, for they relate directly to needs for improving quality and productivity. When the setting is an educational institution, equally critical measures of student learning, retention rates, and school reputation are affected.

When large variations in individual performance exist, there is need to intervene to improve group functioning. Proper diagnoses of problems are essential. If differences in performance result from variations in capabilities that are hard to modify, a selection program with a built-in winnowing process is called for. Frequently, inadequate training and supervision may be the cause. Dissatisfaction with working conditions, lack of interest in the work, frustration with obstacles standing in the way of getting the job done, hostility toward the boss, or annoyance with rules and policies may also indicate the root of poor performance. By whatever method they select, leaders must become informed and deal with such issues.

CHAPTER SEVEN

A Test Battery Used in a Leadership Development Program

It would be great if future leaders could be identified early so they might be given opportunities to improve through appropriate training and experience. Countless organizations would embrace with enthusiasm recommendations for ranking potential candidates for leadership positions. Young persons would pursue the discovery of their aptitude score for leadership, if such a score existed. They would be intrigued by a profile of measures comparing them with known leaders on given traits.

In general, test scores do not help much in picking persons who will perform well as leaders. However, test scores have proved useful in career choices, in employment decisions, in school and college admission programs, and in predicting the likelihood of promotion to higher levels in an organization.

Psychologists interested in measurement have been collecting data for decades on persons aspiring to enter many lines of work. Measures have been developed for abilities, special knowledge, skills and aptitudes, preferences for types of people and activities, personality characteristics, values, life-styles, and for biographical histories. Purposes for collecting the measures have included identifying persons who would succeed in some activity, show promise for learning skills or acquiring information, or be adept at solving problems or getting things done. Measures have been collected on individuals in leadership positions and on those persons holding specific positions within identified groups or organizations; they identify those who are more likely to get promoted but are poor gauges of leadership success.

How to identify leadership talent has been studied systematically, but only since World War II have successful methods been developed to identify effective leaders. Methods used to study leadership differ in important ways from those used to predict success in a given occupation. Usual test batteries work because an individual can demonstrate possession of the knowledge and skills required for success in an occupation, can describe preferences for types of activities, or can describe thoughts and attitudes in a paper-and-pencil test. These measures can be compared with later success in the occupation. Such predictor tests have been developed for many occupations. Predictor tests for leadership need to measure traits that individuals cannot assess well for themselves. People cannot report accurately on what others think and how others react to them. The best measures of leadership have come when the presumed leader is described by others, especially by others who have observed the leader in an active role.

Training programs can reproduce the context of leadership and can provide a variety of experiences that reveal the usual modes of behavior of each participant. To make the experience most effective, comparison of the description of the individual's behavior in the daily work setting as a leader can provide a test of the accuracy of descriptions obtained by observation in exercises. Usually, additional items of personal information are obtained prior to the training experience in order to provide evidence of the differences that exist among people and their styles of work and to establish a base for counseling on how better to behave in order to become more effective. When such information includes descriptions by peers and subordinates of critical aspects of leader behavior, the difference between self-image and other-image becomes a critical item for discussion.

Tests, assessment procedures, and training programs abound for use by organizations in developing their supervisors, managers, executives, and leaders. Programs differ for each group. Those designed especially for middle- and higher-level managers, including the top leadership of the organization, are more plentiful and appear to be current pacesetters in the field. The description of one typical individual taking a test battery used in one leadership development program follows. The name and some items are changed to protect his privacy.

The Story of John Miller

John Miller, a newly appointed vice-president of MacMillan and Hartford, an electronics firm in Riverton, Missouri, exemplifies a person who decides to participate in a well-known assessment and training program. Miller is an engineer promoted to manager, one of a very large group of persons who prepared for a life in a technological field who then moved into management.

John Miller decided to change jobs after seventeen years of work with one company. He accepted an attractive offer from a firm he knew well and moved with his wife and three children from Indiana to a suburb of St. Louis, Missouri.

John, age forty-eight, is an electrical engineer with a bachelor's degree from Purdue University and a Master of Science degree from the University of Illinois. He joined MacMillan and Hartford, a successful electronics firm, as their vice-president for research. John's prior job included no management responsibilities.

When John worked on his own, he regularly came up with some highly innovative and classic solutions to problems. When he changed positions, he was aware that he had new skills to learn and was assured by his new employer of lots of help in getting started in his new role. John took this offer because it seemed such a great opportunity, and the CEO had been persuasive and personable. Besides, he realized the children were getting older and he wasn't getting any younger, so he really needed to think more about his salary. Tuition costs for educating the children were getting higher every year; also, this new job had an attractive retirement program. But he was forced to admit to himself that he hadn't felt this nervous since he took his first midterms at college. He couldn't stop asking himself whether this risk was greater than he should have assumed.

John knew that he had always been considered by others to be a little shy socially and not exactly the life of the party. He believed that was partly because of his overriding interest in his work, which seemed to absorb a greater portion of his mind and effort than it did for most people with whom he was acquainted. Besides, when he was young his mother always had a quick answer ready and, since his marriage, his wife, because she was so articulate, was always able to carry any conversation. So he had generally felt he was able to ride through almost every social situation silently, as long as he maintained a knowing expression and didn't show any signs of boredom.

On the old job as an equal to all the others in his team, John would adopt a somewhat distant attitude to avoid small talk that he thought a waste of time. His quick, sometimes smart-aleck retorts or sly jabs were considered by his buddies to be normal and OK. Most of his colleagues acted and spoke that way.

They all knew how to take it or hand it out. And when he had to report on how his work was getting on, he could usually write the report quickly and clearly or, if necessary, state it briefly to the boss. He had a special skill for getting to the heart of a problem and unsticking the gluey parts.

But how was he going to relate to a team of which he was the acknowledged leader? How was he going to act when he knew they were waiting for him to set the pace and keep them on track? Would they start saying things about him among themselves the way he had when he was criticizing his prior boss? This was a new game. He was playing a new role. He couldn't just close the door of the lab and forget how the rest were working on their projects. Wow! It was almost as difficult as becoming a father for the first time. Only this time he didn't have some years to plan ahead before the kid grew up.

The Whisper from the Wings

John Miller was exhibiting the typical anxiety associated with expanded responsibility. The other members of his family were having similar problems coping, but John was too preoccupied with his new job to notice. John Miller's experience is common. Newcomers rarely find the support they believe they need in early stages of adjustment. It is easy to see in individual lives how the routines of our institutions can produce stress in ways that are entirely overlooked. The problem is especially acute among those who have responsibilities of leadership thrust upon them, especially when they have no peer group with whom they may share concerns and experiences.

The selection of persons for leadership positions is difficult. MacMillan and Hartford had spent eighteen months finding John Miller. Even though John seemed perfect for the job, he needed training and development. Excellent organizations not only hunt for good people, they also expect to invest heavily in preparing them for their role.

Billions of dollars are spent each year by corporations to train their best prospects. Military services explicitly assign their academies the task of developing leadership qualities in all their cadets or midshipmen. Community organizations have much less money to spend. They often rely on volunteers whose talents were developed by business and the military. We criticize our political leaders because they are ill-equipped to be leaders, but we have done little to assure that they are educated appropriately to meet the challenges of governing offices.

Several months passed as John gradually became acquainted with his team members, of whom there seemed so many, and with the organization, which seemed so distant. He still was not feeling comfortable at his job. Instead of spending his days in a laboratory with three others, he was now spending his time in his office reading stuff dropped by his secretary into his in-basket and talking to one after another of the fifty-eight research persons in the organization. He attended meetings in which persons presented reports about which he had too little information, and he was formulating policies that he wasn't sure applied to his people.

John also discovered that he was expected to solve every problem, resolve every argument however petty, and yield his own time for his special projects to almost every person on his team whenever they wanted to see him. He wondered why his subordinates appeared to have more free time than he did. To keep his own projects going, he started to come to work earlier. He found himself staying later in order to clear the paper work from his desk and to answer urgent telephone calls.

Arriving home tired and frustrated, he found little of interest in the reports from each of his family about their difficulties in finding friends, their feelings of loss about the friends they had left, and their complaints against schools and services in the area, and he failed to notice the increase in stress and anxiety in his wife.

John felt that maybe they had made a mistake in moving. Finally, he decided to talk it over with Mark Jason, the CEO, who had been very supportive and had expressed enthusiasm for what John could accomplish in the company. He hesitated to open the discussion on this topic for fear he would be considered a failure or show irreparable weakness. He did not want to be laughed at or be told that his problems would just go away.

What John learned in the meeting was enlightening. Jason welcomed the discussion and said he appreciated how John had been feeling; he had been waiting for the opportunity to make some suggestions. Jason described a few of his own earlier problems and those of others, far less qualified than John, who had assumed added responsibilities. Jason said the company had used a number of training programs for its managers and executives and he had hoped that John would come forward and show interest in the possibility of such an experience. Jason's suggestion was for John to enroll in a leadership development program and get ready to accept some help.

John's secretary made a call to a well-known leadership center to arrange for his enrollment in a development program. She was surprised to find that the earliest opening was in the following April—about six months later—and that was possible only because of a cancellation. She was told that he might find an earlier opportunity in a similar program offered elsewhere. John's reply was a speedy "No, April is OK." He felt a sense of relief. He recognized how apprehensive he was feeling about joining a group of other managers when he was so unsure of his own status. With this delay, he might be able to cancel later on. He then put the matter out of his mind.

Leadership Development Program

On a cold, wintry day in January, John received a hefty packet from the center. He opened it to find a letter from the registrar that began, "We are looking forward to your participation in the April 14–19 LEADERSHIP DEVELOP- MENT PROGRAM. In preparation, please complete the enclosed packet of assessment instruments (approximately 6–7 hours will be required) and return them by March 1 in order that they can be processed and ready for your personal feedback session." The letter ended, "I hope you will find these exercises a stimulating prelude to the Leadership Development Program."[1]

He looked closely at the first few pages then began glancing at those that followed, moving more quickly through them as he felt a growing annoyance and some anger overtaking him. Somehow, he just couldn't believe that he needed one more task to do with everything else that was piling up in the office. Besides, it looked like he was going to have to give some more thought to his own insufficiencies, and he had been chewing on that regularly for several months. He put the pile of papers on the back right side of his desk, after considering and rejecting the possibility of stashing it in the hall cabinet, and decided to think about it for a while. That pack of papers could represent a remedy. It could be the support he needed. It could be the answer, or it could be so much hogwash. Whatever it was it wouldn't be entertaining, and so it rested for two and a half weeks.

Early in February, trapped at home on a Friday by a miserable ice storm, John reluctantly moved the packet of test materials to the front of his desk and began reading the instructions, filling out the forms, and answering the questions. He noted with some disdain the statement that the center was engaged in research in leadership; he was sure from his own research experience that leadership and management could not be developed in the same way electronic devices are designed and wondered just how "soft" the field was. He was pleased to see that even though he was going to be a guinea pig, he was assured that his responses and all data about him would be kept confidential. He wondered if his boss knew that the sponsoring organization received back no report on any person going through the program.

Completing the Test Battery. The instructions asked him to complete the LEADERSHIP STYLE INDICATOR and the MANAGEMENT SKILLS PROFILE immediately. He found these forms at the bottom of the packet he had received. He hadn't noticed them during his first look at the stuff. John was shocked to see that he was being asked to distribute the Leadership Style Indicator to six subordinates. This was "to get a better idea of how you are viewed as a leader." John had never thought of himself as needing to please or satisfy any subordinate; his goal was to get the job done and to please his boss, the CEO. He questioned the propriety of the whole process; after all, his team was made up of really smart people, but they knew nothing of the responsibilities of managers, to say nothing of leaders. So he looked with some qualms at the form he was to fill out. He discovered that his subordinates were to be asked to fill out an identical form. The instructions read, in part:

> Consider each of the 48 adjectives on the right. If the adjective does not describe how you relate to others while in a LEADERSHIP and/or INFLUENCING ROLE, mark N for NO—DOES NOT DESCRIBE ME. If the adjective describes how you relate to others while in a LEADERSHIP and/or INFLUENCING ROLE, mark either Y for YES—DESCRIBES ME or Y! meaning YES—STRONGLY DESCRIBES ME.
>
> Go back over each of the 48 adjectives. For each word that you marked Y or Y! decide whether this behavior usually makes you MORE EFFECTIVE or LESS EFFECTIVE and fill in either M for MORE EFFECTIVE or L for LESS EFFECTIVE.

The list of adjectives was repeated on the back of the sheet, with these instructions:

> DO NOT MARK EVERY WORD LISTED. *Mark ONLY* the adjectives that you SHOULD KNOW MORE OR LESS of to be more EFFECTIVE when taking a LEADERSHIP ROLE and/or trying to INFLUENCE OTHERS. Mark M for MORE and L for LESS.

John decided he should fill out this form first, before deciding which of his subordinates to ask to do the rating of him. As he moved through the adjectives, he was relieved to see that no adjectives seemed very negative and that few were actually positive. It seemed his subordinates were to be asked to describe him, rather than to grade him. "Effective" was not on the list. "Smart" was not on the list. But "decisive" and "fair" were included. He decided that it might be better to give the form to persons whose feelings he knew little about rather than to those whom he believed were on his side. Maybe he would learn something.

The cover letter for the rather imposing set of materials of the MANAGE-MENT SKILLS PROFILE read, in part:

> The Management Skills Profile (MSP) is a developmental tool that will provide you with constructive feedback about your managerial performance as perceived by up to seven other people in your organization.
>
> We suggest that you give the MSP to your immediate superior and at least two subordinates and two peers. Try to select a representative sample—people you trust to give you an *objective* evaluation.
>
> The feedback that you receive from subordinates and peers will be anonymous because the ratings are summarized. *However, if we receive only one MSP in the "superior" category, those ratings will be reported separately; and, therefore, will not be anonymous.* We suggest that you make that fact clear when you give your superior(s) the MSP.

Still feeling cautious, John examined the MSP before deciding on the people he would ask to complete it. He noted the instructions:

> Please be candid when you fill out this questionnaire. Evaluate the actual behavior of the individual as you have observed it. Then make your ratings carefully, one item at a time.
>
> Your open assessment will help the manager gain a clear understanding of his/her management strengths and development needs. Your feedback will serve as the basis for this person's focused professional development and career direction.

What followed were sixteen pages of questions. John examined the list with misgivings—he was not sure he needed people to give him that sort of going-over. Again, he gave thought to dropping out of the whole process. But he had been asking others about their experiences in such programs and remembered their glowing words. And Jason had said this was certain to be a special benefit. So he started reading the questions in earnest.

This person:

1. is willing to listen to subordinates' concerns . . .
   To a very great extent
   To a great extent
   To some extent
   To a little extent
   Not at all
   Does not apply

John skipped to the bottom of the first page:

11. Is good with numbers . . .
    To a very great extent
    To a great extent
    To some extent
    To a little extent
    Not at all
    Does not apply

"Not very threatening for me, regardless of what people say," thought John. Now he was beginning to feel the pressure of the time it would take, and he decided to stick it out and show just how good he was. After all, he was smarter, had accomplished more, and had a more complete life than most, so why should he be fearful? (He remembered that "fearful" had not been one of the adjectives in the prior form, but "cautious" was. He wondered whether anyone saw him as cautious.)

He had now spent two hours working on the set of materials. He had completed two of the forms and had picked the persons to complete ratings of him. Each person was to be given the form and an envelope so that it would be mailed directly. He planned that distribution for the following Monday and turned to the remainder of the stack to see what was left.

The PARTICIPANT BACKGROUND FORM was easy. He completed that in about five minutes. The SUPPLEMENTAL BIOGRAPHIC INVENTORY was eight pages long and asked detailed questions about his job, educational background, past employment history, and a few questions of self-description. He had trouble finding three "weakest points" and too little space (only three lines?) to answer the question, "Digging deep down inside yourself—where only you can see, what pressures would you say are at work on you?"

John thought it time to take a break but looked with curiosity at the next booklet, the FIRO-B®, and read the directions:

> This questionnaire explores the typical ways you interact with people. There are no right or wrong answers.
>
> Sometimes people are tempted to answer questions like these in terms of what they think a person *should* do. This is *not* what is wanted here. We would like to know how you actually behave.
>
> Some items may seem similar to others. However, each item is different so please answer each one without regard to the others. There is no time limit, but do not debate long over any item.

The questions, fifty-four in all, were on one side of the sheet. The first question was easy, "I try to be with people." John knew lots of persons who would respond "usually" to that question, and sometimes he envied them. But he had learned that he was happiest when other people left him alone in his laboratory, so he debated answering "rarely," thought better of it, and marked "occasionally." The rest of the questions were also easy; he finished the page in less than ten minutes, feeling he had been asked the same question all the time. Now caught up in the spirit of the tests, he looked at the next form, the KIRTON ADAPTATION-INNOVATION INVENTORY. This inventory had thirty-three questions, each asking him whether it was hard or easy for him to present himself as a particular kind of person. He wondered how anyone would be able to use the answers to such questions to make him a better leader but filled out the form anyway. It took him less than three minutes.

The next form, the MANAGERIAL JOB SATISFACTION QUESTIONNAIRE, had only twenty questions. John thought that finally the questions were getting relevant, and wished there were more than twenty to answer. He had a lot of things to write about as a manager. He was a little disappointed in the questions asked. They were not in the form of questions but were presented as statements, and he was expected to indicate the degree to which he agreed or disagreed. The first statement was, "The managers I work for back me up." He marked that "strongly agree" and spent the next couple of minutes wondering what it would be like to have the responsibilities he had and a boss who wasn't wholeheartedly supportive of his efforts. He felt pretty good about that and sorry for those few managers who had bad bosses. How could they survive?

The twenty responses came quickly, but John felt deprived. Where were the questions he had hoped for—the price of managing and leading that makes me give second place to my own work, my own family, my tennis and golf? Does anyone know how much it takes out of me to spend time with one of my team helping to solve his problems with a new design or how often I'm picking up the pieces because the purchasing office ordered the wrong materials? Why do they come to me with their personal problems? Am I the one to tell them whether a mother should live with them or go to a nursing home? Am I always going to have to come to work early and stay late? When will some of my team grow up and accept some responsibilities? Don't other people know about the burdens of being the boss?

The next form, the MYERS-BRIGGS TYPE INDICATOR®, had a vaguely familiar title. There were 166 items, each with a choice of (A) or (B) as a response. He looked at the directions and the first item:

DIRECTIONS

There are no "right" or "wrong" answers to these questions. Your answers will help show how you like to look at things and how you like to go about deciding things. Knowing your own preferences and learning about other people's can help you understand where your special strengths are, what kinds of work you might enjoy and be successful doing, and how people with different preferences can relate to each other and be valuable to society.

Read each question carefully and mark your answer on the separate answer sheet . . .

The first question was:

1. Does following a schedule
   (A) appeal to you, or
   (B) cramp you?

John looked at the remaining stack of forms to complete after this one: still four to go—one short form but three pretty formidable ones. He decided to complete the Myers-Briggs and then take a break for lunch.

During lunch John reflected on the questions he had been asked and wondered if he had given the best answers. What would people think of him when he had said that he really didn't like some of what he saw as essential obligations of his job. Did he really like to be boss—wouldn't he be happier in a more solitary role? Had he really meant it when he said he didn't like helping other people, that he liked giving first priority to his own work? Was he a success at what he was doing? Maybe he should not pass out those forms for his people to complete—he might learn something he did not want to know. Maybe they would think he was weak and had no mind of his own. After all, he didn't need to consult with them in order to do a good job.

By the end of lunch, John decided to watch the news on TV and put off until Sunday afternoon the completion of the rest of the forms. He also decided that he really was beginning to like his job; he enjoyed the ability to influence the way projects developed in his unit, and he had a very good team and a wonderful boss. So he would continue this process of answering peculiar questions; after all, some of them had made him think about himself in ways he had never done before. There must be some worth in the process after all.

When he started again two days later, John found that the next form on the stack was different. Its title, LEADERSHIP DEVELOPMENT PROGRAM, did not reveal its purpose, but the directions did:

To what extent do you expect to obtain the following benefits as a result of the Leadership Development Program?
   5—very definite expectation
   4—definite expectation
   3—some expectation
   2—slight expectation
   1—no expectation

John's first impulse was to just write across the form "YOU TELL ME!" After all, he wasn't planning the program, and he wasn't very knowledgeable about what could be learned.

However, the first question changed his mind. It read: "1. Learn about new management techniques." If there are such things, I sure want to know about them! John put a "5" in the blank. He then read the rest of the items and had an impulse to mark them all "5." But he remembered a speaker at his son's school who had said, "Adolescence is the period of unrealistic expectations." He didn't want to be seen as adolescent, and he thought that maybe his responses would affect the way in which he was dealt with in the program and so elected to mark only ten of the items with a "5" and ten with a "4," maybe to force some priorities in terms of what he saw as his greatest interests. He was beginning to get excited about the forthcoming session and curious about what he would be told about his answers.

The next form, the CALIFORNIA PSYCHOLOGICAL INVENTORY®, was a whole book, with an answer sheet crowded with little circles to fill. The directions read:

> This booklet contains a series of statements. Read each one, decide how you feel about it, and then mark your answer *on the special answer sheet*. If you *agree* with a statement, or feel it is true about you, answer TRUE. If you *disagree* with a statement, or feel that it is not true about you, answer FALSE.

The first item was: "1. I enjoy social gatherings just to be with people." John wondered why the people who made up these instruments put so much emphasis on relations with other people. He figured most persons were like him: Sometimes you like being with people but lots of the time you want to be left alone. He soon forgot about this point as he answered the 480 questions about everything from how he liked his father to putting worms on a fishing hook. He scarcely noticed that he spent a full hour on this one form.

John could see the beginning of the end on the next questionnaire, the LEADERSHIP DECISION STYLES SURVEY, and saw at a glance that he was to answer TRUE or FALSE on the answer sheet. The directions were:

> Here are five styles which you, acting as a leader, might use in reaching a decision. They differ only in the amount of participation which you allow your subordinates and thus the degree to which they can influence the final decision. "Subordinates" refers to those workers who report *directly* to you.
>
> Note that with each style you take full responsibility. IN NO CASE do you give up either authority or responsibility for the final decision.

Style	Description
L1	*You decide alone.* You make the decision without discussing the situation with anyone. You rely entirely on personal knowledge or information available in written documents.
L2	*You seek information and then decide alone.* You seek additional information from one or more of your subordinates to arrive at a decision. You may

or may not describe the problem to them, but you solicit information only, not solutions or suggestions.

LF1   *You consult with individuals and then decide alone.* Here you share the problem with selected subordinates, individually. You gather additional information from them and seek their advice about possible solutions to the problem. Still, you make the decision.

LF2   *You consult with your entire group and then decide alone.* Using this style, you meet with your subordinates in a group and discuss the possible alternatives, essentially using them as consultants. You may use their feelings and opinions as additional input, but you retain the final decision power.

M   *You share the problem with your group, and you all mutually decide what to do.* Here you give your subordinates full participation in the decision-making process. You may define the problem for them, provide relevant information, and participate in the discussion as any other member, but you do not use your position as leader to influence them. The group is the decision maker, and you accept not only their decision, but also the responsibility for it. Your description to others will be, "*We* decided to . . . ," not "The *group* decided to . . . ," or "*I* decided to . . . ."

Following this page were sixteen "cases," each approximately a one-page description of a situation in which a decision had to be made. John's task was to select the best way to make the decision. For most of the cases it was easy, for John could see what the right decision should be. Sometimes he wondered if he had been told enough; sometimes he wondered whether the group would agree with his view. He ended the exercise wondering if there were any "right" ways to handle each of these situations.

Relieved at being done, John put all his papers together and planned to have his secretary mail them off on Monday morning. He was, as usual, ahead of schedule in finishing this job and so promptly forgot about the whole exercise. But he did remember that he was going to complain about the amount of time he had spent doing this. Could the center program prove it was worthwhile?

The Use of Tests in Training Programs

The portfolio of tests and inventories sent to John Miller illustrates the wide use of tests in training programs for business and industry. Tests of this sort, and even these same tests, are used in many settings with a wide array of persons: employees, community leaders, college students, noncommissioned and commissioned officers in military and police organizations, government employees, executives, and volunteers. Each group of tests varies with regard to objectives. What did the training staff at the center have in mind when these tests were selected?

The test data are collected for one main reason: to provide self-information to each person who participates in the program as an aid to that person's development. The planners designed the assessment part of the program to support the development of the participant: to find information on each participant that would help each participant know himself or herself better, to learn what the various tests and devices tell them about themselves, and then to assist the participant to use that information in order to perform more effectively and to grow as a human being and as a person dedicated to a set of well-understood goals.

Tests, then, are selected to inform about behaviors that can be changed and about factors that are understood and accepted by each participant in terms of accepted purposes. This principle may explain the absence of many of the tests that students and managers take in order to compete with each other and to learn where among all other persons they stand. For example, the only test of intelligence that is given during the training program has a very low ceiling. The center does not routinely collect aptitude or ability measures.

Confidentiality was mentioned previously; individual data are not reported to anyone other than the participant. The results of various tests and exercises and the observations of performance in this leadership development program and most others are not reported at all to the sponsoring organization. Therefore, each participant can feel "psychologically safe" in sessions aiming to help them develop. Each person in a session is encouraged to act in a normal and natural fashion and engage fully in activities that relate obviously to everyday work activities. Learning better ways to perform and then "transferring" this to the home turf is the goal.

The purposes for including each test in the battery taken by John are provided by the persons who selected them for inclusion. Tests are listed in the same order in which John took them. These purposes, as given below, may not necessarily fit the purposes of the participant. We will observe that later John discovers what scores he made and how these scores might relate to his own career development plans.

Uses Made of Each Measure

Leadership Style Indicator

The Leadership Style Indicator (LSI) is an adjective checklist, a common form of inventory used to help individuals give descriptions of persons and their usual behaviors in a format designed so that most people will understand. By having both John and his subordinates complete the form, John is provided a way to literally have the gift "to see himself as others see him." Even the same event, when described by others, varies. Our perceptions of others differ from how they see themselves. The relevance of the description to the Leadership Development Program (LDP) exercises is shown during the program. The LSI is scored in ways to help accent this relevance.

An effective leadership development program includes a major unit oriented to providing feedback from subordinates. The LSI provides dramatic evidence that the views of subordinates differ from the views of their superior who is being rated.

Management Skills Profile

The Management Skills Profile (MSP) follows the purposes of the LSI but becomes more specific in content and involves responses from peers and superiors in addition to subordinates. The usual behaviors that John ascribes to himself are summarized in a series of scores, which he may compare later to the scores given him by his associates. Some discrepancies in descriptions may emerge: John will find especially useful the scores he gets in areas where he thinks he is strong and where he thinks he is weak. Part of the plan John will develop for use when he returns home will rely heavily on the MSP and the LSI.

Participant Background Form

Becoming acquainted is one of the first activities of a newly formed class of LDP participants. These data are also accumulated over groups to provide demographic information about managers and leaders with whom the Center works. John will quickly find that he is a pretty typical member of his group. He will discover a number of others in his class who are transiting from important positions in which they used their technical and professional abilities and now are having to learn how to lead, motivate, train, and direct others.

Supplemental Biographic Inventory

This form is used by the staff of the program to get acquainted with each participant before the program begins, to make certain no area of interest, expectation, or strength or weakness is overlooked, and to prepare for the individual feedback session. Much of the six-day program provides individual feedback about how each person behaves in relation to others of the group. If there are special issues, advance warning is helpful.

FIRO-B®

The FIRO-B® is an unusual test, examining a special dynamic of human relations. The letters stand for Fundamental Interpersonal Relations Orientation-Behavior; the two aspects that are measured are: (e) expressed social behavior and (w) wanted behavior in others. These behaviors have three dimensions: Inclusion, Control, and Affection. The FIRO-B results are presented in a group discussion of ways in which people differ in their relations with others.

The importance of the FIRO-B to the development of a leader relates to teamwork and team building. The way human resources can be utilized depends upon the unfulfilled hopes and dreams of very human people. John is struggling to change from a model based on the physical sciences; the FIRO-B gives him a different insight into human behavior, an insight necessary for all leadership. The FIRO-B serves as an entry into discusssion of principles.

Kirton Adaptation-Innovation Inventory

The Kirton Inventory was devised in order to measure a postulated difference in creativity among persons. Michael Kirton had observed that although all persons had varying styles of creativity, some made changes so as to improve a current operation while others preferred to change the system as a way of achieving improvements. Kirton's inventory measures the degree of creativity and the direction in which it is usually exercised. Scores of each person are used to help a participant in the LDP to think through better methods of leadership in order to use the creative capabilities of members of their teams.

Many organizations look to their leadership for the initiatives for change to meet new conditions. How the leader addresses issues depends in large part on the dispositions that are revealed in the Kirton. Knowing one's own place on a scale such as the Kirton helps the leader to understand why others take different positions on concrete proposals.

Managerial Job Satisfaction Questionnaire

The Managerial Job Satisfaction Questionnaire is a widely used question-naire designed to pinpoint good and bad practices in work relations among managers, their superiors, and subordinates. The items speak for themselves and in the training session are used to stimulate discussions about ways in which groups may be helped to work together more effectively and with greater collaboration. The scores help to identify areas where participants like John may need to focus in order to reduce stress and improve the balance between work and other parts of life that relate to personal, family, and community life.

Myers-Briggs Type Indicator®

The Myers-Briggs Type Indicator® (MBTI®) may be the most widely used psychological measure at this time. It is easy to take, there are no wrong answers, and there are no unpleasant surprises as one gets the results. The device aims to show an individual where, among other persons, one's scores fall in four dimen-sions. Scores become more meaningful when two persons find they are different and explore the differences. The training program builds on discovered differ-ences and uses them to show how lack of awareness that others think differently, analyze things differently, and value things differently can conspire to interfere with interactions among persons. Large numbers of persons have taken the MBTI®; their scores are analyzed and available for study by sex, occupation, level of organization, nationality, and many other variables.

The MBTI® is also useful in increasing self-awareness. Knowing one's own preferred styles helps in interpreting the results from the LSI, the MSP, and the FIRO-B®.

Leadership Development Program—Expectations

This form does just what it appears to do; it asks about the expectations of the program that participants bring with them. Knowing what persons expect is useful in planning. It is also a test of the appropriateness of the Center's promotional literature describing the program and the care with which appli-cants' questions are handled in the registration process. Analyses of responses provide an interesting summary of the felt needs of quite successful and well-functioning members of our society.

California Psychological Inventory®

The California Psychological Inventory® (CPI®) is a widely used personality inventory. It differs from most other personality inventories in that its dimen-sions for scoring deal with the variations in patterns of behavior of normal, well-functioning persons rather than of persons with mental disorders. Interpre-tations require professional preparation and knowledge of the vast literature of studies that have been made using the CPI®. Interpretation of John Miller's scores in this instrument will be given to him as part of a half-day session of feedback provided by a well-trained professional person near the end of the six-day session.

The CPI® is a well-developed personality measure. Its scales provide a depth of self-awareness that is especially useful to persons with engineering backgrounds like John's. The scores provide insight into the meaning of the adjectives that John would learn were used by others to describe him.

Leadership Decision Styles Survey

The Leadership Decision Styles Survey (LDSS) is based on the leadership theory developed by Vroom and Yetton, and Vroom and Jago. Leadership is assumed to be exercised when decisions must be made. The degree of involvement of subordinates must consider various factors such as the need for a quality decision, availability of information, and time constraints. The LDSS provides a series of instances in which a decision must be made and asks respondents to select their preferred way of making the decision, taking into account the circumstances as described. The training session starts with information about dispositions to act in natural ways for each participant and discusses implications and effects of each mode of response.

Assessment for Development

This battery of tests was selected for use in a leadership development program in order to begin a process of self-examination by participants in the program. Because the program aims at development of the participant and has no intent to appraise or to predict, the battery is slanted toward those measures that emphasize styles and behaviors rather than aptitudes and abilities.

As might have become apparent, the battery of tests taken helps to prepare the participant for the program by increasing the amount of self-examination. This is especially useful with those persons who tend not to be particularly introspective and those who think in rigorous terms about causes and effects only with regard to material things. John's participation in the course is described in the next chapter.

CHAPTER EIGHT

A Sample Leadership Development Program

The second Sunday in April, John Miller of MacMillan and Hartford stepped off the plane not quite certain how he felt about beginning the Leadership Development Program for which he had registered. Leaving the hotel, he boarded a van with several others who looked curiously at each other and then formally introduced themselves. He did not know it at the time, but he was about to participate in the most widely used training course in the world, one that had repeatedly earned awards as the best of its kind.

The Leadership Development Program

The van was noisy as persons around him began to get acquainted. They all seemed comfortable and relaxed; he felt anxious and wished he were alone. They all agreed that everything that had ever been said about the South in the spring was right. It was balmy and beautiful, the dogwood trees were blooming, and the sky was blue, so even if the program turned out to be a disappointment, at least it would be pleasant and a welcome break from work and problems at home for a week. Again the group introduced themselves, but only a couple of first names stuck. Of the eight participants in his van, the third in a caravan of three, John could remember only three names; it would be impossible to get to know all twenty-four in such a short time! His mind was still spinning from trying to remember the names of all the people back home who reported to him, let alone trying to look friendly when he passed others who worked for the company.

The van passed through a mix of widely separated homes and small farms, rolled past two lakes, one with a couple of fishing boats, and turned into a wooded area where the road curved around to a sprawling stone structure. They were greeted and escorted to a large room outfitted with a U-shaped table and surrounded by twenty-four *very* comfortable swivel chairs (John vowed to find where those chairs could be obtained—he wanted one for his office in Riverton).

A man about his age appeared at the front of the room and introduced himself: "I am Phillip Carlson, and I will be one of the persons who will help you get the most out of this week in the Leadership Development Program. I am a sociologist, which puts me among the minority in this place—most are psychologists. That gives me an advantage, for I know what they know and they have not the slightest inkling about what a sociologist knows.

"You have all told us a lot about yourselves by filling out the forms we sent you. During this week, you will learn your results and what the results mean. In addition, we will learn a lot more about you and will use that to help you learn. Everything we learn about you we will tell you. And we will help you understand how you can use such information.

"You may think that what will happen this week is that you will be discovered. Finally. For you may feel that you moved into a managerial or leadership position not knowing enough and that only your ability to conceal your shortcomings has helped you survive. But, finally, you will be found out. That you are really flawed at the core, a sham, concealing your own uncertainty and inability behind a facade of ease and self-confidence. But now you will be revealed as our methods peel layer after layer off your true self and, like an onion, you will be taken apart.

"Not so. First—we will not intrude into your private self. We will not discover anything that you are not already revealing to others, if not to yourself. We will not press you to say things you do not want to say. Further—we treat everything we learn about you as *your* property. No one will hear from *us* about your experiences here, save you. In addition, we will keep in our computers and files only coded information that will be inaccessible to anyone except in ways in which your identity is removed. You therefore may feel *psychologically safe* during your stay here. Even as we talk about your scores and what they mean, as we will in this group, we will give your scores only to you. You own those scores and may show them or talk about them to anyone here, or you may keep them entirely to yourself. When you go back to your organization, you need not show anything to your boss, your peers, your director of training, or even to your spouse—unless you, on your own, decide to do so.

"What we will do in this program will seem to you like many of the things you do back home. Do your best in each exercise. Behave normally. Act as you usually do in your home setting. You will be observed by the professional staff. We will ask you to observe more than one person in this group as you work together. Feel free to comment about the way the program goes. In fact, we will ask you each day to tell us how we are doing and will teach you how to tell others about how they might improve in ways that will help them, not offend them.

"Part of the process involves the use of well-trained professional persons who observe you in action and give you *feedback*. Feedback is an important word in this program that draws on an important principle in the psychology of learning: Knowledge of results is essential for learning. Feedback gives you the responses of others to the efforts you make to persuade, to make decisions, to show understanding, to motivate, and to support. From the feedback you receive from peers and professional staff, you will get a better idea of your strengths and weaknesses in interpersonal relations. You will also be able to get a better idea of how you come across to others—do you command respect, do you seem sincere, do you show concern for the needs of others?

"Notice on the side of this room there is a mirror. It is a two-way mirror, usually called one-way. People on the dark side can observe the people on the lighted side. There are people in there watching you now. There will almost always be persons behind that mirror observing and taking notes. You need to know that, but you will quickly ignore it because the action will be on this side of the mirror. But maybe sometime you will wonder who saw you—or that fool across the table—do something stupid. If at any time you get curious, walk out this door, enter the next door to the left, and you will see the observers. Ask who they are—they will already know who you are from their seating chart. Stay a few minutes and then come back.

"Let us ask the persons who are back there to come out and introduce themselves and say what they are doing watching you. Will all of you behind the mirror please come and join us?" Four people entered the room, two men and two women.

Late that night John fell into bed, tired but wide awake and reliving the day.

Many things had surprised him. He had expected to feel uncomfortable and not prepared. He reflected on the Hidden Figures Test that he and the others had taken. He had been the best in the group on that test and so had listened with interest to the interpretation of scores, which indicated that high scorers are better able to avoid undue influence from distractions. He felt good about that—he was sure the score was accurate—and was beginning to feel that he was picking up ideas faster than most in his group. Some of those who seemed to be more experienced were no better than he in some of the games they had played. In many ways, he felt he had as much to offer as any. The boost to his self-esteem also surprised him; he had not been paying much attention to the anxiety he was experiencing about this program.

He had also discovered that he was different from many of the group. The Myers-Briggs Type Indicator results for the group showed him to be a visionary INTJ, more of an introvert than most. He had also felt that some group members did not realize that subordinates could be smart; he had learned early on that good ideas could come from anywhere and that every idea was either good in itself or would lead to a better one. He seemed to have more respect for the members of his team back home than did most of the group for their co-workers or subordinates. He certainly did not consider them the enemy, the way that fellow from the construction firm—Fred something—did.

With this feeling of well-being and satisfaction, John drifted off to sleep. He dreamed that night of being called upon for a major address, but he couldn't find his papers, his suitcase had been left in the last town, and he couldn't find the room where he was to speak. As the appointed time approached, he became more and more frantic, until he noted that all of the people in his dream seemed not to care whether any event even occurred, let alone occurred on time. He awoke wondering what *that* dream meant.

Pete Emerson led off the morning sessions with an impassioned discussion of leadership. Somehow he made the work of each person in the room seem more important. They were not only to be leaders, but also *creative* leaders. There were several phases to such leadership, all directed at problem solving, beginning with assessment, formulation of the problem, transformation, goal setting, planning and organizing, control and evaluation, implementation, and reassessment. John had never before thought that his ways of approaching problems were disorderly; he wondered whether he could continue to be creative and original if he had a pattern for solving problems. But what Pete Emerson had described did make sense and helped him to think more about what *his* processes were.

That afternoon he learned about how he had performed on the Leadership Decision Styles Survey. Emerson described the underlying logic of the survey—called the Vroom-Yetton model. He received a computer printout that began:

> The Leadership Decision Styles Survey (LDSS) is an exercise in decision making. A person, acting as a leader, is asked to indicate which one of the following five styles he or she would use in various problem situations. In each case, the leader has the responsibility, the authority, and the need to make a specific decision. The available styles differ mainly in the degree that the leader involves subordinates in making the decision. They range from the one extreme where the leader makes the decision completely alone without any consultation, to the other extreme, where the decision is essentially turned over to the subordinates.
>
> L1   You, as leader, make the decision alone.
> L2   You seek information and then decide alone.
> LF1 You consult with selected individuals, then decide alone.

LF2 You consult with your entire group, and then decide alone.

M   You share the problem with your group, and you all mutually decide what to do.

John learned that each person's responses are scored against a model primarily based on three factors: 1) the technical quality of the decision, 2) the acceptance of the decision by subordinates, and 3) the time efficiency of the decision. He did not like the summary of his answers, which showed that he involved his subordinates in less participation than the model suggested. As the group discussion proceeded, John felt enough courage to challenge the model, and stated, "Most of the cases involved essentially trivial stuff. Employees are hired because they have special skills. They should be freed to spend their time in the things they are good at and not have their time taken with decisions others can make for them. Most of the cases dealt with the petty stuff that people with time on their hands like to grumble about."

To John's surprise, others joined him in challenging the model, and Pete Emerson seemed to think the criticisms were OK. Maybe the nature of the group with whom you are working makes more of a difference than abstract principles.

John found himself thinking that different people have different needs. Different people think differently. The Myers-Briggs kept coming up in the discussion. It was all right for him to be a visionary INTJ as long as he knew others would think differently. Being reflective was OK. Not being as social was OK. Rational, for him, was good. Let others be empathetic. He could live with that, and it made sense of some curious relations he had had with some of his team back home and even with his kids.

The Monday afternoon program began with a report of the ratings participants had given for the Sunday activities. Ratings were on a scale of 1 to 5 for value and for enjoyment. He had given all 4s and 5s, but some of the others had been less impressed. The distribution of ratings for each topic of the day were passed around. Averages were from 3.6 to 4.6, with the results each person received on the Myers-Briggs being rated highest. John mused that it would be easy to have his gang rate him on everything if he could be sure of being rated so well.

Pete Emerson again took the rostrum to present another set of ideas about leadership, this time the Hersey and Blanchard model of situational leadership. This model helps leaders evaluate the behavior of the group and choose the most appropriate response. It is based on two factors:

1. The amount of direction and structure (task behavior) and/or the amount of personal encouragement, support, and recognition (relationship behavior) a leader must provide.
2. The level of "development" apparent in the followers' behavior.

Pete described the ways in which situations differ for leaders. When members of the group do not know how to do their tasks, they need coaching. When they do not want to work hard, they need motivation and a different relationship. The Hersey and Blanchard model provides an outline to help decide when specific behaviors are needed. It is called a situational leadership model. John was told that a book had been written about it, so he could look it up sometime if he wished.

Evidently Pete had little confidence in the ability of participants to apply this model in a sensible and obvious way and announced a practice session in which small groups would decide how to handle a given case, described briefly on cards he provided. John was sure this would be a waste of time. The groups moved outside into lovely warm weather and began the competition. John's group came to agreement quickly and reported their results before any other group was finished. Emerson then reported on group performance. John's group had the poorest score of the lot.

What had gone wrong? Why had they not done as well as the others? John's group retreated to a corner of the lawn and reviewed their efforts. Two problems arose in the group which they addressed immediately and with a certain heat. First, in the written assignment, the situation was described in two or three sentences. Each group member had made assumptions not warranted by the sentences, and all had agreed that more information was needed. This was no different than work situations: Often the leader does not have some critical items of information and so misreads the situation.

The second issue that gradually became clear to the group was that they had been too polite in their discussions. The first idea presented was agreed upon quickly. Yet each person had brought to the discussion a full but hidden agenda about how groups should be led. Each had a set of assumptions based on experience with various groups and with what had worked. Somehow, these assumptions were added to the short descriptions on the cards so that one person would assume that the team members were comfortable with each other and with the leader, but other team members would assume some tension. Some would assume lots of training had been completed; another would assume innocence and naiveté. The comfort level of the group increased considerably as these differences were talked about. They all agreed that they would be more open in expressing differences in views.

The day had started with breakfast at 8:00 a.m., after a twenty-minute van ride from the hotel, and kept going until 6:00 p.m., when a happy half-hour was planned. Only a thirty-minute break for relaxation—stretching exercises and a brisk walk—had been scheduled. Dinner was provided, gourmet but healthy, followed by one more group exercise. By the time vans were leaving for the hotel, everyone was pretty tired and yet somewhat reluctant to quit. The vans were at their disposal; some talked about what they would like to do. John elected to head for his room, call his wife, read a bit, and get a good night's sleep.

Thursday was the day when John would meet with a professional staff person to find out all that had been learned about him. Phillip and Pete had referred to this day as the peak day. John wondered whether anything could exceed the benefit he had gained from talking with all the other participants. By now they were all good friends, but he had found two who were special. One was a man who had a job much like his; they had shared stories and problems and had found themselves with similar views in many of the group discussions. The other good friend was a woman vice-president of a large insurance company. They had disagreed on many points but every argument had been rational, challenging, and fun. He had not met many bright and articulate women like her and was fascinated. He even wondered whether it might not help for him to watch for some women to recruit into his team at work. He had always assumed that not many women electronics geniuses exist, but maybe he could find one.

Thursday was also the day in which they were to practice their abilities at criticizing each other. Emerson used the word "feedback" rather than "critique"; the idea was to get a message through about how to improve performance without arousing so much emotion and resentment that no message could be heard. He had never felt bashful about telling a person when a mistake had been made or when performance was not up to snuff, except with his new secretary. Any hint of criticism with her and she would start to cry. If he said something direct, she would turn hostile. Anything John could learn about giving feedback sure would help!

He met Alice Whitmore, the trainer who would provide his feedback, in the participant lounge. He had seen her around, in breaks between sessions and at a couple of meals. She had not led any of the discussions he had been in so he did not know what to expect, but he hoped she knew how to give feedback without embarrassing him.

Their meeting was in a small office, this time with no mirrors but with a desk, a cassette recorder, and a notebook full of paper. Alice Whitmore quickly got down to business. "I remind you of our policies and the way in which we will conduct this session. We have all morning. I will tell you in language as specific as I can muster what we have learned about you from watching you in sessions, from the tests and inventories you have completed, and from the observed reactions of others to you. In addition, I will record on cassettes everything I say for you to keep and will give you back every test or inventory you have completed. These are yours; *you* may reveal them to anyone you select, but *we* will reveal them to no one unless you ask us to. Further, I will qualify my descriptions to you by calling upon my knowledge of the limitations of all the measures and observations we have collected on you, so that you will not be tempted to assume we have the "real truth" on you. Our ways of learning about you have their limits. You need to know them.

"You may interrupt at any time; you may ask any questions. What we discuss here is as confidential as are all your test scores. Further, we are not limited by the topics that have been covered in the LDP you are completing. Questions of career, of family, of health, of the balance among activities in your life are as relevant to your superior functioning as a leader as are all of the direct items we have on our program. Indeed, we have often learned from the sponsoring institutions that send people here that such broader issues need to be addressed; they hope we will encourage such self-examination."

John: "All right—let's start with my most serious question. Am I cut out to be a leader, or even a manager? Do I show the right qualities? I know that I was in many ways happier when I was working on my own projects and not responsible for the work of others. Would I be better off going back to what I know best?"

Alice: "You have asked one of the most common questions we hear. Let me give you a straight answer first: We cannot tell you where you will be most happy. But we can tell you that leadership can be exercised in many ways by persons with quite different qualities and quite different styles. I can also tell you that in the many things we have learned about you, there is no quality that stands out that would prevent you from being an effective leader or a fine executive. Sometimes we do find what are called 'stop items.' Handicaps prevent excellence in certain areas: A deaf person cannot be a violinist, a blind person cannot be a dentist. Some personality types hamper performance in some areas: A severe paranoid does not make a good insurance salesperson. Absence of skills closes some pathways; with no mathematics, one cannot be a good physicist. We see no such 'stop items' in all we have learned about you. The decision then, must be made by you on other grounds."

Three hours later, John left the room with an armload of materials, a feeling of exhilaration, and a sense of purpose he had not felt for months. He knew he could be a success at what he was doing. He also knew that he didn't have to give up so much of his life to succeed. He had a plan for self-improvement, for more family life, and for improving his physical fitness and health. He could hardly wait to call his wife. Maybe he would even call his boss. Maybe he should talk to the kids.

John's euphoria is a typical reaction to the comprehensive assessment report given as part of an excellent leadership development program. In part, this reaction is produced by the intensive attention given to one person; after all, the most interesting topic of conversation is one's self, isn't it? And the course is designed with the study of different dimensions of leadership to build up to this day, to the point where each person questions the degree to which he or she can live up to the ideal. To get around—finally—to some resolution of the uncertainty is mighty comforting. Typical comments from participants about this day, the high point of a six-day leadership development program, include:

"The staff feedback was effective and appropriately structured. Delivery was highly professional."

"Enjoyed feedback comments from Laurie—handled in positive manner— allowed me to see/understand that I am better at most things than I perceive myself to be."

"The session with Sullivan was one of the most valuable experiences of a lifetime. He did an excellent job and helped clarify some of the things I knew about myself."

"Very, very good. Needless to say, the best part of the course! Jeanne did an excellent job of helping me to pull together all the information about myself."

"This was my first experience with a psychologist and I found it a unique experience. It was not as hard to be open with a 'stranger' as I had anticipated. I appreciated the insights and feedback. It was very valuable."

"The most valuable self-improvement experience in my entire work career. Will be of great value both at work and in my personal life."

"I had been looking forward to the tie-in of all the different inputs. I was pleased at how it all came together in such a believable way."

"On the money. Nonthreatening."

"Quite worthwhile session—well presented."

"Staff feedback raised some interesting questions about the high level of tolerance I had for work and personal situations I am not happy with."

"Don't be afraid to give negative feedback. Positive is good, but we are all mature adults and should be able to handle negative feedback. More negative feedback would have been helpful."

"This one day provided a rare opportunity to learn about oneself. I appreciated the time involvement and insight that was apparent in the staff feedback and the sincerity and kindness of the peer feedback."

Goal Setting

The final unit in most development programs asks the "So what?" question. If this program has provided insights into better modes of functioning and if you have learned more about yourself, what difference will all of this make on your work, your life, and your relations with family and community? If you have learned more about your capabilities, what effect does that have on your aspirations? If you have reorganized your priorities, what changes will become obvious to your associates at work, at home, and in the community? If you have uncovered weaknesses in your modes of behavior, what reeducation and change do you plan? If others have noted your strengths, have you? Do you have plans to build on those strengths?

Any well-run organization must have forward-looking plans and programs. So, also, must each individual. The last discussion sessions in a program should focus attention on plans for change and improvement. All plans include work related goals. But improving one's life was sought by most program participants, including attention to problems at home and such basic matters as quitting smoking, losing weight, developing better eating habits, spending less time at a desk, spending more time with family, and creating a better balance in one's life.

Participants found out about the interesting work at the University of Texas where psychologists have learned to separate workaholics into two groups: those who spend an excess of time in the work setting to reduce anxiety and sometimes guilt or to escape less pleasurable circumstances at home, and those who work excessively for the joy of the tasks. The former are true Type A persons who usually develop cardiac and vascular problems. The ones who find sheer joy in work tend not to develop such disorders.

Goal setting is a group activity in a leadership development program. Just as participants practice criticizing each other in the peer feedback settings, so now they practice advising each other about ways to develop greater strength in their work setting and to achieve greater happiness by enriching their lives. As expected, great individual differences are found in willingness to reveal personal matters; staff in the program guide the discussions to permit the retention of privacy by those who cherish it. Talk, early on, about differences in modes of thought and behavior provide a good base as this discussion progresses.

Leave Taking

John came to the conference worrying about his ability to assimilate such a large group as twenty-four participants. On Friday afternoon he experienced, to his surprise, an anticipatory feeling of loss as the group was disbanding and sought out a number of persons to arrange some means for keeping in touch. He was also pleased that so many persons were seeking him out and expressing interest in keeping in touch with him. That some of them described the great contribution he had made to the group was exhilarating and gave him great satisfaction, but he wondered if they were really talking about the person he perceived himself to be. He wondered also if maybe his ideas about himself needed a little re-adjustment. How could such closeness have developed in such a short period?

John Miller represents a typical person participating in a leadership development program. Although the report is sketchy, many of the experiences are actual. How each person reacts depends on the specific program attended. What has been described is intended to be a brief snapshot album rather than a summary. To recount the total impact of a development program on the lives and careers of participants would be nearly impossible and perhaps misleading. However, each experience demonstrates unique effects and conveys the importance of learning more about one's self. The willing individual can benefit from having the opportunity to change and improve.

Significant learning occurs when a program takes advantage of the differences among participants in order to challenge each to reexamine usual ways of working with others. Through exercises, the program can provide the opportunity for self-reflection to clarify differences in styles of behaving in leadership roles, insight into one's strengths and weaknesses, and reexamination of personal values. Good programs teach how to receive and give feedback on performance and also provide practice in self-assessment and goal setting.

Programs of this sort abound, each with its special emphasis. Many emphasize increased knowledge of finance, law, labor relations, marketing, or some such specialty. Some provide an escape from the day-to-day pressures and spend the time outdoors or in perusing the classics. Some are essentially therapy sessions and allow for exchange of experiences by participants. The programs that receive awards from professional organizations and accolades from users are those that feature many of the elements in the program just described.

CHAPTER NINE

Education and Training for Leaders

A wide variety of courses and programs are offered currently by training centers, colleges, and universities, as well as by business and industry, to train and develop leaders. The Leadership Development Program described in the previous chapter is one example. The titles of these programs often suggest their content, but they cover such areas as strategic planning, team building, putting creative ideas into action, preparing for the executive suite, bringing about change, today's woman in a man's world, modeling and mentoring, living up to a high set of values, why others count, motivation for action in the real world, putting changes into focus, making an organization work, keeping goals in view, systems leadership, and many others. These subjects suggest ways leaders and managers need to change their behavior to be more effective. But to understand them fully and to get a feel for how they may be useful, detailed descriptions must be read. Many programs deal with specific problems while others are customized training courses designed to fit the requirements of clients.

Training Programs for Leaders and Managers

When we think of training programs, the image comes to mind of the new employee being readied to start a new "hands-on job." Often training programs in industry and business are formulated to assure that a specific set of goals is reached or a specific task is accomplished. But beyond these are numerous training and development programs for every level of organizational structure. These are usually short courses offered within the organization or by training centers to meet the needs of those in charge of groups. One such program that targets persons in positions of leadership at a high level is a worthy place to begin a brief review.

Leadership at the Peak is the name of a program for top-level executives that is offered about ten times a year. It is an intense five-day program attended by CEOs, presidents, executive vice-presidents, managing directors, senior officials from government and the nonprofit sector, and others charged with overall direction of an organization. The participants take a fresh look at themselves, learn how others see them, share problems with others in like positions, learn more about what is expected of them, and step back from their day-to-day problems to work on ways to change the climate of their organizations. Tests are given and interpreted and trained observers and professional staff members assist them in all sorts of analyses of their behavior. The size of each class is limited and breakout groups are small. Those who take part discover the strengths of feedback—to give and to receive—and the rewards and complexities of being innovative; during it all, they are able to practice sharpening their listening and communicating skills. They set and examine their own goals and struggle with their own ethical intentions; they learn the advantages of good health and means for coping with stress, and they attempt to gain insight into their capability to deal with small as well as large groups, especially with other individuals with whom they must interact.

Evaluations are done on each session, and the ratings for this program tend to be high. In response to the question, "What did I learn about myself?" one person said, "I thought that I was sensitive and caring in my life style and in my work relationships, but I don't communicate well enough for this to come through. I can change." Another said, "I need to pay attention to health and find a way to elevate the feeling of trust in subordinates." Still another, "I must learn to care for people."

Many reports from participants indicated that they believe it is never too late to learn and change. How dramatically this kind of program affects individuals in leadership positions is a signal that there may be great benefit in starting an educational process of this kind much earlier in the life and development of each person.

Leadership at the Peak is offered by a center specializing in the research and training of leaders. Many business firms offer training programs for their own managers and leaders. Each year, *Training Magazine* reviews the training practices of large corporations; reports reveal the enormous cost of the training enterprise. In 1989, it totaled more than $45.5 billion. Within this total, $2.87 billion was spent on "Seminars and Conferences," with training provided by outside agencies. The largest portion of total expenditures is on salaries for training staff. This item increased by $1.4 billion from 1989 to 1990, from $12.1 billion to $14.9 billion. The total training hours delivered in 1990 is estimated to have been 1.38 billion hours, up 10% over 1989. Production workers received the largest number of hours of training with 305 million hours, up 22% from 1989. Middle managers received 103 million hours; executives, 27 million hours. These percentages did not change from 1989 to 1990; they still represent the highest per capita investment in training hours for any group.

In mid-1991, an article in *Personnel Journal*[1] reported a survey done by the American Society for Training and Development (ASTD) indicating that leadership training is ". . . offered by more than 60% of the nation's largest companies." It went on to report the following findings:

> Only 18% of the survey participants reported that leadership development was not a priority at their company, but 67% reported having a set of recognized leadership values, many of which are defined in writing. Among the companies providing leadership training, 93% offer it to middle management, 66% to top management, 48% to executives, 79% to supervisors and 33% to non-supervisors. The survey also found that more than half of the leadership development programs are designed by training departments within corporations, and nearly two thirds are presented through these departments. Outside vendors and consultants account for the design and presentation of about a third. The rest come from off-the-shelf and university programs.

Detailing the variety of organizations providing training would take more space than these pages allow. The professional organization, the American Society for Training and Development, provides a national arena in which these organizations communicate with clients and with each other. Their publications, annual exposition, and mailing lists provide a network among providers and users. They do not, however, provide a basis for selection of programs, of benefits associated with internal versus external providers, of merits of video and other training materials, or of bases for choosing one training approach over another. With many options available, the rule is *caveat emptor*.

Training Systems

Training of employees is a calculated investment for the employer. It also is a boon to the person entering the world of work for the first time, shifting from one level to another, or reentering in a different role. The training industry has flourished in response to these interests and to the willingness of organizations to invest in their products. When the programs are well designed, trainees acquire new skills that are needed on the job, learn to perform new functions, and expand their usefulness demonstrably to the employer.

A review of seventy studies on the effectiveness of management training by Russell, Wexley, and Hunter[2] showed behavior modeling to be among the most effective training methods available. One reason for this superiority is that modeling helps the person who is ready to learn to be able to recognize that he or she has the competence to do it—the task is clearly doable. Recent development training programs have emphasized self-management or self-regulation in order to increase feelings of self-efficacy, with goal setting at the core of the program. Goal setting works by clarifying for the trainee what is to be attained.

Behavior modeling was used and evaluated by Richard J. Ritchie and Joseph L. Moses[3] in enhancing the interpersonal skills of AT&T supervisors in dealing with their employees. The data showed that people who had been trained through the use of filmed models were rated by judges as more effective in role-playing simulations than people who had not received such training. Another investigator reported that supervisors at General Electric who participated in behavior-modeling training also received higher ratings on role-playing simulations than untrained supervisors.

Latham and Saari[4] studied first-line supervisors at the Weyerhauser Company. Before training, they developed multiple criteria for evaluating behavior modeling and selected a control group to provide a follow-up measure of performance on the job. The trained group improved performance substantially. Subsequent training of individuals in the control group raised their performance to the level of the initially trained groups. This study strongly supports the use of behavior-modeling training programs in industry for bringing about a relatively permanent change in supervisory behavior. Fundamental to the effectiveness of behavior modeling are learning points for the trainee, which are stated in concrete behavioral terms such as: make the praise specific; give the praise immediately after the behavior occurs; focus on the issue, rather than the employee; and focus on the future rather than the past.

An example of a training program that relied on the use of a video tape to demonstrate learning points is provided in the work of Melvin Sorcher and Rod Spence in a South African plant.[5] Supervisors from parts of the plant not involved in the study of effects performed as actors in the video tapes. The situations included in the supervisor training were *How to Welcome a New Employee, How to Give Instructions, How to Recognize Dependable Performance, How to Correct Unacceptable Work/Work Habits, How to Take Corrective Action, How to Respond to an Employee Complaint, How to Introduce Change,* and *How to Encourage your Employee to Express an Opinion.* Situations included in employee training were the reciprocal of these: *How to Clarify Instructions, How to Ask Your Supervisor About Your Performance, How to Respond to Constructive Criticism of Work/Work Habits, How to Respond to Unfair Criticism of Work/Work Habits, How to Make a Complaint, How to Cooperate in a Changing Situation, How to Express a Different Opinion,* and *How to Ask for Help or Guidance.*

Dramatic changes resulted from the training. For example, employees were asked: "Does your supervisor think you are clever and know your job?" Pretraining answers were: "He says we are baboons and he plays the music and we must dance," and "We don't know . . . because he doesn't say." After the training, employees answered: "Treats us like we know our jobs," and "He delegates a task, leaves me to do it, and appreciates good work."

Emphasis in recent development training programs has been on self-management or self-regulation. This training has proved especially effective in increasing self-efficacy. The core of the training is goal setting. Goal setting improves performance because of its specificity and simplicity. It makes clear to the employee or trainee what is to be attained and provides an obvious tie between behavior and its consequences. It works best when the worker participates in setting goals or is persuaded that they are fair and achievable.

Frederick F. Kanfer,[6] professor of Psychology at the University of Illinois, has developed training programs designed for obtaining commitment to an attainment of self-generated goals. In brief, the training teaches people to assess problems, set specific goals related to those problems, monitor ways in which the environment facilitates or hinders goal attainment, and identify and administer reinforcers for working toward (and punishers for failing to work toward) goal attainment. This training teaches people skills in self-observation; it teaches them ways to compare their behavior with the goals they set and to administer reinforcers and punishers that will bring about and sustain good goal commitment. The reinforcer or punisher is made contingent on the degree to which the behavior approximates the goals. Reinforcers and punishers are viewed in terms of informational and emotional feedback in order to take account of cognitive as well as motoric and autonomic effects. He has found goal-setting training especially effective in teaching people to overcome alcoholism and substance abuse.

The power of goal setting has been demonstrated many times. Frayne and Latham[7] trained unionized state government employees to increase their work attendance. Training consisted of goal setting, writing of a behavioral contract, self-monitoring, and the selecting and administering of rewards and punishments. Training in self-management and emphasis on self-efficacy developed skills in overcoming personal and social obstacles that affect job attendance. As a result, employee attendance was significantly higher in the training group than in a control group that received no training. Higher perceived self-efficacy was related to better subsequent job attendance. This increase in job attendance continued over at least twelve months. The control group was then given the same training. Both self-efficacy and job attendance increased to a level parallel to that of the original experimental group.

Leadership Courses and Programs in Schools and Universities

The preceding studies exemplify those that have provided guidelines for the explosive increase in training and development of persons at all levels in business, industry, the military, and government worldwide. This has been in response to the expressed need of many to meet the competition of global commerce and a surging international economy.

However, interest in leadership education is not confined to those who are seeking new markets or promotion and greater responsibility in the workplace. Students in high school and college, volunteers in community organizations, directors of agencies in urban and rural areas, graduate and professional degree candidates, and teachers, professors, and administrators at all levels of the educational enterprise have begun to recognize the benefits to be gained by formally studying leadership and by engaging in leader development courses and programs.

This is not an entirely new happening. Education for leadership has always been a direct or indirect purpose of education. In the United States, it has been a goal of public schooling since the founding of the new colonies in America, a heritage based on many traditions. The educational practices of every group of persons in the world have been influenced by the persistent necessity to train for leadership. What differs is the form and sometimes the content.

In earlier days in the United States, college attendance reflected a commitment to a life of leadership and influence; college graduates represented a small and elite portion of the society. The objectives of educational programs included developing the ability to inform and persuade, to argue logically, and to engage successfully in debate. The readings in history, literature, and philosophy presumably enabled students to cite precedent, to perceive the errors of certain ways, and to guide decisions based on the highest moral standards.

Today in the U.S., a large proportion of secondary school graduates attend college. Community colleges have multiplied. Curricula have changed. Although liberal arts curricula are advised for all students, many students become more oriented toward preparing for specific vocations or for increased specialization as they pursue advanced degrees. Still, colleges aspire to have a critical influence on their students. The introductory pages of college bulletins laud liberal arts programs as leading to greater commitment, preparing students for lives of responsible citizenship, and enabling their graduates to join the select group able to make informed and value-based decisions. Few colleges can avoid citing famous alumni as evidence of the merits of their programs.

As more and more people decry the lack of leaders in our society today, more and more colleges and universities, an occasional high school, and many professional schools are offering explicit courses and programs on leadership. Most courses are designed either to teach leadership or to train and develop leaders with varying combinations to serve both purposes. Some courses show evidence of being compromises with traditional curricular patterns, their descriptions suggesting that they exist within departmental offerings under duress, whereas others are clearly well thought out and take advantage of many academic disciplines.

The stated objectives of each course often reflect the disciplinary background of the instructor and the general mission of the organization of which they are a part. Syllabi generally state the purposes, sometimes the underlying philosophy, the conduct of the course (expectations, projects, research, formal presentations, seminar meetings, discussions, workshops, etc.), the requirements (attendance, participation, exams, papers, observations, personal experiences with mentors, etc.), required readings, supplemental texts, schedules of classes, grading, topics, fieldwork, and so forth. Some courses use biographies, research studies, and texts and apply them to contemporary organizations, social change, and critical pertinent issues.

In many programs and courses, students are encouraged to accept membership and leadership in causes that will sensitize them and lead them to an understanding of problems that pertain to intercultural differences. Because the solutions to these problems will be their charge in the future, it is stated that they would do well to learn about them early. To prepare women for leadership roles there are courses that deal with the history and impact of the feminist movement and what it has or has not accomplished in recent decades. Ethics and value systems are frequently emphasized. Research is reviewed, and writings on leadership are assigned.

Several examples follow to acquaint the reader with the variety in content, scope, curricular intent, disciplinary background, intended audience, and time spans of courses and programs. They have been selected because they are excellent models. They represent but a few of hundreds currently offered in the United States and in other countries to serve students engaged in standard academic programs or those readying themselves to be better leaders in their communities.

The State University of New York at Binghamton

A seminar course, "Leadership and Supervision," is taught in the School of Management at the State University of New York at Binghamton by Bruce Avolio, Ph.D. Courses vary depending on the level of sophistication of students and the instructor in charge, but the following brief description of this course provides a useful example.

> Learning objectives: to provide a broad overview of topics relevant to the concepts of leadership, with a primary goal of showing how effective leadership can be nurtured in organizations. Leadership skills will be practiced to develop leadership potential. Pertinent research will be connected to practice.
>
> Goals include: to survey, critique, and understand models of leadership; to examine definitions of leadership and means for measuring it; to understand strategies for helping to systematically learn more about the construct of leadership; to discover how leadership can be developed; to explore links between leadership and other fields such as motivation, learning, organizational effectiveness, culture, TQM, etc.; to learn about one's own leadership style and practice effective leadership skills. Texts, newspapers, and popular journals are assigned and recommended for producing papers.
>
> Topics for papers include: Ethics, Moral Values, Leadership Development, Application of Leadership Models over Multicultural Settings, Leadership Development for Profit versus Nonprofit Organizations, and Linking Leadership to Total Quality Management Efforts.
>
> Teaching methods employed are: brief lecturettes, discussions, case reviews, videotapes, exercises, projects, and a final exam. Students work in teams and individually. In one project, each student "shadows" a leader in action who is interviewed and observed. An individual critical incident log is required as well as a team summary observational report based on models of leadership reviewed in the course.

In addition to teaching traditional courses in leadership, the Center for Leadership Studies at the School of Management at the State University of New York at Binghamton is supported by the W. K. Kellogg Foundation to train and evaluate community leaders to become more effective transformational leaders. The Kellogg Leadership Program develops transformational leaders who: establish goals and objectives with the intent of developing followers into leaders; raise the consciousness level of followers about the value of specific goals and how to reach them; inspire followers to go beyond their own immediate self-interests for the sake of the mission and vision of the organization; and motivate followers to do more than originally expected.

The assumptions about leadership are: effective leadership is a key factor in community development; community leaders can sharpen their leadership skills through training, resulting in more effective community leadership; transformational leaders contribute more to effective community development and appear to generate consistently higher levels of effort and effectiveness from followers; and community leaders can be trained to be more transformational and thus collectively more effective.

The program is applicable to any organization. It is conducted in two three-day workshops and includes a preassessment, a three-month planning interval between the two workshops, and follow-up upon completion of both workshops. It uses a variety of teaching methods that include: the presentation of an identifiable leadership model; videotaping; various forms of feedback; case studies that emphasize delegation and development of followers as well as awareness of values that underlie decisions; and the solving of a real time problem submitted by participants using the Decision Support Center, a network of twenty-one personal computers, and new problem-solving tools learned in the program.

The University of Richmond

Another example worthy of description is the Jepson School of Leadership Studies established in 1992 at the University of Richmond in Richmond, Virginia. It is the first higher educational college in the U.S. devoted to leadership studies, and it is the first to offer an undergraduate degree in leadership. The programs are designed to prepare leaders in all fields, thus the curriculum embraces all the disciplines offered by all the schools and organizations of the University. The faculty, selected to cover areas such as political science, history, philosophy, organizational behavior, experiential education, ethics, communications, psychology, and sociology, is encouraged to explore innovative teaching and learning techniques. "Foundations of Leadership," a required course for all who intend to major or minor in leadership and open to all students, is described by the Jepson School Dean, Dr. Howard T. Prince, as "part of preparing for service and living in the 21st Century." An assessment instrument has been devised to evaluate the course; the ratings of the course by students are reviewed by the faculty who teach it, and improvements are made accordingly.

> The course has five class sections, with an average of 18 students in each section. Professor Thomas Wren teaches three sections; Professor William Howe teaches 2 sections. In this third iteration of the course, student evaluations and general faculty assessment were the basis for redesign. The course occurs over 14 weeks (28 class periods of 75 minutes or 42 classes of 50 minutes) and is divided into seven modules: 1) History and Theory of leadership; 2) Critical Thinking; 3) Leadership Contexts; 4) Leading Individuals; 5) Leading Groups; 6) Moral Dimensions of Leadership; and 7) Leadership Competencies.
>
> The purposes of the course are: 1) to help students understand and apply the "foundational knowledge" of leadership in the course and in other contexts, and 2) to prepare students for more in-depth study and practice of leadership encountered in the more advanced curriculum of the Jepson School. The course covers the modern theoretical perspectives of leadership including charismatic authority, situational leadership, and transactional and transformational leadership. It

includes the ways women lead, leader-follower relations, race and multicultural aspects, and ethical issues. The nature of critical/creative thinking is considered in terms of understanding and practicing leadership. In the third module, the focus is on formal organizations, political systems, social movements, and community organizations. Understanding individuals and the phases of adult development as well as motivation lead into the study of group processes. Moral and ethical dimensions of leadership are the subject of Module 6 with the final part of the course focussing on specific leadership competencies, such as communicating well, handling conflict, providing a vision, effecting change, and analyzing/implementing policy to address problems. The bibliography is drawn from many sources and disciplines, and the assigned readings are sophisticated.

The faculty evaluate the course with the intent to discover whether the clearly stated objectives for each module have been met and to provide information for improving the course as the basis for the curricular model they are offering.

Preparing Leaders for Nonprofit Organizations

Preparation for leadership will continue to be a requirement because of the large number of groups seeking leaders. There are somewhere between 800,000 and 2 million nonprofit organizations in the United States. Seven million people are employed in nonprofit organizations in the U.S. and nearly that many persons volunteer to assist their efforts. Although business firms have developed many formal programs for training persons for promotion and leadership, little formal education and training is available to help nonprofit organizations select and develop their leadership.

An exception is the Mandel Center for Nonprofit Organizations in Cleveland, Ohio, a university-wide academic center sponsored by three prominent professional schools of Case Western Reserve University: the Mandel School of Applied Social Science, the Weatherhead School of Management, and the School of Law. These schools have joined in partnership to address the growing need for professional education of managers and leaders of private, nonprofit organizations and to encourage and disseminate research on the nonprofit sector.

The programs of the Mandel Center are guided by principles that demand excellence in the educational and research programs for the nonprofit sector, responsiveness to the special character of these organizations because they differ from business and government, and interdisciplinary study that brings to bear the most advanced knowledge and techniques of management, law, social sciences, and the cultural and helping professions. The various offerings of the Mandel Center include:

> The *Masters of Nonprofit Organizations* (MNO), an advanced professional degree for managers and leaders of nonprofit organizations offering 45 credit hours over 17, 24, or 33 month sequences set in intensive formats scheduled to accommodate working professionals or those otherwise employed. The curriculum recognizes concerns such as management of volunteers and professionals, resource development and fund raising, governance by boards of trustees and directors, funding management, legal framework, values of service in community, and character of leadership required.

> The *Certificate in Nonprofit Management*, a set of five graduate credited courses offered for practicing managers and leaders in human service, fine and performing arts, cultural, educational, civic, religious, and nonprofit organizations who hold or aspire to senior-level executive positions.

The *Executive Education Program*, workshops and training to meet the needs of nonprofit groups and organizations, a Public Lecture Series, a Conference Program for current research discussion, a Research Program, and a Publication Program that publishes and distributes a newsletter, an international journal, and a series of research papers.

Teaching Resources for Leadership Training

A thorough review of the available training programs and courses in leadership illustrates limitless numbers and variations of teaching methods and formats used to advance learning. Among them are journal keeping, oral and written exposition, assessment with self- and other-inventories, observation and critical analysis of meetings and organizational processes, and interviews of persons in leadership positions. Subject matter and teaching devices used in each course or training program vary depending on the disciplinary background of instructors and facilitators and the composition or career interests of the student body. The components are easily adapted to specific purposes and thus appear in many varieties of courses and programs.

Keeping a Journal

There is good reason why so many courses require students to write journals. Journals can be a path to self-understanding, a means for recording one's observations, a technique for improving writing skills, a method for conveying one's own understanding of the lessons learned in the course, a memory tickler for writing more significant papers or essays, a means for evaluating the course and/or the instructor, a technique for clarifying one's goals, a measure for checking on one's own commitment or on how much and how many others are responding to the writer. For young students or mature adults, journals are an invaluable asset in setting down evidence to discover whether or not leadership behavior is becoming a part of one's active life.

A journal, unlike a diary, is likely to be a part of one's public rather than private life. It is a tool for retaining one's thoughts in less than polished form, but it does not play memory tricks. Starting a journal with the question asked by Kouzes and Posner, "When am I acting most like a leader?" as a running theme, makes the journal a useful tool for recognizing what leadership is and whether the writer is committed to undertake the challenge. The journal can help define leadership behavior, teach something about feedback, introduce the importance of social reactions, reduce ambiguity, sensitize persons to each other's unvoiced attitudes, lay out the importance of rational thinking, and highlight ways to change one's own and others' behavior. Using presentations of several journals or parts of them can assist students of all ages to deal with issues such as the extent to which a position of leadership exposes one's private life and how much can be delegated to others to accomplish. Understanding the differences in the way that even a simple situation is viewed by someone else is a lesson to be valued by all.

Self-Testing Instruments

Using *The Campbell Development Surveys* as the basis for aiding in self-understanding is a valuable experience.[8] Persons read their inventory scores as if they had gone to a fortuneteller. It is exciting to hear more about yourself and, what's more, it sticks. Tell a person that he or she is destined to be a leader and you have someone trying to act like one. Using the survey forms and teaching others how to read them is a great way to absorb important theory and research that would otherwise be mere statements. Application to oneself clarifies the intent.

Mentors and Mentoring

Writing journals and receiving feedback from a person concerned with your development provides for a reflection on experience that is critical to changing one's behavior for more effective leadership. The determination of where vision leaves off and reality begins is an excellent topic to pursue. Indications of how literature can shape values and extend capacities to envision improvement and better conditions should not be overlooked. The influences of a friend, a teacher, a film, a parent, a sticky situation, or a startling experience can open the door to leadership interest. However, it is not necessary to live forty years before shaping experiences have their effect. Mentors and models leave their mark.

Mentors: Good or Bad? Every organization must worry about whether or not its mentoring program works to preserve the status quo or addresses current problems and supports innovation. Often the opening for discussions about leadership may come about with questions concerning the importance of responding to change in the external climate.

Loden and Rosener examined many organizational practices that relate to fuller use of human resources and have recorded their observations on mentoring:

> Historically, within homogeneous institutions, mentoring has been the dominant group's method of informal succession planning. As such, those in power routinely selected others of similar core identity, shared insider information with them about unstated rules and norms, provided one-on-one counseling and, generally, helped select individuals to move ahead. Like some traditional father-son relationships, mentoring helped to preserve the established order by concentrating organizational power in the hands of the dominant group. While this process of "natural selection" went on in virtually every institution in America, it was seldom discussed or challenged.
>
> Then, during the 1970's as culture clash increased and *others* began to challenge mainstream traditions, this mentoring process came under intense scrutiny. By the 1980's mentoring came to be viewed as a critical ingredient in the formula for career success. Therefore, in many organizations it was deemed crucial that *others* be given mentors to assure their future success.
>
> Since then, diverse employees, researchers, change agents, executives, and many institutions committed to valuing diversity have tried to reconstitute the original mentor relationship of old—with limited success. The inherent contradiction in old versus new values is underscored in mentoring. Organizations that did not value diversity used mentoring to help the dominant group preserve the status quo, share insider information, and perpetuate the homogeneous ideal. It was an exclusive rather than inclusive strategy that promoted elitism, secrecy, and manipulation. As such, the essential purpose behind mentoring worked *in opposition to* the philosophy of valuing diversity. For this reason, it is time for organizations to abandon mentoring as a strategy for valuing diversity and acknowledge it for what it is—a vestige of the past and *not* the key to a more productive future.
>
> Unlike mentoring, informal coaching and tutoring programs do not hinge on the

creation of exclusive, one-on-one relationships. They do not presume that there are unstated "rules" or norms in the organization that only a select group of insiders should know about or discuss. Instead, they are inclusive mechanisms for individual change that focus on technical, interpersonal, and managerial skill development.[9]

The recommendation of Rosen and Lodener seems too strong when they propose abandoning mentoring programs. The method is a good one. The use of more senior persons in an organization to counsel junior individuals has proved highly beneficial to many women and ethnic minority members, as well as white males, as they have struggled to gain recognition. Every organization needs to reexamine its programs for providing such mentoring services to assure that they are in accord with organization-wide policies and values. Many persons with sufficient experience in an organization who appear to be good prospects as mentors may still carry with them vestiges of past policies and practices that disqualify them for such service.

The Lessons of Trauma

Are there lessons to be learned in having one's plans for a lifetime disrupted? What do traumatic events do to one's image of the future? How adaptive should one be? Is flexibility something that can be taught? In what ways do unexpected experiences shape our future? We must continue to question. For example, what can be learned from the women serving in the military in the Middle East who came up sharply against a culture for women they never could have envisioned? How will that change their thinking? What roles will they want to play as women leaders? What have the emerging leaders in the eastern European countries learned from the catastrophes resulting from suppressed hatreds? Will they have a different view of political life and how to achieve peace after such experiences? What was the effect of the coup on Russia's Mikhail Gorbachev? Or the later victories and struggles on Russia's Boris Yeltsin?

None of us lives in isolation. Leadership has everything to do with followership; power and authority are enmeshed in the whole process of acting and being acted upon. There are consequences to accepting responsibility and plunging forward with courage and compassion. There are differences between taking risks for the benefit of others in order to improve the quality of life of society and taking risks for the sheer excitement that violent behavior can bring. All individuals have choices to make; decisions depend on our readiness for assuming the roles we play and the experiences that resulted from past choices.

The analysis of a single life to determine the effects of all of the influences that have affected it would take the lifetime of an investigator. Currently we have only primitive methods at the disposal of researchers interested in such study. Perhaps new research tools in this area will improve as interest in the topic increases.

CHAPTER TEN

Learning Leadership Through Experience

Lifetime experiences can affect the development of persons and produce for some those qualities we admire in the best of our leaders. Living through multiple experiences cannot be enough to nourish leadership; if it were, our best and wisest leaders would be our most adventuresome and our oldest. But we know that some people, as they age, become more sensible, more committed, more involved, and more effective while others deteriorate and become less able, more cautious, less interested in their work and careers, and less energetic. Learning lessons about leadership and having experiences in leading and following seem to assist in developing a style of leadership and the capability to deal with problems so as to avoid egregious errors.

Early Experiences

Many autobiographies of eminent persons recount early experiences that shaped their lives. Most of them refer to events that took place long before they were launched on a career or the schooling to prepare for it. Recalling their early days makes them appear human, vulnerable, and more like the rest of us. Sometimes these accounts provide insights into good methods of parenting, teaching, and perhaps leading. Clarence Thomas reflected on the early childhood influence of his grandfather during his Senate confirmation hearings for appointment to the Supreme Court of the United States. Many persons recall the influence of a particular teacher in shaping their lives.

The advice of a parent or a friend or a teacher that is long remembered may tell us why we took a particular direction. The origins of high aspirations, of a strong sense of duty, and of values that guide decisions can often be assigned to early influences of parents, grandparents, and other models. We should take these accounts seriously, for they suggest ways in which parents and families can engender values and beliefs during a critical period in development. Yet we have little evidence that such accounts, however accurate, describe the actual basis for a successful and satisfying life. We lack control groups, and we do not know that all of the persons whose early experiences fit similar models have had equally satisfying and successful lives.

The studies that proclaimed the success of "Head Start" programs examined the effects of enriching the intellectual and social experiences of young children before entering school. It was proved that these programs increased the likelihood of success in primary school classes to such a degree as to warrant a considerable investment in their continuance. It may be that the effects will be long term; the results are not yet known. But even these studies are unlikely to provide any empirical evidence indicating that those persons involved in the program will demonstrate greater dedication to the common good or heightened attitudes and beliefs that epitomize ideal leaders.

When populations were differently dispersed, three generations of a family

110

might have lived in one domicile in a community tiny enough so that all persons were acquainted, where the school population was small and neighborly. Such a society could establish standards of conduct, values, and beliefs that would be sustained from generation to generation with only a few dissidents. Not so today. The influence of family life is reduced when schooling begins with a bus at the corner and when parents and family, for whatever reasons, spend shorter times with the offspring. It is at this time that not only the teachers but also the school peer group begin to have an impact on interests, goals, preferences, and previously learned values. At younger ages the need to be accepted is high, and children are easily influenced. Not to be overlooked is the effect of the mass media on youths, directing their attention to sports, entertainment, music, material possessions, and unfortunately, to the chilling thrills of violence. Adapting to fads and fashions can become a way of life for many. Because higher-order value and belief systems are continually bombarded, the stability for maintaining them that was taken for granted in earlier generations has just about vanished.

In spite of this, many young persons are able to develop and sustain commitment to more desirable moral and ethical values no matter how hard pressed they are to conform to beliefs and behaviors that might undermine them. Some parents manage to hold on courageously to the precepts they learned that were useful and can demonstrate to their children the importance of emulating them. Subgroups form within the school and within religious and neighborhood communities to reinforce treasured values. There are still noble teachers, coaches, and counselors adept at playing the roles of ideal models and mentors who are remembered wistfully by their students long after these unselfish persons believe they have been forgotten.

There is another side to the effects of peer pressure. Frequently the family values that are being eroded are values no longer appropriate in a changing society. Young persons often need an alternative to a rigid or dysfunctional family or community setting, and frequently it is the peer group that provides the necessary outlet and support for developing a more meaningful life.

Tryouts in Leadership

The qualities that make some individuals excellent prospects for becoming leaders often emerge at very early ages. At first it may be attributable to their having been propelled or selected into it by their siblings, parents, teachers, coaches, or friends. In many settings, a group begins as a leaderless group and gradually turns to one person who acts in an executive role, planning, making arrangements, assigning tasks, and taking responsibility.

Watching children play "tag" over a period of time is revealing. They will often yell out the same name over and over to be "It" first. To be "It" first is not to be the butt; rather it is the person who sets the tone of the play or has previously earned the reputation as the best runner or most artful tagger. When choosing up sides to play a team game, kids will point out Charlie or Mary to be the captain and indicate their enthusiasm, either by jumping up and down or by some other obvious body language, for serving on a particular team. Hasn't something been learned about leadership and followership when one does not remember the profound and giddy pleasure of being the popularly chosen one to be first or be in the captain spot, but instead has only felt the sinking discouragement of being the last to be chosen for the team?

Those who find satisfaction in executive roles sometimes also discover the pain they will have to endure as their actions are criticized or even as they have to make choices about whom to befriend and whom to shun. For others, the uncomfortable "hire and fire" syndrome—with its accompanying attacks of headaches and sleepless nights—may occur at a later time on another stage.

By trying out the leadership role, some learn about the sensitivity of others. Whatever the age, it is not easy to watch someone cry when you are the person who had some responsibility for that reaction. What lessons there are in considering how to avoid hurting others or in dealing with them in ways that provide a healing antidote should be reported in boldface. Not picking a poor player for a team may appear easy when you are ten years old, but somehow it becomes a different matter and the pain is piercing when you have to tell someone he or she is an incompetent employee or that his or her bungling means that the company faces bankruptcy or that a platoon of soldiers has been wiped out.

It is possible to learn methods to reduce intragroup conflict. Everyone has experienced the bewilderment of facing multiple strongly held ideas in a small group discussion that turned into a heated argument. It is especially confounding when it is unexpected and when the ideas do not appear to contradict each other and when the persons involved have impressed you as fairly sensible. Often part of the memory is vivid: You remember where you were when the argument took place and even most of the faces—if not the names—of the discussants, even though you preserve little about the subject under discussion or how you reacted and how the experience shaped your later behavior.

What Must be Learned in High School and College

For most young people the first steps into high school are fearful yet exciting. The school building is larger than the one attended the previous year, the students too, are taller, and most of them seem to know where classes are located. The academic subjects begin to have titles that sound as if the grades for them are the keys to open college or career doors. Moreover, parents seem to know less about how the learning process functions and what is expected from each student, so seeking advice from that source brings vague responses. And what is most confusing is the need to make choices. Apparently there are counselors available to help, but first the system for making appointments and learning to ask smart questions has to be worked out. It will get worse in college, but most high school students do not know that. It will get even worse later on for most people, and far too many are unprepared to acknowledge that.

Assuming responsibility to clarify goals and to set priorities for meeting them, learning the skills that will be needed in the "real" world, establishing satisfying relationships, and joining clubs or trying out for teams or groups that will be enjoyable are difficult challenges for adults, but they are present and almost overwhelming problems for high school students. These decisions take more emotional stamina than signing up for English I, social studies, or the right level of math. Figuring out how to fit schoolwork and the assignment for learning new plays for football or a new piece of music for band practice into an evening when you hoped to watch a game or a show on TV is almost too much to handle. It is not much help to get parental feedback that amounts to "Just get your work done!" It is almost impossible to believe that learning how to bring some order into some of this perplexity will be the stuff you can use to plan your future and establish some important goals.

Leadership programs and courses are now being offered on many college and university campuses. When the purposes and objectives are examined, it becomes clear that, in somewhat different versions, they could be established as part of the high school curriculum, as well. Some topics that compose the syllabi of these courses include: how to deal with self-doubt and criticism, how to make decisions, how to deal with stress, how to maintain one's dignity, how to learn from failure, how to get along with others and encourage their ideas, how to deal with ambiguity, how to sustain one's courage in the face of adversity, how to give and accept feedback, and how to set goals and assess one's progress toward them.

A stronger case could be made for the importance of including leadership education and leader development in the high schools by adding other topics, also found in most college leadership courses, such as improving one's comprehending and communicating skills and examining one's own and society's ethics and values and finding ways to promote their improvement.

Whether in high school or college, young persons should be made aware of the likelihood that they will be asked to accept important leadership responsibilities at some time. Excellence in speaking, writing, and analytical skills relates to excellence in leadership. The ability to persuade and to assure others of one's own integrity and sincerity of purpose are rare abilities. Usually a person seeks a job that uses basic skills and abilities and learns easily how to hunt for the job. It is less easy to predict when the challenge will come to accept the responsibility of leadership. Those who have the potential and the interest should be prepared to respond affirmatively.

Learning to Become a Leader in the Adult Years

Very few young persons who complete their schooling and enter the workplace think of themselves as leaders. They may hope some day to own their own business, or to become president of the local Boy Scout council, or to be a leader of the community band. But when asked what they expect to do, they will describe a specific occupation. If asked how their life will progress, they will give few responses that go beyond the age of fifty. After that they will be old, over the hill, on the downgrade. Clearly in this mistaken and shortsighted view of one's life span, most people engage in far too limited goal setting and career planning.

The years of life in which adult learning occurs—the "middle years"—have received less systematic study by sociologists, psychologists, and other researchers than have the developing years and the declining years. What is known is not often widely communicated to those who ought to be informed. As a result, many notions that are false or only partly true about the years from thirty to sixty-five are widely accepted. These include beliefs about a "midlife crisis" that can be expected in all careers, convictions about a plateau in learning ability and intelligence that will appear shortly after the end of schooling, the mythical signs of early decay in memory for recent events in persons over fifty, and stories about the loss of many benefits of education as the mind gradually divests itself of useless memories. Each of these widely held notions is wrong in some way; those that are partly true apply only to some persons or to special circumstances.

These misconceptions can shape one's view of leadership, turning it into something that will happen much later—becoming the frosting on the cake of success. First one must establish one's self in a specialty, so it is thought, before the prospects of playing a larger role may be considered. The work of Kouzes and Posner[1] suggests a different interpretation. They asked young managers, "When were you at your leadership best?" Every person had an example. Two persons experiencing the pleasure of acting as a leader said:

> "We set three objectives. . . . First we planned to grow the company profitably. Second, to share the wealth among employees. And third and equally critical, it was important to have fun—not just the two owners, but all our employees."

The other answered:

> "I think good people deserve good leadership. The people I manage deserve the best leader in the world. If you could see them, you would understand why somebody would want to work sixty hours a week to make those people more successful."[2]

These experiences are harbingers of later leadership involvement. Many incidents occur in the lives of each of us that have a long-term effect on our behavior, which at the time may have seemed commonplace and not especially extraordinary. We do not recognize them as direction setting. Often such experiences do not seem to portend changes and improvements in leadership behaviors. We have to ask ourselves, *when does experience produce learning*?

Most active performers in all walks of life tend to improve as they practice, whether that practice be in work or play. But do leaders improve with practice? If they do, we can ask, "What is practice for a leader?" Is it true, as many say, that each leader needs to have made at least one serious mistake in order to learn how to cope with failure and to avoid supreme arrogance? Are some CEOs of industry more effective as leaders because they progressed up a career ladder that involved many varieties of experiences? Does commitment to an organization increase with experience, or does the long climb to the top cause leaders to lose touch with followers, burn out, or become preoccupied with the perquisites of office? How widely do persons differ in their changes through the middle life span? These questions have been studied and are worth reviewing.

Psychological research into the learning process emphasizes the law of effect. B. F. Skinner, a prominent Harvard psychologist, studied the effects of reinforcement on the behavior of many organisms. Using such rewards as bits of corn or pellets of food, he and his students were able to shape the behavior of birds, rats, and other animals in amazing and fully predictable ways. When psychologists have collected evidence on the effects of more subtle rewards in humans, demonstrating the effects of a word of praise, a nod of approval, a token, or an M&M candy, the results are impressive. One important point emerges from all this work: It is necessary to have knowledge of results in order for learning to occur. Does all of this laboratory work on learning apply in the real world? Let us see.

Ann Howard and Douglas Bray,[3] studying AT&T managers, found advancement motivation, orientation to work, and a strong self-development theme were the best predictors for attainment of a high-level position twenty years later. Measures of effectiveness were obtained in the course of an assessment program, with assessments repeated after a considerable time interval. Some managers had improved a great deal, but others had not. Many had lost interest in working for high positions and were focusing their energies in other directions.

We can assume that the same differences would have been found if the measures of effectiveness had been collected on the job rather than in an assessment center. Those who do well enjoy their work more and receive more rewards and recognition. Their interest in continuing on the job increases. Those who are not doing as well receive fewer rewards, lose motivation, and look to other areas for fulfillment. This observation should not be surprising.

Managers and potential leaders may all start out with high ambitions for advancement. However, they quickly get sorted out on the basis of their performance in their current jobs and their promise for growth. Members of the fast-track group are assigned to exciting jobs in which they enjoy many challenges and opportunities to show how good they are. Others receive more routine assignments where they have few chances to learn or to show their merit; fewer of them are selected for the next round of challenging assignments, partly because their achievements were less and partly because they were given less of a chance to show their merit.

The assignments that provide substantial challenge, opportunities for growth, and demonstration of potential are the assignments that are sought after by those with drive and ambition. Receiving such an assignment is highly gratifying and reinforcing: The behaviors that led to that advancement will be repeated. Those who do not receive these assignments do not get this reinforcement; they are often left in ignorance about what they did wrong or did not do. They usually receive few cues about those parts of their performance that were ineffective. After several rounds of being passed over, the best persons in this group will be the most disheartened. Yet, in a sense, this group was exposed to less risk than those given the tough jobs where failure was more likely.

This process of progressive job assignments for career development and for learning was examined by Morgan McCall, Michael Lombardo, and Ann Morrison with a team of investigators from the Center for Creative Leadership.[4] This group enlisted the cooperation of a dozen Fortune 500 companies in a review of learning experiences that seemed to teach important lessons. The basic question was: "We don't have enough executive bench strength for the future; how can we grow enough talent to lead this company in the years ahead?"

That question started a research program that went from interviews to open-ended surveys to mailed questionnaires, that started with three but eventually involved twelve major corporations. The core data used for their major report[5] encompasses 191 successful executives from six major corporations who responded to some version of the following question:

> When you think about your career as a manager, certain events or episodes probably stand out in your mind—things that led to a lasting change in you as a manager. Please identify at least three key events in your career, things that made a difference in the way you manage now and answer these questions: 1) What happened? 2) What did you learn from it (for better or worse)?

Analysis of the answers received yielded descriptions of 616 events and 1,547 corresponding lessons. The experiences could be broadly described as assignments (specific jobs they were given to do), bosses (other people who had impact in their own right), and hardships (setbacks and rough times).

A list of the specific kinds of lessons that executives described is shown in Table 1. These are *potential* lessons, presumably producing changes in the way in which these executives interpreted events and changed their behaviors. What were the circumstances that caused these lessons to be identified? Table 2 lists information that can be given to an individual or an organization about types of experiences that are reported as developmental—that usually lead to learning.

We have no way to estimate the amount of selective forgetting, of conclusions counter to facts, or of the highlighting of consequences that would have occurred anyway. To understand fully the way in which events produce lasting changes in behavior patterns, we should be collecting data on events in process, on careers

Table 1. Lessons Learned by Executives[6]

Setting and Implementing Agendas
Technical/professional skills
All about the business one is in
Strategic thinking
Shouldering full responsibility
Building and using structure and
control systems

Handling Relationships
Handling political situations
Getting people to implement solutions
What executives are like
How to work with executives
Strategies of negotiation
Dealing with people over whom you
have no authority
Understanding other people's
perspectives
Dealing with conflict
Directing and motivating subordinates
Developing other people
Confronting subordinate performance
problems
Managing former bosses and peers

Basic Values
You can't manage everything all alone
Sensitivity to the human side of
management
Basic management values

Executive Temperament
Being tough when necessary
Self-confidence
Coping with situations beyond your
control
Persevering through adversity
Coping with ambiguous situations
Use (and abuse) of power

Personal Awareness
The balance between work and personal
life
Knowing what really excites you about
work
Personal limits and blind spots
Taking charge of your career
Recognizing and seizing
opportunities[7]

that are not yet fulfilled, and on relationships we can continue to examine with
self-reports augmented by reports from bosses, peers, and subordinates.

Even so, the reports from *Lessons of Experience* are enlightening. This report,
for example, comes from an engineer just promoted to his first management job:

Table 2. Experiences That Teach

Setting the Stage
Early work experiences
First supervisory job

Leading by Persuasion
Project/task force assignment
Line to staff switches

Leading on Line
Starting from scratch
Turning a business around
Managing a larger scope

When Other People Matter
Bosses

Hardships
Personal trauma
Career setback
Changing jobs
Business mistakes
Subordinate performance problems

When I first became a supervisor of a group of development engineers, I looked at management as an engineer would. I read all about performance reviews, and boy was I ready to give performance reviews. I told them in detail all the things they did wrong, and all the things they did right. No one had ever given them that kind of feedback before. But I just about killed those engineers, and nearly crushed the morale of that organization. I was clearly not a skilled coach of people. So I went out and got some help. I finally learned that just as you had to know the laws of physics to be a good engineer, I had to know the laws of psychology to be a good manager.[8]

Some experiences establish a lifelong pattern. One executive described his experience this way:

I was a marketing guy sent to start up the first computerization project our company had ever attempted. In those days, adding machines were our most sophisticated tool. I walked in, not really even knowing what a computer was and faced this group of computer fanatics ready to revolutionize our operations. Maybe my ignorance saved me because how could I posture when I knew nothing? Anyway, this is what I said: "Let me tell you guys three things. One, you've got a leader who knows nothing about computers and a lot about marketing, so we've both got a lot to learn from each other. Two, I'm not afraid to say 'I don't know' and ask stupid questions, and don't you be either. Third, let's not worry about our differences too much. Let's see what we can do to set up this system and while we're at it let's move the art of marketing twenty years into the future."[9]

What does experience teach? Not surprisingly, different persons report that they learned different things. One said, "When I was a kid, I thought that most decisions were a matter of choosing right over wrong. I'm still looking to make a decision like that. It seems that all my decisions are between two goods or two bads."[10]

McCall, Lombardo, and Morrison interpret their findings to indicate that significant learning, as experienced by mature, well-functioning adults, must occur "on line," that is, in the process of getting the job done. Learning occurs as problems arise that have significant consequences. When stakes are high even the most confident persons experience a rise in anxiety level and pay attention to ways that work or do not work.

These findings of McCall, Lombardo, and Morrison need qualification for a variety of reasons. First, the objects of study were fast-track executives, picked as such by their superiors and by astute observers. Second, the report of their learning experiences came from their own memories. Third, there was no control group of less successful executives with whom to compare although the researchers did examine a group of "derailed" executives. Fourth, there were no data collected from followers. Did some of these "successes" include some of the intolerable bosses or those described by their subordinates as "the most stressful part of my job"?

Why do some events produce learning and others not; why do some persons learn and others not? Why do some need to have a failure before any change occurs, while others see the need for a different approach almost immediately? Are such differences modifiable? In other words, are there ways in which vicarious learning could prevent some of the failures? If we are to concur with the study's recommendation that calls for better use of on-the-job experiences to produce desired changes in behavior, we must also learn to identify developmentally significant jobs, to identify people who are ready to learn and change, and to develop more effective ways to help talented people learn from these experiences.

Learning from Seminars or Learning from Experience

Ask any successful executive what event triggered the most valuable learning. The most common answers are: being promoted to a more challenging job, taking a job with greater scope, handling a task that looked impossible, confronting a challenge that required me to go it alone, and producing a failure that shook me up (and maybe some others, too).

Ask successful executives about their college experiences. They remember a few exciting professors and some interesting fellow students. But often their memories of great learning experiences are not classroom memories but out-of-class events. The number of life-influencing interactions with memorable faculty is small compared to the number of unforgettable and often painful events they experienced elsewhere.

Does this mean college is a waste of time? Not at all. During the college experience one learns a great deal about how society and the world work, one learns factual material and develops abilities that are not easily accessible elsewhere, and one stores up many domains of knowledge for use later. With luck, one learns to calculate and communicate, discover something about the meaning of life, make some lasting friends, and fall in love. One learns that many people can come to a particular place with an infinite variety of beliefs and values but one can, with persistence, learn something about one's own distinctive characteristics.

Colleges and universities assert that their effects on students are substantial and lifelong, saying, "Little wonder so many of our graduates do well, we gave them a good education." Maybe that is not so. The work of Alexander Astin[11] enunciates that differences among average achievements of alumni from different colleges only reflect differences in the quality of the entering freshman classes. Good students in—good graduates out. The value-added effects of so-called "good schools" have not been documented. Learning a lot can occur on any campus, although there are some campuses on which it is harder to find well-taught courses and dedicated faculty.

Much of the learning reported by successful executives concerns *compensatory* learning—insights *not* acquired during earlier education and experience, the absence of which causes problems of every kind. They report their need to realize that they were viewed as self-confident even when they were most uncertain; that sometimes they appeared uncaring when their hearts were bleeding; that often they were perceived as not paying attention during times when they wanted to act but their hands were tied. Learning these lessons while young can make a big difference in early success. Many college students who graduate with excellent grades have learned too little about themselves and how they are perceived, yet these are essential ingredients to achieving success in relations with others and bringing satisfaction into their own lives.

Executives' memories to the contrary, some college experiences emphasized in the classroom have direct relevance to a successful life. Think about these valued assets: the ability to digest information quickly from a printed page, to speak and write in clear and persuasive ways, to listen and to remember, to analyze and restate a problem in ways that make it amenable to resolution, and to know something of the laws that govern the natural world and the principles that guide the world of humans.

It is curious, though, that college grades have so little relation to success in life—at least to the definition of success as measured by economists. The lifetime earnings of the average college graduate are markedly higher than those of persons who have not attended college or have not graduated. The lifetime earnings of those who get good grades in college courses is not appreciably higher than those who graduate with poor grades.[12] One possible explanation exists. A study of executives who derail concluded that managers who take their agenda from the expressed wishes of their bosses—boss pleasers—succeed for a while but fail when they have to develop their own agenda. Good grades are earned by some students—teacher pleasers—who listen carefully to what teachers want. Such a pattern does not lead to lifelong learning.[13]

These observations about college learning are directly relevant to our discussion about lifelong learning. A much more proactive response to an item learned is required when that item relates to an important aspect of one's life, work, or anything held valuable. New information made available to the leader is processed in terms of the action required. As one executive remarked: "When I was younger, every time I learned something new, I was thrilled; now, when I learn something I had not known, I would rather not have learned it." Why should that be? When leaders acquire information, there is a corresponding need to decide its meaning and whether or not it requires action. Does that make learning painful? When does the energy required to act become so burdensome that it retards learning? How can leaders be enabled to analyze information, determine its relevance to other information, and order priorities for action? After formal schooling there is no classroom teacher to state a problem in a solvable form. Nor is there a textbook showing the "school solution" to every problem. Clearly, the search for a support system is continuous. As leaders gain experience, do they become less interested in new knowledge or do they learn more about acquiring better support systems?

Sometimes week-long seminars are faulted for providing too little behavior change that can be carried home by the participant; many persons report that what they learned, however impressive, does not apply to their jobs or within their company. Several training programs have been developed that provide for teaching and training spread over time, with certain projects assigned for application on the job. These programs are gaining wider acceptance and may presage a new relationship between learning from experience and learning in the seminar room.

Clark Wilson and his associates in the Wilson Publishing Company in New Canaan, Connecticut have developed a form of training that seeks to achieve some of the objectives just described. These training programs also do not rely on single-seminar training exposure but include follow-up training and evaluation. Program content includes the exercise of organizational roles that depend on skills at influencing others. Part of training includes differentiated roles. One report of the team's work by Wilson, O'Hare, and Shipper[14] includes the following questions to identify the steps necessary to complete one task cycle: 1) What do I do? 2) How do I do it? 3) How do I carry out the plan? 4) How do I know I am performing? and 5) How do I fix my mistakes? These questions, when answered, lead to satisfaction derived from achieving the task and to increased interest in the task itself. At this point, the work of the team must be recognized and rewards shared.

Wilson uses a cognitive learning paradigm to underlie his training plan. The task of the training staff is to generate events in which problems are presented, signs of success are provided, preferred behaviors are reinforced, and the learner becomes more aware of the interrelationships of events. Wilson's training methods have led to improvement in job behaviors of employees of a multinational bank, a nuclear power plant, and a health care facility, as well as greater work output in a government bureaucracy.

We noted earlier that many executives reported that most of their significant lessons were learned on the job. We have also seen off-site learning settings increase performance of employees. There are ample data to suggest, however, that many workers given challenging assignments do not learn from the challenge. Are there data to suggest that some persons are better prospects for learning and change than others? Can we spot such persons early?

Yes, we can, but not always. Ann Howard and Douglas Bray,[15] in their study of AT&T executives, found many managers at middle levels who showed reduced commitment to the company and less aspiration to progress to higher levels. So there may be a factor of *motivation*.

Joseph L. Moses, also at AT&T, ran modified assessment programs at the time of AT&T's divestiture process to identify those middle managers who could cope with the anxiety, uncertainty, and ambiguity prevalent at that time within the company. He found only about one manager in four—all presumed still on track for further promotion—who showed enough *adaptability* to cope with the change, the stress, and the new problems that surfaced.[16]

Robert Hogan of the University of Tulsa has studied for many years the personality characteristics of various executives and high-level managers. He reports discovering clues to later performance in the *personality characteristics* of many potential executives that make them appear to be promising candidates likely to be selected for advancement.[17] Yet they become almost certain disasters for the organization if given responsibility in certain important leadership positions. Persons of this sort often have private agendas, gross overestimations of their own achievements, and deep hostility and resentment toward others, toward organizations, and toward society; they have power needs and status needs that continually influence their actions. When these characteristics are combined with insensitivity to the needs of others, less than a full commitment to the organization's goals, or overvaluing of the perquisites of position and authority, enormous mischief can be expected.

How can such persons be discovered before they cause great harm? Background checks often fail, for traits of the sort described do not appear early in careers when the surface manifestations are most attractive. Some of these types are exceedingly impressive in interviews. Somehow the provocative questions are never asked, or responses are allowed to slip by. Assessment programs may provide clues, just as questionnaires and inventories may be suggestive. Risks are highest when recruitment is from outside the organization, but even reviews of inside candidates sometimes fail. Tryouts of persons in developmental positions may be planned. However, as positions carry more responsibility, power, and authority, these undesirable qualities emerge more readily.

Is there any way in which behaviors generated in closely observed work situations might help in assessing the qualities of candidates? Is there any way to improve behaviors that are appropriate and eliminate those that are not appropriate?

Elliott Jaques[18] has studied many hierarchical organizations. He asserts that wisdom has to do with the soundness of a person's judgment about the ways of the world, about what people are like, and about how they are likely to react. Acquisition of wisdom is one of the areas that shows that action without sound theory and concepts can be debilitating. Wisdom and tact can be evaluated and developed in people.

Jaques has examined closely the natural growth of working capacity and time horizon with age and has collected data and plotted the growth of persons at various ages. He believes that his system makes it possible to identify by age thirty or thirty-five those persons who have potential for developing into very high levels of cognitive capability, and says:

> These maturation bands were first deduced from the discovery of a regular pattern of progression of the real earnings of individuals over a period of years, like the lines of force you can see in iron filings on the surface of a sheet of paper with a bar magnet underneath. Their validity has been established in studies tracking the careers of individuals over a 30-year period. One study followed a group of nearly 200 individuals for periods of 18 to 25 years. It was found that they felt comfortable with their level of work so long as the growth of time span and level of work stayed within the time horizons in one of the maturation bands.

In the follow-up studies of up to twelve years, the maturation bands were shown to be accurate predictors of future potential. Other investigators have not yet provided independent verification of Jaques's methods, though his related work is highly respected.

Simulations provide an interesting middle ground between the job and the seminar room. They are popular in the military services where the cost of training on high-technology equipment is prohibitive. They have proven worthy for teaching principles of management and leadership; participants find them "just like home" in replicating problems and ambiguities of the job and produce in each participant the characteristic behaviors evidenced back on the job.

Learning Requires Knowledge of Results

Many of the studies that have counted years of experience or that have asked successful persons to recall the lessons they learned overlook a basic principle of learning. Learning progresses only when the learner can discern how well any action succeeded. A golfer who does not watch where the ball lands is not likely to improve. A manager who only sees his or her side of the effects of a new rule will not learn the faults in that rule. Even pointing to a word on a printed page requires coordination of eye and hand, with minute corrections to hit the right word.

Many training programs emphasize *feedback*. Exercises are provided to help the participant discover things not known about how the participant's behavior affects others. Time after time in these programs a participant will say, "I never knew I was coming across like *that*!" Experience per se does *not* teach. The feedback from a given action provides cues about whether to change or not change behavior. With little or no feedback, behavior can settle into a fairly rigid form with the actor feeling comfortable, mainly because there are no ripples. Prior behaviors of this person may have taught subordinates not to make waves—to accept their lot and not complain or make suggestions. Within each group of persons with ten years of experience in a management role, there will be some who have learned a lot and changed a great deal, some who have learned only a little, and some who have learned some very bad habits. This means that counted time in a job means little. Some independent method must be employed to provide information about how much was learned. Perhaps that is why we commonly hear that a failure is the best learning experience—it is hard to ignore the fact that something was done wrong.

Subordinate Judgments

We referred earlier to programs that use subordinate judgments as part of a program to identify leadership qualities. Subordinate judgments are also exceedingly useful in providing feedback to managers and leaders. Most managers do not collect data from subordinates to determine how well they are performing their functions as managers. They do not know when peers and subordinates question their commitment and integrity. Most managers do not try to obtain such information. Most subordinates are pretty cautious if asked by a superior to give candid appraisals, for the boss has power to fire, change assignments, shun, or turn a deaf ear. So some method is needed that provides the information without confrontation.

One of the best methods is to use an outside organization to collect data from all units, supplying to each manager data for his or her unit. Top management then gets summary data. When anyone gets a rating that displeases, what is recommended is some private searching out among subordinates to discover what behaviors or policies or procedures caused the low ratings. Such a method requires clear support from the total organization to be effective.

Corporations have learned to use challenging assignments to promote the growth of important abilities in their most promising managers and prospective leaders. The lessons learned are critical to good performance: confidence in one's ability to work independently, knowledge of one's limitations, the need to rely on others and to delegate, humility, a strengthening of values, and the courage to act. Greater self-knowledge is central to many of the learning experiences.

Such learning must produce observable changes in the behavior of managers and leaders, but the documentation of changed behavior is rarely demonstrated. Since we know that self-ratings of leadership behavior are much less accurate than ratings by others, we must view with caution what results we have been able to attain. It does appear, however, that leaders who receive abundant feedback from their peers and subordinates perform better than those who are ignorant of their own behavior or those who continue to ignore the effects their behaviors have on others.

CHAPTER ELEVEN

To See Ourselves As Others See Us

Leaders achieve positive results through processes of influence and persuasion. The test of their effectiveness comes in changed behaviors among their followers. Examination of what is done by successful leaders shows that whatever the cause of their achievements, it is not some magical force. Rather, hard work, knowledge of what is needed, and consistent enforcement of important operational principles are essential. Engendering trust in the leader's vision and capability, as well as demonstrating confidence that followers have the ability to help solve the problems articulated by the leader, are integral to a positive outcome of a leader's program. It takes easy communication and frequent interchanges between a leader and a follower to build confidence that goals can be attained.

Attitudes of followers, their opinions about the organization and its leaders, and their confidence about their own future are of great concern in all well-run and successful organizations, regardless of size and purpose. Every leader of whatever role or status must seek to maintain the commitment and the motivation of group members to achieve the organization's goals.

Loss in productivity associated with reduced worker motivation is often cited as the main cause for the loss of America's competitive position worldwide. The work ethic that produced greatness for the U.S. appears to have been lost. It is said that other nations are replacing the U.S. in the top ranks on productivity charts. Whether or not this is true, any evidence of disaffection among followers or workers must be taken seriously. It takes a long time to establish trust and confidence; erosion of relationships occurs quickly. Organizations must heed early signals of opposition and lack of loyal dedication, often preceded by a total breakdown in communications. To know early that followers are becoming disenchanted reduces the likelihood of serious conflict and undesirable outcomes.

Many methods are available to organizations and institutions for keeping them in tune with the opinions and attitudes of all members and followers. They are used widely by those who know that the commitment of followers is important and that the empowered and enthusiastic worker is a better worker. But not all persons in positions of power are sufficiently impressed by the value of motivated and loyal followers and workers. Often persons with aspirations for rapid promotion believe they will prosper and move ahead more rapidly if they please their immediate superior and that the road to mediocrity is taken by those who support their subordinates and help them improve and prosper.

Unhealthy practices flourish when an organization is in crisis, when the number of middle managers is being reduced, when takeover of corporations is the mode, or when plants are being closed. Frantic executives forego good practice and make hasty decisions that produce fear, anger, and disloyalty, effects that take years to overcome. Articles offering advice about how to behave find their way into the media, but ruinous effects are certain for some who choose to heed them. An example is given in the following article from the *Wall Street Journal*:

HOW TO GET AHEAD AS A MIDDLE MANAGER BY BEING RUTHLESS

Executive Strategies Monthly Offers Tips, But Its Editor Truly is a Kindhearted Soul

Sometimes *Executive Strategies* gives such outrageous advice that even the guy who writes the newsletter bridles. "Personally, I find it totally abhorrent," says editor Thomas Weyr of his recommendation to managers that they snoop on their underlings.

". . . Invasion of employee privacy is becoming a routine tool of management," the advice reads. "Savvy executives make sure to get real career mileage from the videotape and the camera. This is revolting stuff," Mr. Weyr concedes. "I'd quit a job in a minute if they put in a camera."

Survival Tactics

But that is beside the point: The purpose of *Executive Strategies* is to tell middle managers how to survive the "downsizing" of corporate America, not to serve up platitudes about making the workplace of the 1990s more congenial.

The essential message communicated by the 65-year-old Mr. Weyr (pronounced Wire): Be as ruthless as you must with subordinates and rivals while toadying to the higher-ups.

How brutal do managers have to get?

"Make a visitor stand in front of your desk. . . . Lean back and look at him coldly with a frozen smile. The body language of contempt can cut your opponent like a razor. . . .

"Tantrums should be sudden, scary, and seemingly irrational. . . . Throwing a tantrum can be fun.

"Everybody cheats at one time or another in order to advance their careers. . . . Dirty tricks are part of the game."[1]

The assured outcome of tactics of this sort is a marked increase in job stress and a significant decrease in commitment to the firm. Yet this type of advice continues to appeal to many managers. If judgments about retention or promotion are made on inadequate knowledge about performance and if executives are impressed by those who seek to curry their favor, then others in the organization get the message that their main job is to please the boss. This demeans subordinates and reduces their contribution to the organization.

Improved performance can be expected when leader attention focuses on the needs of the persons who perform the tasks. The broad categories used to summarize what leaders do include such words and phrases as "motivated work force," "worker satisfaction," "intellectual stimulation," "inspiration," "vision," "commitment," and "extra energy." Followers then speak of "trust," "respect," "opportunities," "challenging work," "kept informed," and "being respected."

Workers expect to be treated fairly and watch for evidence to reassure themselves. When sources of information are scarce, rumors fill the vacuum, and worker anxiety increases. When specific evidence of harmful or suspicious activities emerges, reactions can be serious. When a corporation is not making a profit and its future well-being is in doubt, high pay to executives who are in charge can be infuriating to the rest of the organization, as noted in the following excerpt from *Fortune* magazine:

THE TRUST GAP

Corporate America is split by a gulf between top management and everybody else—in pay, in perks, in self-importance. Here's how to regain employees' confidence.

Today, as CEO's waken to the new dawn of participatory management and even slugabeds are heard to murmur "empowerment" in their sleep, there is reason to believe that their hithertofore faithful retainers, the employees, would like nothing better than to push a butter knife slowly through the boss's well-intentioned heart.

Relations between employer and employed are not good, and at an especially dicey moment. Just when top management wants everyone to begin swaying to a faster, more productive beat, employees are loathe to dance. Observes David Sirota, chairman of the corporate polling firm Sirota, Alper & Pfau: "CEO's say, 'We're a team, we're all in this together, rah, rah, rah.' But employees look at the difference between their pay and the CEO's. They see top management's perks—oak dining rooms and heated garages, vs. cafeterias for the hourly guys and parking spaces half a mile from the plant. And they wonder: "Is this togetherness?" As the disparity in pay widens, the wonder grows.

People below the acme of the corporate pyramid trust those on top just about as far as they can throw a Gulfstream IV, with shower. Hourly workers and supervisors indeed agree that "we're all in this together," but what "we're in" turns out to be a frame of mind that mistrusts senior management's intentions, doubts its competence, and resents its self-congratulatory pay.

Just about everyone who keeps tabs on employee opinion finds evidence of a trust gap. And it is widening. One example: The Hay Group, drawing on ten years of survey data—hundreds of companies, thousands of employees—concluded in a 1988 study that the attitudes of middle managers and professionals toward the workplace are becoming more like those of hourly workers, historically the most disaffected group. . . .

What's the problem? Is it just pay? Working conditions? Benefits not good enough? None of these rank high in the new pantheon of gripes. If that surprises you, you are not alone. When Lou Harris & Associates polled office workers and their managers on behalf of the Steelcase office furniture company this year, they found a growing "perception gap" between what employees really want and what top management *thinks* they want.

Managers assume, for instance, that job security is of paramount importance to employees. In fact, among workers it ranks far below such ethereal-sounding desires as respect, a higher standard of management ethics, increased recognition of employee contributions, and closer, more honest communications between employees and senior management. . . .[2]

The *Fortune* article continues with results from other surveys conducted by national agencies and by individual organizations. The results are useful, for they show time after time that top management believes that their messages and policy statements are well understood by all, while the surveys show that the rank and file never got the word. The results are often humbling, as employees show their disdain and note the ineffectiveness of decisions made by top management.

Worker Satisfaction

Can measures of worker satisfaction indicate that workers are motivated and are performing appropriately? From the attention given to such measures, one would assume so. Worker satisfaction is viewed by top executives of major corporations as an important indicator. Employers enlist public opinion organizations to provide information about changing worker attitudes. These data are studied carefully in executive circles. But they are also misinterpreted or overestimated. Differences of any magnitude are considered significant. Of enormous interest is the controversy that can arise over interpretations, as illustrated by the following accounts.

A Lou Harris poll reported in *Industry Week*[3] in July 1989 shows that job satisfaction was slipping: "Happy workers work harder. Based on that assumption, managements have been pouring a lot of money and effort into raising their employees' satisfaction level. *It isn't working.* In fact, pollster Louis Harris, after surveying 1,500 office workers and bosses, concluded that fewer—41% vs. 46%—admitted being 'very satisfied' with their job situation than did so a year ago."

A Gallup poll reported in *Training*[4] in March 1989 concluded just the opposite: ". . . It may come as a surprise to learn that a recent poll says Americans are really quite satisfied with their jobs. But that's the conclusion of a survey conducted by the Gallup Organization Inc. . . . According to the survey, 46 percent of the respondents were very satisfied with their jobs, and another 41 percent were somewhat satisfied. . . . The results echo those of similar surveys done by the National Opinion Research Center from 1983 to 1986. In those polls, 44 to 48 percent of respondents said they were very satisfied with their jobs."

It is disquieting to find two such markedly different analyses of job satisfaction of workers appearing almost simultaneously, especially when the data collected are remarkably similar. Why should this be? The questions asked are fairly standard. We would like to be able to trust these national polling agencies and believe that they are not biased in reporting their results in order to please their sponsors. Perhaps the differences seem greater depending on the perspective of the person doing the interpreting.

In the newspaper comic strip, Blondie asks her husband, Dagwood, as she works a crossword puzzle, "I need a six-letter word meaning boss." Dagwood responds, "Grumpy—cranky—unjust—crabby—ornery—tyrant—brutal—despot—absurd—stupid—crazed—insane—." Blondie, looking quizzical, responds, "Oh dear, I may have asked the wrong person." Perhaps levels of job satisfaction differ depending on whom you ask.

Indeed, differences emerge when we select for study a single occupational group, as illustrated in the following article from the *Wall Street Journal*:

NOT HAPPY TEACHERS—BETTER TEACHERS

Education is in serious trouble in this nation. The parade of reports documenting its ills seems endless. The causes of its decline include such things as lack of parental involvement, disruptive students, drugs, racism and so on. Yet one area that persists in getting kid-glove treatment is the teaching force.

Rather than raise the possibility that some teachers may actually be part of the problem, that there may very well be some teachers out there doing a poor job, experts in education persist in enumerating the complaints of disgruntled teachers. The obsession with documenting the misery index of current teachers and suggesting that we should focus our attention on making them happy by giving them more authority, more money and more respect may be a waste of time.

The fact is, we may not even want many of these people teaching—and the bigger problem may very well be how to get rid of them.

With all the talk about teachers feeling no control and working under autocratic principals, 80% of teachers surveyed said they are satisfied with their relationship with their principal. . . .

From 1986 to 1990 [teacher's] satisfaction with their jobs dropped to 77% from 90%. . . .[5]

Public reporting frequently omits attention to key details. Should we compare teachers' job satisfaction percentages that dropped from 90% to 77% with the drop from 46% to 41% reported in the *Business Week* article, or with the 87% (46% plus 41%) reported in the *Training* article? These numbers are often used without adequate comparative figures. Writers interpret them in ways consistent with their thesis of the moment, without adequate background information to give them meaning. Eric Sevareid, noted reporter and television newsman, described the major sin of the media not as bias, but haste. Too often the superficial account is considered sufficient.

There are so many polls and so many figures available that one may choose among the various results to prove almost any point. The points to be proved often depend on the perspective of the viewer, rather than on the data conveyed by poll results, especially when issues of worker motivation and productivity are at issue.

More than 800 executive-level managers in federal government were asked about their work experiences under five presidential administrations from Johnson through Reagan.[6] Every measure of working conditions used—organizational climate, job recognition, clarity of purpose, feedback, decision making, job design, organization of activities, and influence—reflected a steady deterioration through this period. Is such a decline a particular feature of federal employment, or is it more general?

Organizations that collect such data tend not to publish their findings. Some company exchanges do occur informally, however. One survey of middle managers and first-line supervisors cited lack of teamwork and a dog-eat-dog atmosphere in their organizations. They objected to the paperwork, the endless meetings, and the bureaucracy. They complained that their efforts are not acknowledged. These managers suggested many changes: "Abolish titles," "Work as a team," "Provide more recognition," and "Have a boss who cares." These findings clearly suggest the need for changes in practice and more top-level attention to lower levels of management.

Different work settings produce different results. Managers in management information systems reply in surveys that they are generally satisfied with their work and with their salaries. Frustrations with ineffective management is reported by 32%. Most managers wanted more recognition and deplored living with unrealistic expectations and deadlines.

Surely top decision makers must feel better about their work. Yet the trend toward decentralized organizational forms, loose structures, and generally less hierarchical designs has increased the pressure at the top. Top executives are more comfortable with hierarchy and structure, a framework that reduces the high information loads on them as decision makers and obviates the necessity to process highly specific information. With less structure, the complexity of decision making increases immeasurably.

Work satisfaction is a complex phenomenon. It is not possible to make simple statements about the effects of the work environment, a person's place in the structure, relationships with superiors and subordinates, and the effect of the work on feelings and moods as reported in questionnaires. Each of these has components that may have different effects. For example, some features of the work environment may be adored, others despised; interest in some specific task may be great while there is distress about one's position or pay; and there may be both attractive and unattractive features of organizational policies. Evidence about morale, satisfaction, and measures of motivation is difficult to interpret unless data are collected in a way that enables comparisons and unless questions are written so as to make comparisons possible.

General Purpose Surveys of Worker Satisfaction

Surveys conducted outside an organization frequently address questions of little interest to the leadership of a particular organization. Many organizations therefore devise their own questionnaires and administer them within the walls of the organization. Some companies incorporate "standard" items that are regularly used by other firms so that responses may be compared. There are also standard survey forms that organizations may use, supplied by a consulting firm or available as a published questionnaire. We report on one general form recently developed.

David P. Campbell, Smith Richardson Senior Fellow at the Center for Creative Leadership, developed the Campbell Organizational Survey™ (COS™)[7] so that measures of various dimensions of worker satisfaction could be made across and within organizations. The COS™ is a 44-item, 13-scale standardized employee attitude survey. Items are relevant for employees or members at any level in any type of organization; scales have been standardized for "the typical employee in the typical organization."

When an individual completes the COS™, a profile containing the numerical scores for each scale is produced, with each score reported both numerically and graphically. Group profiles are produced by averaging the scores for members of the group and reporting them both numerically and graphically. The thirteen COS™ Scales are:

The Work Itself
Working Conditions
Freedom From Stress
Co-Workers
Supervision
Top Leadership
Pay
Benefits
Job Security
Promotional Opportunities
Feedback/Communications
Organizational Planning
Support for Innovation

Sample items are:

I enjoy my work.
I work in a pleasing, attractive setting.

When I am under stress, I have someone at work who I can talk to about the problems.

People at my level help each other out when the work load is heavy.

My supervisor believes in helping subordinates grow and develop.

I am proud of the people who hold the top leadership positions in our organization.

I am satisfied with my pay.

Our fringe benefits—such as holidays, insurance, vacations, and retirement plans—are good.

I know that as long as I do good work, my job here is secure.

This job is a good steppingstone for the future.

Feedback on performance for people at my level is timely, accurate, and constructive.

A visible, clearly stated planning process is used to guide our future actions.

New ideas are nurtured and welcomed here.

Responses to each item are given on a six-point scale:

STRONGLY AGREE
Agree
Slightly Agree
Slightly Disagree
Disagree
STRONGLY DISAGREE

Possible applications for the COS™ include use with individuals or with groups. Individual profiles enable a person to compare his/her views of the organization with those of the group. Group profiles help identify sources of discontent in the organization or highlight differences that may call for action. Following are several profiles that illustrate these uses.

Figure 1 shows the profiles of a president and chief executive officer in a public service company—Person D—and an executive director of a manufacturing company—Person E. The two profiles are quite similar, indicating substantial similarities in their overall perceptions of their individual work situations. Person E's low rating of PAY, even with a six-digit salary, is explained: "I produce enormous levels of profit for this company, and my compensation does not reflect that." Even the low scores for these two senior executives were comfortably above the general average, and the individual levels of enthusiasm for their work and commitment to their organization comes through in conversations with both of them.

The COS can also identify the range in satisfaction among members of a group. Figure 2 presents the profiles of the most and least satisfied individuals within the same work group, along with the average profile for all members. Both of these extreme employees were well educated and experienced; they present a real dilemma to the leader of their group, for they obviously cannot be treated in the same way. They differ greatly in their feelings about almost every issue, save working conditions. It may be that the manager's challenge may include keeping the completely dissatisfied person from influencing the entire work group with negative attitudes and behavior. Because data are collected anonymously, the manager can only guess at the person's identity.

Variability among units of an organization would also be expected and can be identified using the COS. Figure 3 portrays the profiles of the most and least

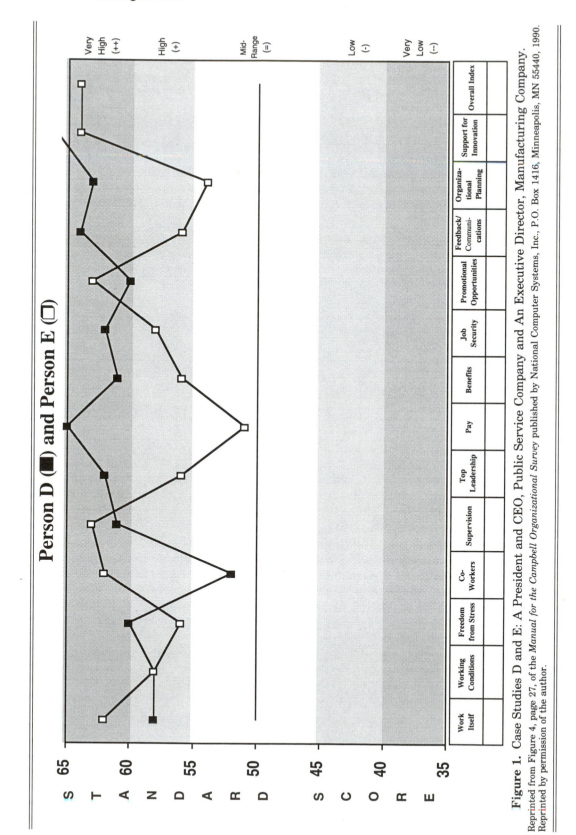

Figure 1. Case Studies D and E: A President and CEO, Public Service Company and An Executive Director, Manufacturing Company.

Reprinted from Figure 4, page 27, of the *Manual for the Campbell Organizational Survey* published by National Computer Systems, Inc., P.O. Box 1416, Minneapolis, MN 55440, 1990. Reprinted by permission of the author.

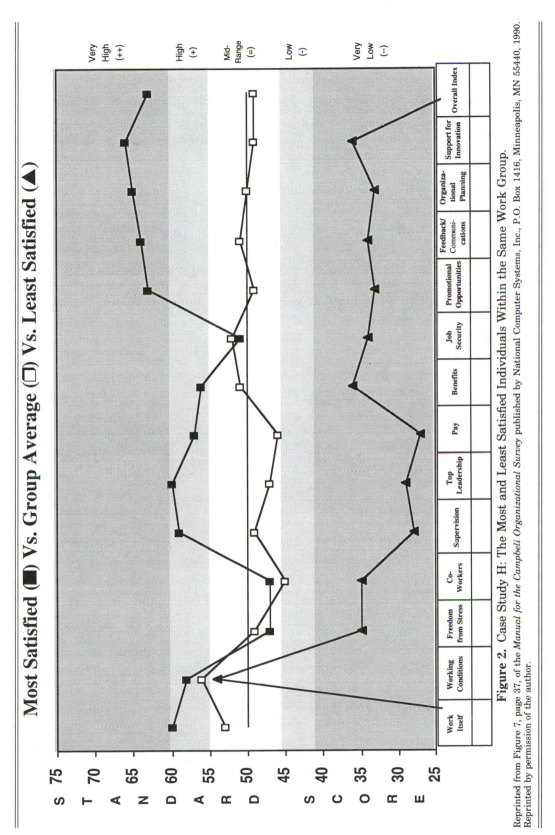

Figure 2. Case Study H: The Most and Least Satisfied Individuals Within the Same Work Group.

Reprinted from Figure 7, page 37, of the *Manual for the Campbell Organizational Survey* published by National Computer Systems, Inc., P.O. Box 1416, Minneapolis, MN 55440, 1990. Reprinted by permission of the author.

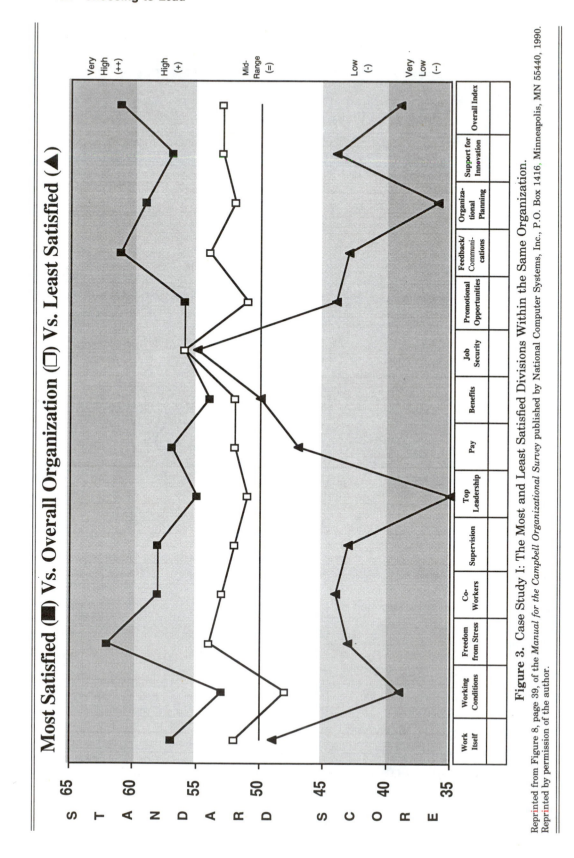

Figure 3. Case Study I: The Most and Least Satisfied Divisions Within the Same Organization.

Reprinted from Figure 8, page 39, of the *Manual for the Campbell Organizational Survey* published by National Computer Systems, Inc., P.O. Box 1416, Minneapolis, MN 55440, 1990. Reprinted by permission of the author.

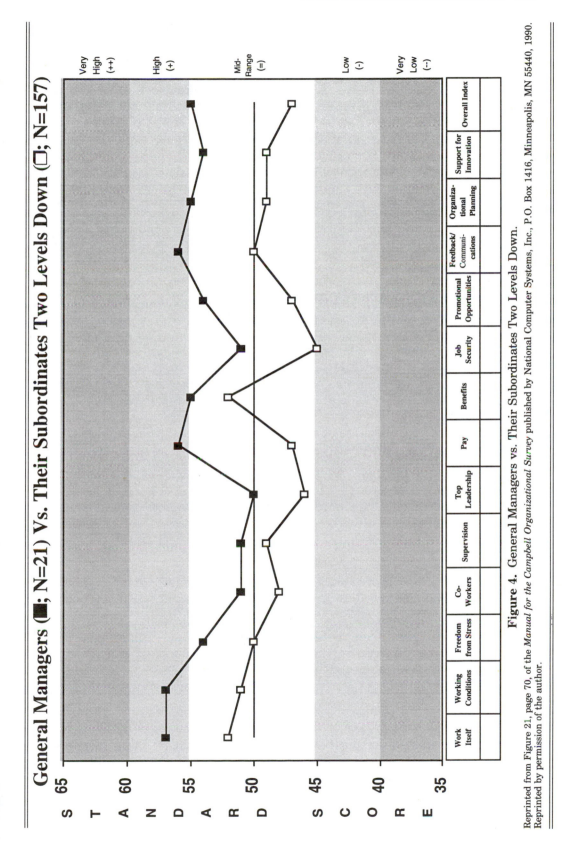

Figure 4. General Managers vs. Their Subordinates Two Levels Down.

Reprinted from Figure 21, page 70, of the *Manual for the Campbell Organizational Survey* published by National Computer Systems, Inc., P.O. Box 1416, Minneapolis, MN 55440, 1990. Reprinted by permission of the author.

satisfied divisions within the same organization and the profile for the entire organization. The divisions were all quite similar, with approximately the same number of staff members, and had about the same status. Campbell reports that the major difference between these two divisions was the difference between the two managers. Yet the differences in profiles are striking not only for areas directly under the division manager's control, but also for those areas relating to the larger organization.

Satisfaction is related to rank in civilian, military, governmental, and voluntary organizations. Greater satisfaction comes with movement to higher ranks. This principle is illustrated in Figure 4, a representation of the profiles of twenty-one general managers in one company and 157 subordinates in the appropriate divisions two levels below. The two profiles are distinct, with no scale average of the subordinate group exceeding the average of the general managers. Although this phenomenon of "rank-related" satisfaction is not universal, it can be observed in most settings.

Inadequate Performance

Some workers get much less done than others. The variability in performance of workers of all sorts and at all levels is well documented. Often the best worker accomplishes more than twice what is done by the poorest worker. The leader who fixes on the accomplishment of the task by the group and sees no difference between the performance of a good and a poor worker loses the trust and respect of followers or subordinates. A recent article makes the point.

WORKERS TO BOSS: FIRE THAT LAZY JERK

Almost half of American workers say their managers tolerate poor performance too long. That's what The Wyatt Company discovered in a survey involving more than 3,500 workers from a variety of jobs and industries.

"Responsible employees are tired of picking up the slack," says John Parkington, a consultant in Wyatt's Boston office. "Even though the number of poor performers may be small, they are extremely damaging to morale and motivation in the workplace."

In addition to tolerating poor performers, 3 out of 10 employees say their supervisors do a poor job of solving people problems. The same number said their supervisors don't give regular performance feedback.

"Employees want to know not only that good work will be appreciated, but also that poor performance will be corrected," Parkington said. "Unfortunately many supervisors don't take the necessary time either to evaluate employee performance adequately or to explain performance standards fully."[8]

Many studies of business organizations demonstrate that selecting and developing people who behave in ways described as characteristic of effective leaders has an effect on productivity and on the attitudes of group members.[9] Most productivity measures were direct measures of output and quality of output. These effective leaders somehow create the conditions that increase the willingness of group members to expend energy. They do this when they become concerned with member attitudes and work motivation, demonstrating specific behaviors that have been described in earlier chapters. For example:

Leadership that is limited to a transactional exchange of rewards with subordinates for the services they render also limits how much effort will be forthcoming from the subordinates, how satisfied the subordinates will be with the arrangements, and how effectively they will contribute to reaching the organization's goals. To proceed beyond such limits in subordinate effort, satisfaction, and effectiveness calls for a leader who articulates a realistic vision of the future that can be shared, stimulates subordinates intellectually, and pays attention to the differences among subordinates.[10]

Collecting information and understanding the implications of various items of evidence is a critical component of the leader's work. Making decisions about a course of action is seldom easy and requires the leader to possess a firm set of values and an understanding of principles of learning and motivation. The leader must know what is required to change the attitudes of employees, constituents, followers, or members so that they exert more effort and meet higher standards. The leader can gauge success by finding out what the followers have to say about him or her and then behave differently in the light of that knowledge. Followers want to be proud of and happy to be associated with their leader. They want personal expression of praise for work well done, help in getting it done, and recognition of the values held by each member of the group. They want to be included in decisions that affect their work and their working conditions; they want to be given problem-solving responsibilities and assistance in growing on the job. They want inspiration; they want to know that the entire operation is important, as is their role in it. They want to be challenged with hard but realistic goals.

When followers' expectations are met, their enthusiasm leads to better performances. The key role is played by the leader, but followers must be receptive and must share the goals articulated by the leader. Although many people are given general instructions in how to lead, only some adopt methods that produce these highly desired results for the organization. This makes it all the more important for the leader to discover the mood, the perceptions, and the attitudes of followers so that appropriate corrective actions may be taken in a timely manner.

CHAPTER TWELVE

Leadership, Power, and Position

The concern about power—its use and misuse—is widespread; we especially have a problem with how other people exercise power. We become anxious when those with whom we disagree have power and may abuse it. Many of us question how we would behave if we were among the powerful and wonder whether we might misuse power if we had it. Angry and agitated persons alarm us when they say that all they need is power and appear ready to use it maliciously.

Children covet the power of their parents over them. Students in classrooms find ways to exert influence on teachers in subtle—and sometimes obvious—ways. Voters use their power not only in the election booth but also in the many organizations they join that lobby actively for the group's special interests. One individual can often delay or prevent an action if willing to take the time and suffer the negative publicity. The bully on the school grounds is replicated in every form of adult activity. Many bureaucrats gain great satisfaction in exercising their small amount of authority over people standing in lines or requiring their attention to pay a tax or meet a regulation.

Perceptions of Power

Perceptions of power are not consistent. Some see money as power; some see military strength, popularity, or visibility as power. Some seek high positions to gain power, while others seek new knowledge or information or rely on numbers—People Power. Some see power simply as directed responsibility, without which there would be no progress.

In his book *Managing with Power*,[1] Jeffrey Pfeffer, at the Graduate School of Business of Stanford University, assigns the origins of our confusion and ambivalence about power to the way we were taught in school. "Interdependence is minimized . . . it is you versus the material . . . as long as you have mastered the material, you have achieved what is expected. Cooperation may even be considered cheating." He argues that in healthy organizations quite the reverse is true. Working with others to accomplish objectives is essential; it is appropriate use of power that makes accomplishment possible.

Classroom teachers and faculty in colleges and universities see themselves with lots of authority but little power. But they, as well as their pupils, see the school administration, the business world, and the government suffused with power that carries high stakes—especially the power to hire, to reward with pay and promotion, and to penalize with layoffs and "downsizing" of the work force. Students, moreover, see many of their teachers and their professors holding real power, especially over them. It does not take many penetrating questions in a conversation with a small group of adults to elicit some horror stories about their classroom experiences or those of their children. They recall some of their teachers as tyrants who not only loaded them with meaningless work but also had lasting and sometimes unfortunate effects on their personalities and views of the world.

Executives in large organizations often see themselves as having much less power than they need to accomplish their purposes. Thus, one important feature of the concept of power is that its perception may be stronger than reality. Of course, power not exercised is sometimes indistinguishable from the absence of power; perceptions of power-holders are surely a consequence of how they do or do not wield it.

However power is defined by others, it is within the context of leadership and leaders that we will examine it. We can view power as a process—she vetoed the legislation; as a tool—he sent three aircraft carriers into the Gulf; as an entity—I have the power to do that!; as a mechanism—the Party will manage to get that done; or as an abstraction to be clarified singularly with each detail pertaining to the situation being described—the power of the press. In respect to leadership we can see power as applying to the achievement of goals or as a means for solving problems, gathering information, or making decisions. Thus described, power can be seen as a positive—even an essential—force when tasks have to be completed, an ideology has to be furthered, or a mission has to be accomplished. If we employ the term power in these circumstances, it can be seen as targeted at achieving definable purposes and not as a way of aggrandizing some persons and degrading others.

If we accept this definition of power, we can observe readily whether power is being used to attain previously outlined objectives or whether it serves to benefit the selfish pursuits of those in leadership positions. Further, it is possible to consider whether power is being used to persuade, to influence, or to coerce. By differentiating these means for achieving ends, we can put ourselves in a felicitous position to judge whether or not the means are acceptable and, if not, to reexamine the ends. This provides for followers, as well as leaders, some method to examine periodically the condition of the "road to success."

In a participative democracy, the potential for using power resides in everyone. It can be employed wisely or foolishly. People with information can use it to make wise decisions to further society's goals or abuse it to achieve personal glory—insider traders on Wall Street, for example. A calming voice to reduce conflict or an unflurried demeanor to soothe those in pain exemplifies a "good" use of power. Loving parents have power to support or spoil their children. The mayor of the town has power, the lifeguard at the beach has power, the newspaper editor has power. In one way or another, we all have power at some time or under some conditions. The proper *use* of power must be addressed by leaders at all levels. Their role includes not only attention to their own use of power, but to the ways in which power is distributed among group members and used or abused in the furthering of the purposes of the group.

In small groups, one person is either designated to serve as the team leader or becomes its de facto leader. When a group is engaged in a common task, there are many times when one person must act for the group, resolve conflicts, and make decisions. These are exercises of power, although group members might prefer to use some other word. When resources are limited, someone—usually the leader—must assure a fair distribution. This, also, is an exercise of power but might be called "acting for the group." Most differentiation of roles carries a distinction in status for one person who is designated as leader, boss, foreman, chairman, or president. Group members usually defer to such a person as long as they see the role being played properly. When they are convinced that the leader has too much power and is using it unfairly, the relationship changes; often the lead person is then replaced. Signals of improper behaviors may provide sufficient ammunition to set in motion an active rebellion.

Speech Patterns and Power

Speech patterns of the leader may provide sufficient clues to inform sophisticated audiences about the nature of the leader. Ian Cunningham[2] provides a novel way to identify those leaders who have an appropriate view of their role in an organization. Such leaders tend to speak in a particular way that reflects their perception of the relationship they have to the total organization. They employ a pattern of phrases that may be detected in speeches and other messages exemplified by sequences of "I . . ." and "We . . .". In the "I . . ." section, the leader states a position, a plan, or a course of action. In the "We . . ." section, the followers are persuaded to play their proper role and are assured that the outcomes will be gratifying for them. This linguistic pattern, when repeated, often suggests that the leader feels a personal responsibility to work for the aims of the followers and the need for all to remain together in pursuit of common goals.

Analysis of speech patterns has also been used in estimating the motivations of U.S. presidents. As the use of negatives ("I will not . . .") increases in the first inaugural address of a U.S. president, the likelihood that the president will use military power in the resolution of conflicts decreases.

Pfeffer, cited earlier, says, "We exercise power and influence, when we do it successfully, through the subtle use of language, symbols, ceremonies, and settings that make people feel good about what they are doing." He contends that part of the job of people interested in wielding power and influence is to make others feel good about doing what needs to be done, using symbolism and value-laden language in the process. To make others feel good about the actions or decisions you require of them is not acting against their interests. After all, if the actions or decisions are important, all parties might as well feel good about them as not.[3]

Structure and Power

Part of the issue of power reflects problems in structure. A properly structured organization allocates power and authority in ways that encourage accountability. Without accountability, priorities are confused and goals are left unmet. In such organizations, conflicts develop among units and between superiors and subordinates; enormous aggravation occurs because obvious remedies are not applied. The works of Jaques[4] and of Byham[5] are relevant.

We noted previously that one in three workers find the boss to be the major source of dissatisfaction at work; most of the complaints are of arrogance, incompetence, or of improper use of power. Hogan was cited as reporting that 60 to 75% of managers in the United States are incompetent. He says, "Incompetent supervision is a primary—perhaps the primary—source of stress and occupational unhappiness for the majority of workers in corporate America." Selection of persons for leadership and managerial positions is often made on the wrong basis. Persons who do good work are sometimes mistakenly promoted although they are not qualified for leadership or supervisory roles. It may be that they relate poorly to others and that working in a solitary fashion is more compatible with their personalities. These persons, when in a position of authority, are often the reason for complaint and dissension.

Status differences are produced not only by the behaviors of the leader but also by the expectations, prior experiences, and behaviors of the followers. Some followers will assign to the leader the role in their lives unfilled by their parents, or they will assign to the leader the hostility they feel toward authority figures in general. They are likely to accord to any new leader the same subservience they have shown to authority figures in other aspects of their lives. In some cultures, the deference given to those of higher status, thereby increasing their power, interferes with proper decision making for the group.

Earlier we described forms of behavior characterizing leaders who develop effective teams. In many ways, leaders of a group small enough for personal contact with each team member have the most rewarding jobs, for their leadership can be exercised face to face, and the behaviors of team members can be modified to increase effectiveness. This situation exists in most athletic teams. The role of leadership exercised by the coach is not only obvious, it is also highly publicized and rewarded.

However, even under the best conditions it is easy for tyranny to emerge. When highly autocratic coaches produce winning teams, most persons applaud. When controls are carried to excess, teams rebel; when their resentment interferes with their best performance, they lose games. It is clear that the leader's power and influence on followers and subordinates must maintain the fragile balance between being neither too permissive nor too controlling; balance can determine the degree to which the leader can implement plans, decisions, and action strategies successfully.

Definitions of Power

Our imaginations and our prior experiences provide each of us with an obvious definition of power and a chronicle of its uses. If we are to benefit from a review of research and analysis relating to power, we must agree upon a definition and on the concepts that surround power and the reactions to its use. We shall begin by restricting the use of the term power to its use within groups and organizations, especially the use and distribution of power relating to the allocation of resources and making decisions that affect the group or organization.

Power is thus the ability, whether exercised or not, to allocate resources, to assign tasks, and to provide, withhold, or withdraw tangible rewards, including the assignment and withdrawal of responsibilities. Although some definitions of leadership and the power that goes with it include the phrase "without coercion," the concept of coercion is not particularly relevant to most acts of leadership with which we are now concerned, for it suggests enslavement, torture, imprisonment, and execution. Our concern is with such matters as working enthusiastically, putting every effort into tasks, and being fully committed to the purposes of the group. Therefore, we will discuss power only within the limits of its use in a society where concerns are with the attainment of lofty goals, not with preserving in power those who restrict the freedoms of others.

Our definition will seem too restrictive to those critics who say we are denying the grave abuses of power by tyrants. They will ask how we can speak of leaders without being concerned with absolute power? It is true we are limiting our frame of reference, but we are also being pragmatic; very few great accomplishments in the civilized world today were achieved by threat of execution, torture, or other excesses of power. B. F. Skinner demonstrated over and over again that positive reinforcement—reward—produces the desired shaping of behaviors. Punishment reduces activity and thus lessens the opportunity for improvement.

The Exercise of Power

But is not the award of a benefit an exercise of power? Of course. This becomes an integral part of the power that the ideal leader exercises. Even a word of praise, a smile, or a nod in one's direction can produce a powerful effect on a follower when the leader is greatly admired or has other favors to bestow. Being ignored after putting forth great effort in "the cause" can be painful, since that is an improper use of power. The persons who fear power should thus not fear the exercise of power, but its wrongful exercise.

A person moving into a leadership position must therefore exercise care not to be misled by fatuous words of advice such as "Show them who is boss!"; "You cannot fraternize with the troops!"; "It's yours, play it your way!"; and, even more disruptively, by paying heed to "Rank hath its privileges!" for this may spell eventual disaster for a person assuming a responsible position. The leader's behavior is watched closely by followers. Small clues that do not jibe with what they have been led to believe cause them to become suspicious and distrustful. Persons who have suffered betrayal of promises have long memories. Arrogance or insensitivity by a leader may signal to followers that it is time to seek a new leader.

Fred Fiedler[6] has found that the effectiveness of different leadership styles depends upon the particular leader-member relations that exist and the nature of the tasks to be performed. A vaguely defined ambiguous task creates uncertainty and thus decreases the leader's situational control. Power conferred on the leader by the organization for the purpose of getting the job done is essential. However, the actual power of a leader is, in most cases, rather limited. Regardless of how much power the leader might have in theory, in practice it is difficult to maintain absolute control over disenchanted followers or recalcitrant subordinates. There are innumerable ways in which subordinates can frustrate a leader, from playing dumb—being "passive-aggressive"—to getting the leader into serious trouble by delaying the completion of the task—a slow-up—or disobeying the agreed-upon rules—a virtual rebellion.

Gary Yukl[7] makes a distinction between power and influence: Influence can be used even if the force of power is not brought to bear. Leadership effectiveness is dependent on the amount and type of power and how it is exercised. It can be used not only to influence subordinates but also peers, superiors, and persons outside the organization. Sources of power derive from individual attributes, the situation in which it is exerted, and the ongoing reciprocal processes of influence. Yukl indicates that the following are required to gain power: expertise in order to promote innovative proposals that are likely to succeed, control over information, the capacity to control decisions and the judgment to recognize their value, and the competence not only to solve problems but also to work with others to do so. It is necessary to understand that credibility is not attained if one is perceived as self-interested or irresponsible; one must be able to demonstrate loyalty to the group. Naturally, it is essential to avoid making serious mistakes.

Demonstration of exceptional expertise may result in attribution of charisma by subordinates if the leader implements innovative strategies that involve high risk of personal loss.[8] Such charismatic leaders use personal power more than position power; they rely on positive reward behavior rather than punishment. Those who exercise power in an arrogant, manipulative, domineering manner engender resistance. Those who succeed develop influence tactics to fit the situation: rational persuasion, exchange of benefits, pressure tactics, ingratiation, appeal to authority, consultation, inspirational appeals, intentional role modeling, coalition formation, co-opting of opponents, gaining of control over key decisions, and institutionalizing of power.

Astin and Leland[9] studied women who provided leadership during the first two decades of the modern women's movement in the United States, roughly from the mid-1960s to the mid-1980s. They documented the experiences, perspectives, and accomplishments of three groups of women whom they called *Predecessors*, *Instigators*, and *Inheritors*. These group titles referred to the generational differences of the three groups. As part of their conceptual framework, the authors identified power as energy, not control, for a leader does not have to exercise power over others but can mobilize power and engage in leadership activities that empower others.

A question posed by Astin and Leland to women in leadership positions in colleges and universities was, "Do you think of yourself as someone who has or has had power?" Respondents viewed power as a relational process and talked about having influence rather than power. Influence was preferred because power was seen in interpersonal and in value-oriented terms. Although others attributed power to them because of their positions of authority, these leaders viewed what they did as using their power base to influence and develop networks that became the powerful agents of change.

Power and Personality

Why is power frequently exercised so as to subvert the leadership process? For one set of answers to this question, we can turn to the study of personality by psychoanalysts, psychiatrists, clinical psychologists, social psychologists, and personality psychologists. However, many mysteries remain even after attending to their reports. It remains hard to figure out why some people who already hold highly visible and responsible positions often engage in bizarre behaviors that aggrandize themselves when the positions they hold provide great opportunities for them to do good and to earn honorable reputations.

Many persons who appear mature and well socialized, confident and successful, are nonetheless often full of anxiety. They are insecure, have strong needs for power or achievement, and require continual overt evidence of their success, status, and worth. Speaking of them as "power hungry" is not remiss. Such feelings may drive such persons to great lengths and great accomplishments. Their energy and single-mindedness are astounding. Often they are impelled to insist on the trappings of office, the deference of others, and the assignment to them of credit for all accomplishments. Such persons, when succeeding to leadership positions, end up with position power but cannot be said to possess the attributes of leadership nor should they be referred to as leaders.

Usually it takes force, excessive compensation, or, in the case of high government office, an election or even a revolution to remove such persons from high position. Robert Kaplan writes of this in *Beyond Ambition*.[10] "No one can argue with wanting to be the best. One can only argue with wanting too badly to be the best. It is only when executives go too far in pursuing their ambitions that trouble comes."

In a somewhat different vein, Robert Hogan has written in great detail about a group of executives he studied who represent the "dark side" of charisma: Engaging and personable, they impress everyone with their skill in dealing with issues—but only in speeches and conversation, never in action.[11] Hogan describes a marketing executive whose psychological profile showed qualities that would virtually assure success in gaining employment, for he seemed to be "bright, imaginative, open-minded, forceful and charismatic." Another angle, however, showed a dark side; he was a flaky, politically obtuse showoff who could not be trusted. He eventually was moved out, but before that he demoralized the marketing department that reported to him.

U.S. presidents represent a unique group viewed as holding enormous power. Their motives are examined constantly. Students of the U.S. presidency have developed measures of presidential motives by "scoring" the inaugural address or related documents. These measures prove to predict such various events as cabinet member turnover, assassination attempts, scandals in presidential administrations, arms limitation agreements, entry into war, and type of persons picked for cabinet positions.

David McClelland[12] asserts that individuals who use "nots" frequently in their writing or their speeches use power for social or group objectives rather than for personal interests. Perhaps this observation applies particularly to persons perceived to have great power: Their commitment to limit its use may be reassuring. Any sentences making such statements would include the words, "no," "not," or the like.

Power and "The System"

Defects in the personality of the leader are only one source of mismanagement of working groups. Frequently leaders, managers, chairmen, presidents, and chief executives exercise power and authority because "the system" expects it. Whether elected or appointed, the new incumbent frequently receives explicit or implicit signals about how to behave. Not behaving accordingly is to be categorized as a "wimp," whereas behaving as expected is described approvingly as a "take-charge person." Even those who find the exercise of power stressful or offensive and who resent every intrusion of the leader into their own private domains will nonetheless expect the leader to intrude into the domains of others when it is to their own personal interest.

Leaders therefore get mixed signals. Pressed to behave in different ways, they frequently must rely on their own prior experiences and their own preferences for modes of response. For many, it can be their favorite advisors or friends or the latest article or book in fashion to which they turn, or they may refer to the management class they attended or the text they studied. And then, when the results differ from the case history reports cited or the advice given, they may begin to question their own coping mechanisms, which, in turn, creates additional problems. These conflicting pressures cause leaders to behave in varying ways that are not only detrimental to them but also to the organization.

Organizations differ in their histories, in their expectations of leaders, and in their explicit rules of conduct. But each leader of an organization finds opportunities to modify the climate, the expectations, and the rules. Those leaders who do not take advantage of the opportunity and responsibility to provide channels for the full expression of views from all levels of the organization will soon find themselves cut off from important sources of information. They will also discover that although they may wish to see greater empowerment for all participants in the organization, there will be obstacles in the way. No more important task resides with the new leader than to open channels of communication and develop and promulgate policies that will allow more autonomy to each work group within the organization and to each individual.

In large organizations this becomes a most difficult task, for most of the action and response to action will come through intermediaries. At each level of the organization the message becomes a bit more distorted. We used to laugh wildly as children when we played some variation of the game that required us to sit in a circle, whisper to the person next to us what we had heard, and add our own item to the long list of items to be packed in the bags we were taking "On Our Trip." It all became so garbled and so incoherent and so irrational and so funny. How much did we learn from that game? One can only say that the real games we play as adults are not such laughing matters. Whether or not the message comes through as a clear signal to all parties must be checked by devices and processes that will not filter and transform the message.

Empowerment

The appropriate distribution of power, authority, and influence is critical to the smooth functioning of an organization. There is a word for it: *Empowerment.* The theme of the empowerment movement is that the power to make decisions should be located at the place in the organization where the optimal amount of information exists on which to base the decisions. A subgroup of the movement sees empowerment as decentralization and campaigns for moving power down. Also central to the campaigns for empowerment is a desire to involve all members of the organization in thinking about ways to perfect the organization and its procedures. Every worker in a plant, every member of a community organization, every citizen in every community should be watching for ways to solve problems; there should be willing participants in any campaign for improvement.

The value of empowering employees is captured in *Zapp! The Lightning of Empowerment* by William C. Byham,[13] president and founder of Development Dimensions International, a human resources training and development company. Byham portrays the value of empowering members of the group in a fictional account of a manufacturing concern. His message is simple: "In a world-class organization, everybody in the company has to be thinking about ways to make the business better in quality, output, costs, sales, and customer satisfaction. In government and other public service organizations as well as in business, there are demands for higher performance." He addresses the principles of empowering members of the group and of helping workers take ownership of their jobs so that they acquire an interest in improving the performance of the total group or the organization.

Walter F. Ulmer, Jr., president of the Center for Creative Leadership and former commanding general of Fort Hood, Texas, and the Third Corps of the Army, stressed principles of "power-down." Although most military commands centralize decision making in order to attain uniformity, General Ulmer argued for decentralization as a means of increasing the feelings of involvement and ownership among his forces. He said that those decisions about operations that would influence the quality of operations should be made by the persons best informed, as long as they were committed to the success of the overall organization. Any decisions made with insufficient information and without dedicated involvement usually led to loss of faith in leadership. So Ulmer asked his troops to call into central headquarters on a direct telephone line to report anything they observed that they thought "dumb." He guaranteed a prompt, personal reply. These reports were taken seriously and formed the basis for change.

Power and Politics

The exercise of power is an important issue in the governance of nations and other political units. Historians have recorded the deeds of despots who have struggled to attain it and patriots who have fought to combat its excesses. Constitutions have been drafted and structures have been designed to make government more responsive to the needs of its people and to control the willfulness of political leaders. These structures are the central focus of study for political scientists. In recent times, even more attention is being directed to the ways political structures are subverted to the special purposes of incumbents and their supporters and how these political behaviors are used and abused. They refer often to the subject of leadership and the exercise of power.

One view about the nature of political leadership and the nature of political leaders is stated by Arthur S. Goldberg. He writes:

> The exercise of political leadership is less oriented toward well-specified goals and missions than is the exercise of leadership in, for example, business or the military. In the political arena, acceptability, rather than efficacy, is the criterion by which leadership normally judges policy.... The nature of political leaders is best understood if one contemplates that conflict over values is the central "stuff" of politics.... Those who enter and remain are people with a high tolerance for conflict, as well as for ambiguity and uncertainty....
>
> There is a second aspect ... the need for leaders to be supported by coalitions.... Coalitions are *not* comprised of individuals with identical goals or even compatible goals. As a result, the matter of conflict confronts the would-be political leader not only in regard to avowed adversaries, but within that would-be political leader's own coalition. Therefore, those who are particularly adept at dissimulation, and who have a tolerance for, if not a love of, duplicity have an increased probability of survival in the Darwinian "natural selection" processes of the political arena.[14]

Edwin Hargrove, professor of Political Science at Vanderbilt University, provides an inside view of the Jimmy Carter presidency in which he notes two ingredients for effective presidential leadership:

1. The range of manipulative skills discussed under the heading of presidential "power": creating bargaining coalitions; establishing authority over subordinates; keeping potential opponents off balance; ensuring alternative sources of information and advice; and, in general, making the most of the institutional levers available to a President to win influence with other holders of power.
2. The ability to define the policy dilemmas facing the nation in terms of an emerging historical situation and suggest solutions that win widespread support.[15]

Robert House, J. M. Howell, Boas Shamir, Brian Smith, and William D. Spangler[16] built on the work of Dean Simonton[17] to obtain an overall rating of presidential charisma for recent U.S. presidents. This measure—operationally defined in terms of behavior, attributions by others, and descriptions by others—proved to correlate highly with cabinet members' level of positive feelings about their role in the administration (r = .51), frequency of compliance of cabinet members to presidential wishes and orders (r = .55), and agreement with presidential policies (r = .37). This finding suggests that charisma may have an important effect on those who work most closely with the charismatic president.

House, Spangler, and Woycke[18] report that the U.S. president's charismatic quality is also strongly and positively related to recorded presidential actions, subjective judgments about presidential performance, presidential economic performance, and presidential social performance. Only in international relations performance is there no relationship. Experiencing a crisis increases the relationship between presidential charisma and presidential performance. The striking feature of this study is that 66% of the variability in measures of direct presidential action was explained by a measure that combined presidential power motives, behavioral charisma, recency of incumbency, and crises. These results may be somewhat overstated because of spurious factors; even so, the analysis suggests a greater orderliness and predictability in presidential actions and performance than most students of the American presidency would have predicted.

The Many Faces of Power

What are the uses of power that characterize such prominent persons as Robert Moses, Lyndon Johnson, and Michael Milken? All three believed in what Pfeffer[19] refers to as the New Golden Rule: The person with the gold makes the rules. They all ". . . realized that various kinds of resources, including allies, are vitally important as sources of power . . ." especially when ". . . coupled with an understanding of how resources can be created, how control over resources can be gained and maintained, and finally, how to use incremental or temporarily unallocated resources in order to build power."

Robert Moses' name was widely known in the middle of the twentieth century. He was parks and bridges commissioner of New York State. During his 44-year tenure he built 12 bridges, 35 highways, 751 playgrounds, 13 golf courses, 18 swimming pools, and more than 2 million acres of parks in New York. His architectural and planning influence was international in scope and multi-generational in time. In the course of his productive life, Moses sat on many committees and commissions responsible for developing sites and building the structures that would be located on them. He was at the core of the financial, legal, contractual, and informational processes that made it all happen. In other words, Moses became a powerful force in his time.

Lyndon Johnson went to Washington, D.C., as a congressional secretary in 1931. He "took over" the almost unknown and ineffective twenty-one-year-old Little Congress, a group that had been formed to sharpen the skills of congressional secretaries. The Little Congress was intended to be modeled on the House of Representatives but, in fact, had not developed into anything more than a modest social club. Johnson turned it into an important source where the invited press could learn about forthcoming legislation and where members of Congress could "meet the press," a distinct benefit for both. The Little Congress was a great boon to Johnson, who was interested in being recognized and in becoming known as a politically astute figure. This was a factor in forming an early power base for him.

Michael Milken, a super salesman and a brilliant financial theorist, came to Wall Street to "make it big" on high-yield securities. Having read analyses of low-grade unrated bonds and being a quick study, Milken did his homework and learned a lot about an area of investment in which almost nobody was interested. With his persuasive personality, he managed to fire the imaginations of those willing to take risks to make money, involving them in deals about which he knew everything. By so doing, Milken was able to charge enormous fees, maintain control, and amass huge sums of money for himself in an essentially unregulated market.

Moses, Johnson, and Milken understood what they needed to know about what others wanted, how to get them to invest interest and/or money in it, how to use their information, and how to keep within their own sights the positions they desired. These examples are not meant to describe leadership. Instead, they epitomize the way in which power can be netted and brought to shore. Each of the persons described took over what was an unwanted and devalued backwater and turned it into a valuable resource to attain their objectives. The fact that Moses was interested in reaching a position of power to build mighty structures, that Johnson was interested in becoming the president of the United States—a position of vast political power, and that Milken wanted to take over corporate America—certainly a position of almost unlimited power—but wound up in jail, can become the basis for examining our own concepts about power.

When power becomes an end in itself it can consume the person who wields it, subvert the purposes of the organization that created it, and disappoint those it is intended to serve. However, when power is understood as a force to be coupled with clearly articulated values and used to attain goals agreed upon by the group, it is a necessary adjunct to effective leadership.

CHAPTER THIRTEEN
Leadership and Cultural Differences

Leaders make a difference in all nations, all cultures, all economies, all political systems, and all ethnic groups. Leadership has been a key element in every major historical change. Now, in the last years of the twentieth century as the world grows smaller, as trade becomes even more international, and as all societies know almost immediately what is going on everywhere in the world, the call sounds even more sharply for leaders who can understand and respond to a populace with greater diversity, who can give increased attention to ethnicity and national pride, and who can assure distribution of economic, health, and educational benefits among the poor as well as the affluent nations.

The challenge presented by incredible progress in transportation, communication, medical treatment, and productive capacities around the world is being met with hesitancy. Those now holding important positions of leadership are trying to respond while encased in priority systems that are outdated economically and politically. The benefits that can accrue to world populations are seen as illusory; leaders are failing to attain the commitment of followers to act vigorously in alleviating poverty and suffering.

The world of the twenty-first century can be a much better place for everyone, or it can be many decades of disappointment. Whether or not institutions adapt to change, change will occur. Increased diversity of populations, heightened stress as highly skilled work forces discover a major need for retraining, and the substantial relocation of workplace settings will produce major relocations of people. Better transportation will diminish national boundaries, resulting in an increased mix in populations, which, in turn, can produce great benefits or severe tensions and ferment. Leaders can influence the outcome.

Differences in culture have, in past years, provided a natural laboratory for examining various forms of leader-follower relations. Because culture is not static, its dynamic quality must be considered whenever it is studied. It changes from time to time, from place to place, from group to group, and from person to person, both in its many forms and in its impact.

A review of studies of cultural differences may provide some insights into a future that portends world interrelationships. Observing how persons interact in cultures other than our own may be instructive.

Culture can be described broadly or specifically. We can speak of the culture of a nation, a community, a race, an organization, a geographic area, an educational background, a factory, a school, a school of thought, and on and on. We can wander even further afield and define it in terms of its effects. We can also define culture very narrowly, as evidenced by different behaviors in specific situations. Strongly held cultural beliefs have been known to obstruct well-intentioned programs set up to combat illness, famine, violence, and war because planners know too little about how another culture will react to action programs. Cultural differences in industry and business, if misunderstood, can often result in failure. Corporate climates and corporate images are influential in an industrialized society; they must be understood if the leadership of an organization expects to be effective and maintain a productive working force. The ability to live peaceably with one's neighbors in a community or a nation and to work together harmoniously requires that we recognize and respond adequately to each other's cultural differences. We must learn more, and we must comprehend how easily a misunderstanding can erupt into violence.

Definitions of Culture

C. Geertz writes: "Culture denotes an historically transmitted pattern of meanings embodied in symbols, a system of inherited conceptions expressed in symbolic forms by means of which men communicate, perpetuate, and develop their knowledge about and attitudes toward life."[1] Other writers consider the definition of culture obvious: One says it is the "man-made" part of the human environment. A more comprehensive definition is provided by the well-known anthropologist, Clyde Kluckhohn: "Culture consists in patterned ways of thinking, feeling and reacting, acquired and transmitted mainly by symbols, constituting the distinctive achievements of human groups, including their embodiment in artifacts; the essential core of culture consists of traditional (i.e., historically derived and selected) ideas and especially their attached values."[2]

Some writers have conceptualized culture as an unexpressed agreement among members of a community to act in certain ways for the mutual benefit of all. Adherence to this unspoken contract is exhibited in U.S. culture, for example, by lining up, by waiting for a green light before crossing a street, by yielding space on a crowded sidewalk, by avoiding loud noises at midnight, and by having change ready when approaching a highway toll booth. Rules change. Men, noting the attitudes of women about their independence, no longer feel required to open doors for them or offer them seats in a bus. Sometimes groups generate their own subculture and become specific in relation to limits set by them and for them. For example, college students in residence halls may find it necessary to make explicit their own values for privacy, quiet, sleeping late, socializing selectively, and sexual activity.

Studies About Culture

In this age of easy transportation and international competitive trade, programs to educate and advise people who must engage in business abroad is fast becoming an industry. Books and articles are being published; training programs are being conducted. Functioning productively in a culturally alien environment can be a harrowing experience. There is great shock in store for those who believe that it is a romantic adventure to work in a foreign country with a native populace. In a new environment, there is no certainty that anything will conform to one's former upbringing. However, sometimes cultural similarities are found when differences are expected, and this is a surprising pleasure. Nevertheless, those who are unprepared to face trauma and ambiguity involved in coping successfully with an unfamiliar culture are likely to be among the many who cannot "make it."

Even those who believe they understand their own cultural heritage can discover that assumptions are insufficient when estimating or measuring the impact of cultural differences and similarities. Misumi talks about the beginning of his research in Japan:

Recognizing the fact that Japanese children of that time had not been accustomed to democratic leadership, I did not anticipate obtaining any result indicating democratic style leadership to be as effective as it is in the United States. To our surprise, however, we found that the major part of our findings were very similar to the findings of the United States' study. While we allow for socio-historical and cultural differences in human social behavior, we cannot help but recognize the general and universal nature of group dynamics.[3]

The vast body of writings on leaders and leadership is in many ways a domain of study of the western world, and particularly the United States. Many of the platitudes voiced about leaders and how their most effective behaviors can be more productive assume that everyone worldwide agrees with some fundamental purposes and priorities about human life. Instead, the principles about leadership that are developed in western countries must be limited to use in western countries; even then, modes of behavior may change enough to make some principles obsolete. When the prescribed "best way" is used in a different or changed culture, the specified procedures that made it best may not pertain. For example, "managing by walking around" does not work in a culture with great class distinctions. In some cultures, an insistence on being on time or an expectation that each person will be ambitious, work harder, and put the work first may be offensive to co-workers and superiors alike.

Definitive comparative studies of the role of culture in the leadership process are rare. But then, renaissance people are rare, too. Few people are reared in more than one culture. Also, few students in the field are able to engage in simultaneous study of groups or organizations in two or more cultures. When such studies occur, inadequate measurement and limited control over extraneous variables limits the interpretability of findings. Often the best studies are little more than intensive case studies.

One way to proceed in a study of culture is to use identical or near identical measures of leader behaviors, follower expectations, and follower reactions to leader performance. These measures can be correlated with indicators of performance of the individuals or the groups under study. But even these studies are difficult to do; they are few in number, and most of them have collected comparable data in only a handful of countries.

The Work of Hofstede

A major multinational corporation with operational components in sixty-seven countries has provided data to help us understand cultural differences. The methods used illustrate one way to study culture and its consequences. The work was done by Geerte Hofstede[4] who designed and analyzed a series of questionnaires completed by over 116,000 employees of this American-owned firm in forty-seven countries around the world. The company questionnaire asked the employees to pick from a list of descriptors the type of boss the employee currently had and the type of boss the employee would like to have.

Hofstede collected and analyzed the questionnaire responses. Analysis of the responses identified four dimensions of work-related values of workers: Individualism versus Collectivism; Power Distance; Uncertainty Avoidance; and Masculinity-Femininity. Scores on scales measuring these four dimensions varied substantially depending on national origins of respondents.

On Hofstede's four dimensions, American workers rank highest on the Individualism scale; this is another way of saying that independence and autonomy are prized by American workers. The Power Distance measure is a measure of expected status differences between worker and boss: Do workers prefer to have distant or close personal relations with their superior? U.S. groups, along with Western Europe, Canada, Australia, and New Zealand, have very low scores, showing a preference for little power distance. Employees in all other countries had higher Power Distance scores: They expect and prefer a great psychological distance between superior and subordinate. The U.S. employees show less Uncertainty Avoidance; in other words, they are greater risk-takers than their contemporaries in other countries. In the U.S., employees get high ratings on Masculinity but not as high as the Japanese; this scale measures such characteristics as ambition, striving, and desire for advancement and success.

The differences discovered were not small. They were large enough to make quite a difference in the effectiveness of a given set of behaviors if applied in each country in the same way. These findings inform us that many of the features of leadership and leadership behavior, which we have been describing as effective in the U.S., may not apply in those settings where leaders are expected to exercise power and authority and where workers prize security more than advancement. The empowering of subordinates that permits greater use of the talents of employees will not be welcomed by a work force that desires to avoid uncertainty.

The power distance norm for a given culture is the perception by the less powerful of the power distance between the boss and the subordinate. The subordinate expects the distance to be maintained and prefers circumstances in which expectancies are fulfilled. Hofstede identifies the power distance norm as the most useful criterion for characterizing cultures, for it appears not just in the work setting but between the privileged class and the subjected class, between the head of a group and a group member, and among family members. Its source may be found in the early socialization process by the family, the school, and other institutions of a society.

Power distance reflects power striving that is only partly satisfied. Power striving is seen by Hofstede as an outcome of satisfaction, not dissatisfaction. Having power feeds the need for more power. This characteristic is much like the need for power in U.S. culture that has been described (see Chapter 12, "Leadership, Power, and Position") by McClelland.[5]

Human pecking orders appear in almost all cultures as part of the socialization process. How the basic fact of dominance is worked out in human social existence, however, varies from one society to another and from one group to another. Hofstede's work is impressive but may actually understate differences among various nations and cultures, for he observed only employees of a single company. These people probably are less like their compatriots than would be found if a random sample of residents had been used.

The Work of Smith and Peterson

Smith and Peterson,[6] a research team with bases both in England and the U.S., have reviewed much of the data available in published studies around the world. Their work leads them to conclude that the heterogeneity of corporate cultures and the impact of national and cultural backgrounds on leader and worker expectancies make the tasks of multinational organizations very difficult indeed. They caution that the making and remaking of cultures is a hard business. Leadership becomes complicated when leaders and followers include a large proportion of persons with different cultural backgrounds.

One common theme emerging from studies conducted worldwide is the necessity for leaders to attend to both the tasks to be accomplished and the needs of the people who perform the tasks. Tasks need to be clarified, deadlines need to be set, and individual responsibilities need to be assigned. At the same time, workers need to see the importance of the work, have their conflicts resolved, and receive individual consideration. These dimensions are not defined in quite the same way in various cultures and do not show equal effects on performance.

The universality of the need to attend to both the work to be done and to the needs of the people who perform the tasks does not lessen the responsibility for attending to cultural differences. Smith and Peterson conclude that all actions must occur within the context of rules and procedures of the organization and within the norms of the culture(s) that supplies its members.[7]

Some, but not all, specific behaviors vary with cultural differences. For instance, talking sympathetically with a subordinate who suffers personal difficulties is seen as considerate in all cultures; talking frequently about work progress is seen as task centered in all cultures. But a supervisor who talks about a subordinate's personal difficulties to his colleagues when the person is absent is deemed inconsiderate in Britain and the U.S. but considerate in Hong Kong and Japan. The supervisor who shows disapproval of subordinates who are latecomers is seen as task centered in Britain and Hong Kong, unfriendly and inconsiderate in the U.S., and neither of these things in Japan.

The Work of Triandis

Harry Triandis,[8] professor of Psychology at the University of Illinois, makes the point that most social psychological theories generated in the western world are culture bound. He cites work done in Japan that shows that positive reinforcement has different effects in Japan than in the United States. In the U.S., an individual who receives reinforcement of some sort after a task is completed successfully is more likely to repeat the success on the next trial. The reinforcement may be praise, recognition, or a material reward. In Japan, there is evidence from research studies that Japanese *adults* respond just as well when another person gets reinforced as when they, themselves, get reinforced. That is not true of young Japanese under the age of fifteen, suggesting that the socialization process in Japan is at work.

Triandis also reports that extroverts learn significantly better from the observation of reinforcement of others than do introverts; subjects in less individualistic cultures and all subjects who are other-oriented prefer to divide rewards equally, or on the basis of need, rather than giving rewards to those who earn them (equity). In individualistic countries, equality is considered "unjust"; the individualism dimension of cultural variation probably underlies this observed cultural difference. Triandis also cites a study showing that subjects in Hong Kong prefer bargaining and mediation over adversarial and inquisitorial adjudication; subjects in the state of Illinois in the U.S. prefer adversarial adjudication and mediation over bargaining and inquisitorial adjudication. In the U.S., subjects divide rewards among those who earn them regardless of who they are, but Hong Kong subjects do this only when some subjects are outsiders and when their inputs—thus rewards—are low. When all are in-group members and their own inputs are high, they divide rewards equally. Triandis concludes that individuals from collectivist cultures treat in-group members with special consideration, bending over backward to give them the benefit of a doubt in interpersonal relationships. By contrast, they treat out-group members with suspicion or even hostility, taking advantage of them when they can.

Both culture and personality may moderate the use of equity versus equality or need principles. All cultures use principles of justice. But cultural values such as individualism are parameters that determine the circumstances under which a principle is to be used. Triandis says, in addition:

> In most traditional societies the individual is a bundle of roles. One cannot interact "properly" with another without knowing the role relationship. That is why some of the Australian aborigines sit down when they meet one another for the first time and go over their genealogies for several days until they finally discover what their proper kinship relationship is. Once they know that they are cousins, even fifteen times removed, they can do business with each other. By Western standards all this is lost motion, and the cognitive load of knowing one's ancestors for three hundred years is something we cannot even carry for the British royalty, let alone for ourselves.

Assignments Abroad

The Work of Ronen. Ronen[9] undertakes to identify the optimal skills necessary for an international assignee and to evaluate the training techniques available for developing such skills. Cross-cultural sensitivity and intercultural competence—sometimes referred to as multiculturalism—is critical. To function effectively in a new culture, individuals must exhibit behavior that reflects appropriate personal characteristics of both a cognitive and an affective nature, such as perseverance, empathy, courtesy, tact, respect, interest in nationals, flexibility, adaptability, patience, tolerance, initiative, energy, and openness.

Few companies have assessed training needs associated with improving effectiveness among managers living or dealing abroad. Unfortunately, corporations that do so rarely report their findings publicly. One firm, Honeywell, Inc., has reported its findings.[10] The company surveyed 347 managers who lived abroad or traveled regularly plus fifty-five local executives who interacted with foreign managers. Two quotations from the interviews illustrate their findings:

> "Time as a cultural value is something which we don't understand until we are in another culture. It took me 6 months to accept the fact that my staff meeting wouldn't begin on time and more often would start 30 minutes late and nobody would be bothered but me."
>
> "Communication can be a problem. I had to learn to speak at half the speed I normally talk."[11]

The most important result of the study was the conclusion that increased levels of training are necessary in international management for both top headquarters executives and candidates for international assignment. Recommendations regarding assignees included:

1. Improve the selection process.
2. Provide extensive culture-specific information.
3. Provide general cultural information on values assumptions, and so forth.
4. Provide self-specific information, including identification of one's own cultural paradigms such as values and beliefs, which shape perceptions about others.
5. Provide language training.

American executives from various multinational corporations have reported their perceptions of the factors contributing to expatriates' failures to function effectively in foreign environments.[12] Following are the factors in descending order of importance:

1. Inability of manager's spouse to adjust to a different physical and cultural environment.
2. Inability of manager to adjust to a different physical or cultural environment.
3. Other family-related problems.
4. Manager's personal or emotional immaturity.
5. Manager's inability to cope with the larger responsibility posed by overseas work.
6. Manager's lack of technical competence for the assignment.
7. Lack of motivation to work overseas.

One of the most significant concerns reported by returning assignees—particularly early returners—regarding their overseas experience concerns the adaptability of the spouse and children to the new environment. In fact, this aspect has been reported as the major reason for failure to complete international assignments.

Ronen tells us that raising the level of intercultural sensitivity means that the individual becomes more tolerant of other value systems, more accepting of unfamiliar behavior, and more empathic to other beliefs and social norms. To achieve this nonethnocentric attitude, we must change the beliefs and value systems that the individual has acquired during his or her socialization process. However, early socialization also contributes to the individual's identity, perception of truth and reality, and preferred ways of thinking and behaving. An individual chooses or accepts his or her reference groups, which reinforced these beliefs and value systems. Can multicultural training threaten the individual with the loss of personal identity? Can it confuse the individual's self-concept or threaten the support of his or her peer groups? To what extent can multicultural training be threatening and stress provoking? Many individuals resist and experience stress when forced to expose personal tendencies such as rigidity, fear of failure, and argumentativeness. Individuals resent exposing their biases and prejudices, qualities that may appear during training. Thus appropriate intervention methods must be devised.

Convergence. Many observers have suggested that we need to pay little attention to the ways in which developing countries adapt their own customs to the pressures of technological advances. The argument is that such countries will be compelled to change with modern times. They cannot expect more advanced nations to accommodate to their idiosyncrasies. So, if we are willing to be patient, many of the cultural differences that interfere with modernization of medical practice, improved agricultural practice, and even population control will be reduced and become more tractable with the passage of time.

No longer is it fashionable to assume that nations with the highest technology are world leaders in all domains. Anthropologists no longer study primitive societies in order to gain insights into the origins of "more advanced" cultures. Increasing industrialization and widespread transfer of technology seems not to have diminished the impact of cultural factors; differences among nations and among ethnic groups do not vanish as technology advances, nor have organizational characteristics diminished as the world views the material success of highly industrialized nations.

Almost fifty years ago, the well-known sociologist, Max Weber,[13] listed time, basic resources, demography, and cultural inertia as the forces pulling toward divergence of nations. He defined cultural inertia as the values, beliefs, and habitual behavior patterns that resist change because of the security they supply. Studies by Laurent[14] and Hofstede[15] have shown that managerial values and beliefs across nations differ significantly. The argument has not been supported that education, and especially business education that is rooted in a philosophy developed in business schools of the United States, would constitute a major unifying force. Laurent's work with values of managers of the same company in different European countries shows that multinational corporations or the business education system have not caused managerial conceptions to become standardized across nations.

Kagitçibasi[16] has a somewhat different view about what will happen. A world change toward more individualistic, competitive orientations may actually come about, he contends, but only because a model of psychological and social change stemming from a Western ideology of individualism is imposed on the rest of the world. Research evidence shows that change toward individualism is not an inevitable outcome of socioeconomic development. Therefore, it should not be imposed artificially. It is important that attempts to understand and to effect change be based on valid evidence rather than on assumptions.

Diversity in the Work Force

The increasing diversity of the American work force in the next couple of decades attracts the attention of many writers, as individual and organizational awareness of related phenomena increases. Loden and Rosener[17] have reviewed common practices and recommend some changed policies and procedures. Using a diverse cross section of employees in public, private, and educational institutions, they conducted a study in 1989 to isolate specific dimensions of the leadership required when the workforce increases in its diversity. They refer to this type of leadership as *pluralistic leadership*. Based on their collective experience, they believe that pluralistic leadership qualities would most often be found by interviewing persons outside the mainstream of the work force. They conducted exploratory interviews with over 200 employees at every level of twenty organizations, using the findings to develop a model with five key dimensions. To refine this model, they surveyed 450 managers and employees from public, private, and not-for-profit institutions. Respondents were asked to indicate the degree of importance they ascribed to each leadership dimension identified in the model and any additional qualities they believed were essential for effective pluralistic leadership. The dimensions that grew out of this effort included the following:

1. Vision and values that recognize and support diversity within the organization.
2. Ethical commitment to fairness and the illumination of all types of workplace discrimination.
3. Broad knowledge and awareness regarding the primary and secondary dimensions of diversity and multicultural issues.

4. Openness to change based on diverse input and feedback about personal filters and blind spots.
5. Mentor and empowerer of diverse employees.
6. Ongoing catalyst and model for individual and organizational change.

The first four of these leadership dimensions consist of values and attitudes that make leaders effective in organizations where diversity is valued. The last two describe specific roles that diverse employees believe must be played by effective leaders.

The importance of these qualities of pluralistic leadership is emphasized by the evidence Loden and Rosener present on demographic change. They cite data showing that throughout the 1990s, people of color, white women, and immigrants will account for 85% of the net growth in our nation's labor force. In 1980, women made up 43% of the total work force; by the year 2000 they will account for more than 47% of the total, and 61% of all American women will be employed. In 1980, blacks made up 10% of the total work force and Hispanics accounted for 6%. By the end of the 1990s, blacks will make up 12% of the total work force, Hispanics 10%, and Asians another 4%. In this same decade, the American work force will continue to mature, with those in the 35–54 age group increasing by more than 25 million—from 38% of the work force in 1985 to 51% by the year 2000. At the same time, those in the 16–24 age group will decline by almost 2 million or by 8%. Also, during the 1980s, immigrant populations accounted for one third of the total population growth in America. Currently, white men are a declining share of the U.S. population, accounting for just 37% of the total. In 16 of the top 25 urban markets throughout the United States, people of color now are the majority population. Over the next twenty years, the U.S. population is expected to grow by 42 million: Hispanics will account for 47% of this growth; blacks will account for 22%; Asians and other people of color will make up 18% of this increase; and whites will account for 13%.

Pervasive Organizational Cultures

The definitions of culture and the descriptions of how cultures impose specific ways of thinking and acting can apply to organizations and have been known to cut across national boundaries. Schein observed ". . . that companies operating in the multinational context sometimes did things in dramatically similar ways, even in widely differing cultures. Companies thus seemed to have cultures of their own that were sometimes strong enough to override or at least modify local cultures."[18] His analysis aims to show how culture can be abstracted into a set of basic assumptions. These assumptions may be unwritten—and even unrecognized—and yet underlie many of the processes and procedures of the organization.

Basic dimensions developed in the anthropological study of culture have been modified and applied by Schein to organizational cultures. He concludes:

> A dynamic analysis of organizational culture makes it clear that leadership is intertwined with culture formation, evolution, transformation, and destruction. Culture is created in the first action by leaders; culture is also embedded and strengthened by leaders. When culture becomes dysfunctional, leadership is needed to help the group unlearn some of its cultural assumptions and learn new assumptions. . . . In fact, the endless discussion of what leadership is and is not

could, perhaps, be simplified if we recognized that the unique and essential function of leadership is the manipulation of culture.[19]

Training the Expatriate

Helping to cross cultural lines is neither easy nor obvious. Yet many organizations have been impelled to do what they can. In fact, such efforts, minimal at the moment, may become an essential part of training for multinational organizations.

Trainers Help Expatriate Employees Build Bridges to Different Cultures

LA HULPE. Belgium—At a training center here, Bob Walsfisz is introducing young managers from International Business Machines Corp. to the mysteries of foreign cultures.

To stir discussion, he asks them to explain the British ideal of keeping a stiff upper lip.

"What is 'stiff upper lip'" asks Daan Kooman, an IBM manager from the Netherlands. Walter Sum, a German colleague, suggests that it means "I can absorb pain without showing emotion." Mr. Walsfisz then expounds on scientific data showing that Britons tend to put a high value on "masculine" traits.

Dave Wilkin, a Canadian, puts up his hand and raises a tougher question: "Why do French women always dress in such a sexy way?" Mr. Walsfisz, a Dutchman fizzing with energy and wisecracks, dances around the question by noting that the French and Italians generally consider it important to project a certain image of themselves by dressing smartly.

Some of the chatter may sound trivial. But Mr. Walsfisz, who heads a training firm based in The Hague, and a growing band of other trainers are persuading big companies that their managers ought to attend such seminars in "multicultural" management.

Don't Pat That Child

These seminars, which began to pop up in Europe in the 1980s, go beyond the traditional short course on how an expatriate executive can cope with the folkways of a particular country. The goal is to help executives come to terms with a wide range of people with different values and ways of solving problems. The trainers try to change attitudes and challenge biases—rather than merely parroting a list of admonitions against, say, patting a Thai child on the head or arriving late for a meeting in Frankfurt.

Multicultural management is "a question of attitude, an openness to human variety, not a question of knowledge," says Fons Trompenaars, another Dutchman who is one of Mr. Walsfisz's rivals on the seminar circuit. These culture gurus have a new sales pitch for their courses and consulting work: Many companies that rushed into cross-border mergers and acquisitions in the late '80s now realize that such projects are more complicated than they appeared. "The missing element is the human factor," says Rudi Plettinx, a training official in the Management Centre Europe in Brussels.

The gurus also tell potential clients that Anglo-Saxon business theories and practice—dominant in many multinationals—are ill-suited for much of the world outside of the U.S. and Britain. David Howell, a culture trainer based in Ashley, England, says that Americans and Britons tend to be impatient to get down to business when they meet foreigners. "Americans say, 'If there is a buck in it, we'll do business with them,'" Mr. Howell says, "but people in other parts of the world say, 'Unless we like you, we won't do business together.'"

Not all companies feel compelled to call in outsiders to explain cultural mysteries. Some use in-house experts or figure that their executives learn by doing. Tony Preedy, vice president, personnel, at London-based Poly-Gram NV, says that many of the music company's executives travel frequently and get used to working with colleagues all over the world. If multicultural management is the wave of the future, PolyGram figures it has an advantage: It already has 15 different nationalities among its top 33 managers.

"No one nationality dominates," says Mr. Preedy. "I think it's the way multinationals will have to go. You can't believe that head office knows best."

Others are eager to smooth over cultural differences, rather than to cultivate them. "We try to build a common corporate culture," says Peter M. Dessau, the head of human resources at the European division of Colgate-Palmolive Co. "We want them all to be Colgaters."

Then there are the true believers in multicultural training. Among them is Knud Christensen, a Danish personnel manager at BP Oil Europe, a Brussels-based unit of British Petroleum Co. "No culture is better or worse than another," Mr. Christensen says. "They're just different. We have to understand that."

Toward that end, the company has put about 250 of its managers through 2 1/2-day courses led by Mr. Walsfisz over the past three years. The cost per manager is around $1500, Mr. Christensen says. Among other benefits, he says, the courses have helped BP Oil managers adapt policies to fit various national needs.

For example, the company promotes "upward feed-back" under which managers comment on their bosses' performance. That works well in Scandinavia, Britain and the Netherlands, where managers tend not to be overly intimidated by their superiors, Mr. Christensen says. But it is more difficult in France, Turkey and Greece, where tradition calls for showing more deference toward authorities. Managers in such countries "might be less direct" in providing their feedback, Mr. Christensen says.

Motorola Inc. has gone so far as to open a special center for cultural training at its headquarters in Schaumburg, Illinois. The electronics company is putting hundreds of its managers through short courses there, using programs partly developed by Mr. Trompenaars. "It is imperative that we understand all national cultures and respect all cultures—and use it as a competitive advantage," says Rs Moorthy, a Malaysian who runs the training center. Mr. Moorthy's goal? To make Motorola managers "trans-culturally competent."

On the other side of the Atlantic, Philippe Alloing is nearly as enthusiastic. A Frenchman who has spent most of his career outside France, Mr. Alloing became convinced of the need for cultural training a few years ago when he was head of human resources at BP Nutrition, another British Petroleum unit, and found himself dealing with "a melting pot in which things didn't melt very well."

Mr. Alloing still uses cultural training now that he is human resources head at CarnaudMetalbox SA, a huge Paris-based maker of packaging, formed by the 1989 merger of rivals from France and Britain. At the moment, he is using Mr. Trompenaars's services to try to resolve cultural clashes between British and German managers whose business units are merging. "In Germany, you are a beginner until you are 38," Mr. Alloing says. "In England, at 38 you are a has-been and are looking at early retirement."

This kind of contrast is a culture guru's bread and butter. During his seminars, Mr. Trompenaars reports a correlation between the number of lawyers in a society and spending on pet food. "This has nothing to do with what lawyers eat," he quips. Rather, he explains, people in the U.S. and other largely Protestant cultures often are so suspicious of humanity that they turn to lawyers and dogs.

Mr. Walsfisz explains all kinds of cultural differences by reference to the writings of Geerte Hofstede, a Dutch academic who devised a way to rank nations according to such criteria as their degree of individualism, respect for authority and aversion to uncertainty. Within an hour or two, Mr. Walsfisz has his students batting around such terms as "power distance" and "uncertainty avoidance." Lest the jargon and data send students to sleep, Mr. Walsfisz keeps jabbing them with humor.

A sample: "In Germany, everything is forbidden unless it is allowed. In Britain, everything is allowed unless it is forbidden. And in France, everything is allowed even if it's forbidden."[20]

The Effects of Context on Leadership

Profound change occurs only when followers who seek change find leaders who can articulate goals that have a chance of being achieved in the context of the times. Sometimes context is the most important variable. Gandhi obviously took into account the nature of the enemy in planning his campaign to liberate the Indian nation from British rule. He not only considered the laws and the traditions of ruling in the colonial empire, but also the existence of a large body of potential allies among the British populace. He was confident that the most severe repressive measures would not be used in the colonies because of the backlash such measures would produce back home. Many an activist has learned that such constraints cannot be expected from most tyrants.

Greensboro, North Carolina, was chosen by civil rights activists for the first sit-in. Jesse Jackson had attended college in Greensboro; he knew the chief of police and the community leaders to be fair-minded and concerned. That community, more than any other, was judged to be the most tolerant concerning the black position; therefore, it was the best locus to hold a demonstration that might remain peaceful yet have the desired effect for change.

The history and traditions of the group will affect greatly the type of leadership that will be effective. Groups cannot become cohesive if conflicting cultures are struggling for dominance. Differing cultures and religions combine to set constraints on the character and the behavior of the leader. These differences in context exist, sometimes implicitly, in most accounts of leadership events and must be factored into any judgments about the effectiveness of leaders and any system of generalization about leadership.

CHAPTER FOURTEEN

Translating Knowledge Into Better Practice

Encouraging the Choice to Lead

We have decried the shortage of leaders possessing the qualities we want. Yet our society does little to identify and educate the best of our prospective leaders. Nurturing and encouraging can assist the young and the not-so-young to use their emerging talents for leadership. Past and present leaders, whatever their faults, are still useful role models. History books are full of examples. Brilliantly highlighted in the best writing on leaders is the importance of commitment to the common good, the capability to take a long view of the future, the advantage of great wisdom, and the benefits of building a strong character. Each person entrusted with leadership responsibilities must learn to deal with exceedingly complex issues while maintaining a solid sense of values and an inherent respect for the worth of others. These qualities are modifiable. They can be taught. They can be learned.

The Need for Better Leaders

Our views about leaders and leadership are shaped by the way we feel about those in charge and how they affect others, how they act, and how they influence their followers. When people internalize high-minded views, they increase the likelihood of becoming respected and effective leaders. However, not all leaders and those in authoritative positions have left a legacy of honor. Some could have done great good but failed for various reasons. Many historical figures failed miserably, sometimes offending and alienating their followers or even causing their suffering and death. Many persons in power were hated and despised because they were cruel, arrogant, or tyrannical.

It is universally accepted that the best leaders are dedicated to noble purposes; they face greater demands and are willing to be held accountable to a greater degree than those who work for self-aggrandizement. Organizations search relentlessly for people who will assume leadership assignments and do well. Not many members of a society are fit or willing to lead. There are always too few persons to exercise leadership to meet every need.

Every society, institution, or group must learn more about how leaders are identified early and how they may develop the qualities we so admire in leaders. We do not know enough about leaders and leadership and must continue to search for knowledge from every source. Reading, talking, and learning about leadership issues in business, education, health care, the military, government, religion, the community, and the world is just the beginning. People must work and become seriously involved in organizations in order to comprehend the dynamics of individuals and groups. Only by becoming involved is it possible to understand the complexity of interactions among group members and the impact on the group of effective or inadequate leadership.

How the Best Leaders Behave

Studies of leadership originate in different settings and contexts and they use different methods. The search is akin to the archaeologist coming across a big bone sticking out of a marsh—there had better be some digging and further uncovering before the animal carcass can be labeled a dinosaur. It can be expected that one's understanding of leadership will change and expand as experience accumulates.

The descriptions of leaders and leadership that emerge from important studies of groups provide descriptions that vary widely and suggest endless and sometimes inconsistent patterns of effective leader behavior. We must move beyond this confusion and uncertainty to embrace proven ways in which leaders can be effective. Leadership, however defined, is studied not only for its effects on outcomes—such as improved prospects for survival of the organization, profitability, quality, and retention of membership—but also for its effects on the relationships among various constituencies. Changes in these relationships influence the functioning of an organization. Study of the benefits of excellent leadership practices also clarifies what leaders do to produce better results. The key to developing better leaders may lie in pursuing these studies.

Sharpening the Definition of Leadership

Because "leader" is a common word that slips easily out of focus and because leaders are followers in some aspects of their lives, specificity is essential as we speak or write about leaders. Samples of leaders must be selected from those who meet our definitions. Although it is easy to list presidents, governors, kings, emperors, or generals, it is very hard to draw up a list of persons whose *principal* achievement was that they exercised leadership. Almost all the persons on any list probably would have been more accurately described as something else. The "something else" occupied most of their productive lives and might have been related to their earlier aspirations and their period of preparation for the future.

Lincoln, for example, was a lawyer. That was the life for which he prepared himself; he probably thought of himself as a lawyer. His leadership role as president came later and was, in a sense, an outgrowth not only of his earlier career plans and his value system but also of being enmeshed in the crises of the times in which he was living. It is difficult to say what role he would have played later, if he had not been assassinated.

Including Leadership in Life Plans

Young people do not routinely aspire to be leaders. Ask a high school senior, "Do you want to become a leader?" and you will hear such responses as, "What do you mean? Is there a job open? Will I qualify?" But if you ask, "Do you want to be a success?" or "Do you want to make a lot of money or achieve fame?" the answers are quick and generally positive. Ask what they want to be in later life and they will speak about occupations, not about leadership. For most persons, becoming a leader seems more of an accident than part of a life plan. Persons prepare to become engineers, chemists, physicians, lawyers, plumbers, accountants, machinists, computer specialists, or philosophers. Only in a few occupations such as religion, the military, and politics are persons forced to consider preparation for exercising leadership because it is clearly part of the job.

Modulating the Criticism of Leaders Who are Trying to Do Well

Because leaders are criticized so often and so intensely, young people do not usually have high opinions of leaders and so have reservations about preparing to be one. They ask hard questions: Do leaders accomplish worthy things? Is leadership among the best or the worst of roles in life? Is it worth it? Would power and status corrupt me? Would my friends continue to respect me? Answers to hard questions require well-thought-out answers, careful study, and a firm grounding in basic principles. Young people are still building an identity that is based on self-perceptions and growing self-esteem. Those who counsel them should highlight the value of preparation for leadership in building feelings of self-efficacy and confidence.

Preparing for leadership will be neglected as long as a society criticizes leaders so harshly, especially during their lifetimes. We tend to be suspicious of reports about leader motives, special privileges, abuse of power, and even accomplishments. We blame much of what we experience in life that is not to our liking on our leaders. Pollution is attributed mainly to greed among corporate leaders. The closing of plants, poor working conditions, and low pay are viewed as a result of mismanagement and unwise planning by those in charge. We view inferior schools, high crime rates, and overcrowded highways as the product of illogical priorities set by political leaders.

The Need for Loyal Followers

Effective leaders cannot function well unless they gain full support of loyal followers. Those who search to replace faulty leaders must look for people committed to high standards who have earned the reputation for accepting responsibilities and fulfilling them. There are many people of high talent who could prepare to lead if they thought they would be supported and could be effective. Opportunities exist now. Even in such carefully constrained societies as existed during and following the Stalin period in the Soviet Union, leaders of the opposition developed and, when the time was ripe, stepped into positions of international prominence. College students generally do not identify with the leaders of the day, yet every college student at some time will have the opportunity to exercise leadership. The study of leaders and leadership, both current and in the past, should therefore be an integral part of every college student's education. Only the foolish will ignore the necessity to get ready for a role that is almost certain to be thrust upon them.

Beginning Leadership Training Early

Persuading young people of the attractiveness of leadership activities is not hard. Those educational institutions that have begun programs in leadership education have found high interest among students. Faculties of colleges and universities are becoming increasingly aware of the value of leadership offerings. Alumni have found leadership programs at their former colleges or universities excellent targets for major contributions. The current involvement of young persons in political activities is a gratifying sign. If our society maintains concerted efforts to increase the appeal of leadership for its younger citizens, our current shortage of leaders may disappear. The evidence is convincing: Leadership behaviors are teachable.

In trial after trial, we have shown that better results occur when leaders behave in certain ways—ways that excite, enliven, and refresh their organizations. Ordinary persons who are in charge at any level can improve their behaviors in relation to others and make their organizations more successful. Followers respond positively when leader behaviors are demonstrated; everyone becomes happier, more involved, and more productive. This cyclical effect fuels progress toward established goals.

Good Leadership Pays Off

Results of studies show at least a 20% improvement in performance, in profits, or in some other measure of effectiveness when leaders and managers exhibit patterns of behavior that have been described earlier as leadership behaviors. With so much emphasis on productivity, profitability, and competitiveness, one would expect that many organizations would invest in selection and training processes most likely to result in an increase in the numbers of desirable leaders. But we have also provided data showing that many supervisors, managers, and executives do not behave appropriately—that bosses are the main source of stress in the workplace and that a majority of members in many organizations find their leaders disappointing.

Learning More About Leadership

Where have we stumbled? What are the stumbling blocks? *Too few persons know the evidence.* Either we do not communicate what we know, or we have failed to put what we know into terms that are easily understood. Leadership is thought by many to be a "soft" subject, less important than finance, production, and sales. With so much pressure from other sectors, issues of leadership are neglected. It appears that many people in power also do not know the evidence.

Individuals are poor judges of their own leadership abilities. Many people have little knowledge of the effects their behaviors have on others. Even when we ask others what they think about our way of doing things or about our ideas, we do not listen to the answers. Most persons appointed to important jobs conclude they must be leaders. They feel no need to learn anything about people and people relationships. Rising to the top as a personal goal often takes precedence over rising to the top to benefit the organization.

Top executives overrate themselves. David Campbell[1] has collected data on chief executives of major U.S. corporations. He finds that *on average*, top corporate executives rate themselves as being much more credible, trusting, flexible, considerate, resilient, and affable than their closest associates rate them. Campbell asks the chief executives not only to rate themselves but also to pick persons who know them well enough to provide meaningful ratings. How receptive to change is a CEO who thinks he/she is right on track? How many people who are in charge of something have this same problem?

Persons in leadership positions see no need to change their own behaviors or to change their style. After all, their qualities, good or bad, got them where they are. Yet as time goes on and advancement adds challenges, change in behaviors and thought patterns must occur. Top persons in an organization are inundated with all kinds of reports but almost no suggestions by anyone that a change in their behavior would make a difference. Persons in powerful positions seldom listen to bad news about their own behaviors. The "death to the messenger" axiom has many adherents. Reliable methods to obtain useful feedback on one's own behavior are essential; only a few organizations adopt them.

No one person can achieve an organization's goals: that requires the efforts of all. Too many persons expect powerful people to exercise power, to make all the decisions, to ride over those who disagree, and to really get things done. This distorted view of leadership as achieving great things by taking charge and wielding power strongly pervades all cultures. However, marshaling the talents and energies of others in order to achieve worthwhile goals is the key role of a leader. Many persons who think they are leaders have never learned this.

New practices are adopted reluctantly. An egregious example was the failure of the British Navy to adopt the practice of feeding limes to sailors until 500 years after it was known that limes prevented scurvy. Illustrations of failure to make appropriate changes in a timely fashion occur every day. Sometimes they capture the attention of the media. More often, those who see the problem are unwilling to act—save to obscure the issue—so that the inevitable disaster appears to have struck suddenly. The comments of one thoughtful observer, Mark Stahlman,[2] on the distress of IBM in 1993 illustrate this point:

Creative Destruction at IBM

The news is filled with laments over IBM's latest round of trouble: another massive write-off, 25,000 more in staff cuts, more plants to be closed, an unprecedented reduction in R&D spending and a threatened cut in its hitherto sacrosanct dividend. One wonders why these events seem so surprising, and even so terrifying, to so many people who don't own the stock and don't collect the Big Blue stipend. Do they assume that, with IBM in trouble, there's no sure thing, no place to hide?

IBM has been unfairly burdened—with excessive praise from decades of excellence seekers and with the overheated scorn of today's scavenger-critics. What has happened to IBM, however, is natural and predictable; indeed, it will happen to scores of other companies. It is nothing less than the marketplace at work.

Extraordinary Management Failure

Forecasting IBM's doom has become a thriving business over the past few years. But the extraordinary management failure that led to the company's well-publicized troubles has never been adequately explained. Put simply, IBM has failed because the company's senior managers have misunderstood the competitive dynamics of the computer marketplace. . . .[3]

Implementing Changes in Behaviors

The problem of finding ways to apply new knowledge bears directly on issues of leadership. As we learn more about circumstances in which leader behaviors result in more effective actions—in a climate where challenges are met more enthusiastically—we discover more about the nature of leadership that made it happen. We also learn that one of the important qualities of leadership is the ability of the leader to encourage organizations to change so that the effectiveness of the group will improve.

How to Start: Endorsement and Support from the Top

Programs that are supported by the top person in an organization are accepted more readily. Support is more than an initial endorsement of an idea. New initiatives create anxiety; the leader must show continuing support for each component and seek ways to exhibit enthusiasm and excitement. When obstacles arise, the leader must be available to help remove them. When problems arise, the leader needs to show that goals and objectives are still the same and just as important as ever.

Start With Yourself

"Model the way" is one of the suggestions made earlier. This is one of the best procedures for producing change and increasing performance. In the technical literature, it is called "behavior modeling" and is one of the key features of many training programs. Fundamental to the effectiveness of behavior modeling are learning points for the trainee that are stated in concrete behavioral terms such as: make the praise specific; give the praise immediately after the behavior occurs; focus on the issue, rather than the employee; and focus on the future, rather than the past. A well-conducted study strongly supports the use of behavior modeling training programs in industry for bringing about a relatively permanent change in supervisory behavior.[4]

Build an Effective Team

A group need not be large in order to teach its members about leadership. A small group allows the practice of the skills of leadership that have been discussed in this book and does not require success all at once. Team building requires the development of a special set of relationships within the group, an excitement about the task(s) to be performed, and an expectation of great success. Watching for the change in dynamics of the group can be fascinating and instructive. Asserting leadership by empowering all members of the group has been demonstrated to produce markedly improved performance. The factors that produce such advances are much easier to discern when the group is working face to face.

Set Goals

Goal setting for the group and for yourself is a superior way to focus a group's attention on objectives and to achieve outstanding performance. Goals need to be specific, attainable, and yet challenging. They have the greatest effects on behaviors of members of the group when they are fully accepted as possible and fair. Having members participate in setting goals is a useful way to assure acceptance. The leader needs to instill confidence in the attainment of the goals and to help the group members feel the goals are important to them.

Collect Data to Measure Change

Sometimes the method for translating knowledge into better practice is to develop a measuring device. Although it is known that people differ in mental abilities and that various tasks require different levels of mental ability, it is possible to improve the selection of students and employees only when tests become available. When Alfred Binet introduced the first measure of intelligence, schools and colleges used the scores to adapt education to the individual differences of learners.

An organization committed to improving the quality of its leaders discovers that competing for a leadership position leads candidates to behave according to the expectations of the examiners. If certain types of behaviors are desired, they will be exhibited. Therefore, those who screen candidates must find behavioral data collected under more normal circumstances. Information collected regularly from all persons in the organization, or that part of the organization in which leadership is expected, might include descriptions provided by superiors, peers, and subordinates, using a questionnaire that asks factual questions about everyday behavior. Respondents mark each behavior description in terms of frequency—Always, Usually, Occasionally, Rarely, or Never. An appropriate consultant can help score and interpret results. Will employees in organizations be willing to do this? In two large corporations, over 85% of persons polled said they were willing to have their behavior described and to describe the behaviors of others using a method of this sort.[5]

Use the Organization's Structure

A hierarchical organization is just that. Many persons hold positions superior to others, and many report to a superior. Rarely is this structure used to its full power in changing the nature of relationships between subordinates and superiors. Yet it is precisely the right structure within which to implant a system that emphasizes leadership behaviors and uses the methods of behavior modeling. Progress in attaining goals can be assessed using measures of leadership behavior. Each person with managerial responsibilities can be assigned to develop the leadership behaviors of subordinates. The person responsible for monitoring the quality of a developmental program can be the manager's immediate superior. Short courses on leadership development—either on- or off-site—help sustain the effort.

The structure may not be helpful every time. Promotions are often made without regard to the views of subordinates[6] and place more emphasis on past performance than on the challenges of the next assignment. When organizations have well established mentoring programs, they may work against the interests of all except white males.

Collect Data

Use knowledge about leadership by continuously collecting data on potential leaders. Picking a person who will be a leader requires basic knowledge of leaders. We know some important things, including:

1. Subordinates know the most about leadership qualities. Superiors know less. Candidates are the poorest judges of their own leadership qualities.
2. The larger the pool of good candidates, the greater the chances for an excellent choice.
3. Organizations that provide varied assignments and experiences for their most promising candidates for advancement will increase the knowledge

about these candidates and the quality of the pool from which later selections will be made.

4. Candidates who have shown a marked ability to learn and change as a result of experience should be given special attention.

Progress through Training

Training programs are widely used to improve the quality of management and leadership. It is thought by many that one training program is as good as any other; thus persons can select the one they want to attend. However, most organizations fail to precede the training with sufficient discussions of goals and do not assist the learner to transfer newly gained knowledge to the organizational setting.

Training programs that are most successful systematically identify specific processes or strategies and provide training in their application to a variety of task domains. They are more effective when the applications of strategies and processes are explained and modeled. A mere description of a strategy is not enough; it must be demonstrated and practiced. Systematic feedback must be provided during practice to assure that learning is progressing as it should. A training program that aims to develop abilities of the participant must encourage active practice and help the participant analyze the underlying purposes of processes and strategies being taught. Success of these efforts decreases as efforts become less focused. Do not try to do too much.

Training programs conducted off-site are widely used. They are most effective when the sponsoring organization provides the participant with the rationale for the training experience, both in terms of the organization's purposes and the interests of the participant. A somewhat different session is helpful after return of the participant from training. The most useful debriefing session focuses on the ways in which the training may be brought to bear on the organization's problems and the effect of application of this new knowledge on the career development of the participant. Some organizations send managers away for training when major changes are contemplated. They report that the off-site experience makes the returning manager more open to new ideas.

Punishment

Most discussions of leadership include nothing about punishment. We are led to believe that leaders can persuade all members of their organizations and do it so well that there will be no incompetents, no disenchanted, and no over-ambitious, selfish, hostile, or aggressive nonbelievers. The question is not whether using punishment is good or bad; after all, it is used in virtually every organization. Punishment can be used effectively to further the purposes of any organization, so long as it is not used in ways that contradict the principles of leadership we have been describing. Procedures must be fair and well known so that they may be applied correctly and humanely.

Many people assert that punishment reduces the occurrence of unspecified acts without providing adequate clues about better behavior. Others see it as producing only temporary and undesirable effects. Yet everyone must learn that behavior has consequences; sometimes if the consequences are dire, an imposed punishment that fits the act can have beneficial effects in the long run.

Punishment can hurt the one administering it more than the one receiving it—an observation all parents will understand. Yet punishment is most effective in modifying behavior when the relationship is close and the reasons for discipline are clearly presented. The highly troublesome employee who always poses a problem in behavior is best dealt with on a continuous basis—every improper act receives its just reward. Effective punishment is enhanced if the employee is made aware of alternative acceptable responses.

Make the Organization Exciting

Exceptional performance produces a "high" within a group that leads to even greater achievement. Those people who have been part of such a group speak longingly about the experience, and their greatest desire is to have a repeat performance. The Apollo mission, leading to the successful landing of a man on the moon, is an example.

A fortunate few have been part of a great team—a group of people who functioned together in an extraordinary way—who trusted one another, who complemented one another's strengths and compensated for one another's limitations, who had common goals that were larger than individual goals, and who produced extraordinary results. Those who live through such experiences yearn for a repeat of the satisfaction they felt.

What they experienced is membership in a "learning organization." The team that becomes great does not start off great—it *learns* how to produce extraordinary results. Senge[7] argues that "Systems Thinking" is the key to producing such learning organizations. Systems Thinking fuses all other disciplines into a coherent body of theory and practice. Senge writes that leaders must view the world as one in which all parts interact with other parts; seeing interrelationships is more important than hunting for cause-and-effect chains, and seeing processes of change yields more insights than snapshots.

Teams outperform individuals acting alone or in larger organizational groups, according to Jon R. Katzenbach and Douglas K. Smith,[8] who studied more than fifty teams in thirty companies to discover how to enhance team effectiveness. They conclude that teams are in general unrecognized for their worth and are underutilized in most organizations. Commitment to performance goals and common purpose is more important to team success than team building, they conclude.

Building a shared vision is not an idea or even an important idea. It is, rather, a force in people's hearts, a force of impressive power. It may be inspired by an idea, but once the vision appears it is no longer an abstraction; people see it as if it exists. Few, if any, forces in human affairs are as powerful as a shared vision. Most concepts of vision as used in the corporate world today miss the point. Most of them are one person's vision imposed on an organization: such visions command compliance, not commitment. A shared vision is a vision to which many people are truly committed because it is their own—their own personal vision.

Leaders in the New Tomorrow

The coming century is forecast to be very different from the century almost completed. Futurists describe it as menacing and fraught with uncertainties. Yet every future puts fear into the hearts of some, while it puts hopes into the hearts of others. As we look forward, we may not see the precise perils, but we must prepare for mighty challenges. By examining the failures that have accompanied the great successes of the twentieth century, we can begin to comprehend the extent of the work and the hard choices that face us.

How Have We Failed?

We have learned that we can feed all the people on earth, but we have neither developed the will of wealthy nations to do so nor the will of the rulers of starving nations to make peace to save their own people.

We have learned how to put words and visions in front of every young child, but we have not learned to empower each one to realize fully his or her potential.

We have learned how to cure many diseases, reduce suffering, and prolong life, but we have neither learned how to influence persons to care for themselves to avoid illness nor have we been able to assist most people to have satisfying and tension-free lives.

We have studied the distant stars and have begun to understand how the universe began, but although we sometimes ask, we cannot answer what puts self-esteem and hope into the mind of a small child or the desire to live a drug-free and crime-free life into the mind of the criminal.

We have learned to produce an enormous variety of wonderful devices to help us travel widely, listen to beautiful music, speed through waterways, or give our words immediate and wide distribution, but our people are no better educated, no more civilized, no more understanding of others, and no wiser than many of our less affluent ancestors.

A society cannot solve difficult problems without organizing to do so. We have not succeeded in our quest to develop extraordinary teams that might find ways to achieve the wonderful world we want. We have not yet learned enough about how to persuade those who might lead such teams to ensure that their effort will bring the dream to reality.

Our failures are failures of will. We fail in so many important ways because we do not set our priorities for action in congruence with our vision. We have not prepared leaders who can articulate a vision that leads to reconciliation of the differences that produce failure or inaction.

Are there leaders who can set our sights on worthy goals to make our lives worthwhile? If they emerge, they will be the ones who choose to lead, who dedicate themselves to leading others so that the failures of yesterday can become the successes of tomorrow. They are the ones who will be the great leaders of the twenty-first century. They do exist: They are *YOU*, gentle—nay, courageous—reader. You can become one of this select group, to make the choice to commit, to prepare, to serve, to lead.

CHAPTER FIFTEEN

Principles of Leadership

As we consider the problems that we face, a major worry is about what kind of a leader we need, where to look and how to identify people who can deliver, and how to persuade the best of them to choose to lead. When personal or group hand-wringing is at its most stressful point, we ask whether the cause is worth the struggle, whether resources are sufficient, whether we have the courage to meet and sustain the challenge, and whether the spirit to succeed is strong enough. It is then we want a leader who will inspire and reassure us.

Even when we believe strongly that what we are trying to accomplish is worth doing, it becomes almost impossible in times of crises to maintain a cool and detached view long enough to think rationally about the problem. When leaderless, members of the group repeat, "If only we had foreseen these problems," "If only we could get agreement on these points," "If only we had a plan." We ask for a leader who will clarify the issues, articulate a vision, and help our group close ranks. We also wish we knew more about leaders and leadership and how each person could play an appropriate role in an effective group. To be ready for crucial decision making about leadership whenever the need arises, it is necessary to know about leadership and about leader-follower relationships and how leaders develop and change with education, training, and experience.

In our society, no elite group is being prepared for leadership; there are no sanctions against any person aspiring to a leadership role. This provides an ever-increasing pool of candidates who could be developed for leadership roles but creates the problem of finding the right person willing to accept the responsibility. It is no help to say, "We will know the leader when we see him or her." How will we know? The experience of so many groups that have picked the wrong person on first impression should warn us. We need better ways to test potential leaders. To provide a basis for judgment we cannot simulate a special experience called "Being a Leader" for every person we would like to designate. How do we tell which candidate will develop into someone special as a leader? What's more, we need to specify. Are we looking for a national leader, a community leader, a leader in fund-raising, or a leader in some specialty like art or physics?

Identifying the leaders of the next generation is not easy. Our selections of those who will be admitted to the formal procedures for early training in leadership will overlook some of the great personages of the next generation. We do not know enough about developmental processes either in leadership or in special talents. Some of it may be undiscoverable in its early stages. Does the life and experience of a great artist or a creative scientist teach us anything about the lives of leaders? Surely not all leaders show similar progression in styles and maturation. Is there any way to find those who will continue to improve? When does an early failure motivate rather than discourage? Can we formulate our principles only by studying persons retrospectively? To understand the phenomena of human personality as it plays out in leadership and followership is challenging and complex.

Leadership is a persistent theme in historical records. Stories of leaders usually carry a maxim worth learning but rarely provide guidance for leaders whose problems are not simply right versus wrong but instead require accommodation to conflicting interests. As people have devised methods to study how groups and complex institutions organize to accomplish their objectives, they have broadened the scope; they have turned increasingly to the leader-follower relationship.

Findings disclosed in research studies have been reported only piecemeal, but they reveal a consistent pattern: When something needs to be done by a group in a sustained effort, there is a formal or informal division of responsibilities with one person, or occasionally several, becoming the leader. Why does this happen? Do all persons feel the need for a leader? What factors determine the qualities of the person who becomes the leader? What qualities—including knowledge, skills, and abilities—must leaders possess to perform effectively? What group outcomes, if any, are due to the leader? How is effectiveness in leadership evidenced?

The questions are straightforward. But useful answers require careful analysis of the context in which leadership is exercised, the nature of the followers or members, and the goals the organization seeks to attain. Answers must be phrased to guide those who plan the programs for leadership development, those who are preparing to assume a leadership position, and those who must identify and select them. Finding answers that illuminate better practice is more complex than just asking successful leaders to report how they did it, for usually leaders do not know why some things worked and others did not. How, for example, leaders engender trust in their followers is puzzling.

The following list of summary statements reflects the content of this book. Each item has been discussed in greater detail in earlier chapters, and supporting evidence has been provided. In this list, each statement is short and unqualified, for easy reading and recall.

Our 127 Statements

1. *Who the leader is, what the leader says or does, and the nature of leader-follower relations have a substantial effect on group or organizational outcomes whether measured in terms of loyalty, productivity, profitability, member/supporter satisfaction, or continued support of the organization.*

2. *The essence of the leader's role is persuasion: to inspire followers to join in an effort to accomplish valued goals and persuade them that the goals are important.* The leader who can only impose penalties or use rewards to assure acquiescence quickly loses leadership status, but the leader who can reconcile differences through effective use of group processes deserves the title.

3. *Being in charge of a group is not the same as being a leader.* Many persons think they have followers when they merely have subordinates, members, or constituents.

4. *An increase in the productive energy of a group is the natural effect of successful leadership.* Followers of ideal leaders put out extra effort for their leader and also feel freer to suggest better ways, to be innovative, and to perform extra tasks.

5. *"Considerate" leadership behavior affects follower or subordinate satisfaction.* Leaders must show concern for the welfare of their followers. Followers need to know that their leader respects them and their work, that good work will be recognized, and that good ideas will be accepted. The leader needs to help them develop self-esteem and understand the importance of their activities.

6. *Leader behavior aimed at structuring tasks to be performed improves*

worker effectiveness. Followers look to their leader to organize the group, define relationships, specify the task, define limits of responsibility, and clarify roles. The importance of these behaviors varies with the culture and context in which leadership is exercised and the nature of the organizational goals to be achieved.

7. *Leadership cannot exist without followers.* Leaders need followers who are ready to listen and be inspired; followers need leaders who will recognize, respect, and use their talents and energies. Followers can, by their actions, make leaders better or worse.

8. *Leadership is everybody's business.* All of society benefits from excellent leadership, and all of society suffers from flawed leadership at every level and in every organization and group.

9. *Leaders emerge from all walks of life.* The notion that leaders come from an elite segment of the population derives, falsely, from the evidence that positions of power are held disproportionately by persons who grow up in advantaged neighborhoods and attend prestigious schools. Many leaders perform noble acts without tangible credentials to aid them in their efforts.

10. *Leadership emerges at every level of every group or organization.* The general view that leaders exist only at the top of an organization is far from reality. Often leadership is exercised more effectively by those without impressive positions or titles.

11. *People differ in their natural abilities to lead.* Ability to think clearly, speak well, inspire others, accumulate and recall large fonts of information, and analyze complex problems effectively are qualities given in unequal measure to all humans. It is important to identify and develop those individuals with natural talents for leadership.

12. *Managers are not the same as leaders.* Managers have a responsibility to see that tasks are done. Often they spend more time attending to the wishes of their superiors than the needs of their subordinates. Managers exercise position authority. Leaders build teams that share the leader's vision.

13. *Qualities desired in managers and leaders have some elements in common.* Both can control large amounts of information, spend quality time with followers or subordinates, engage in activities that are not well defined, decide on the best use of their time, and develop priorities. Almost all managers report instances in which they were exercising leadership. Most leaders acknowledge they spend a good deal of time managing.

14. *Getting any job done requires the group to know both why and how they should do it.* If the why is missing, the group becomes drones. If the how is missing, the group becomes frustrated and hostile.

15. *Different leaders use different methods to achieve their effects.* Persons differ greatly in their styles, their ways of doing things, their strengths and weaknesses, their interests and preferences for activities, their values and priorities, and their goals in life. There is as much diversity among leaders and followers as among any other population segment.

16. *Effective leadership shows in the bottom line.* Well-led teams win more contests, earn more profits, and have less turnover. Schools that have principals who behave like leaders have better graduation rates, higher student achievement, and fewer dropouts. Within corporations, divisions with effective leaders have been shown to outperform units with poor leadership by 20% or more.

17. *Stereotypes about being in charge interfere with communication between persons of different status.* A suggestion from a superior to change behavior produces a sizable emotional response that impedes communication.

18. *An organization would be unwise to select its leaders solely in terms of observed personality traits.* An aggressive and forceful style need not interfere with a leader's ability to achieve remarkable outcomes.

19. *Some persons have less leadership to offer than meets the eye.* A pleasing demeanor does not guarantee effective leadership.

20. *Experience and ability can be dangerous when integrity is lacking.*

21. *Ambition and leadership are uneasy companions.* The leader who needs recognition for accomplishments runs into conflicts, for it is better for the group to say, "We did it ourselves." On the other hand, the leader without a drive to accomplish and advance is unlikely to succeed.

22. *Leaders must have followers, but they do not require formal organizations.* Some of the best examples of leadership are displayed by those who have generated movements to support causes, such as Mahatma Gandhi, Martin Luther King, Jr., Susan B. Anthony, and Clara Barton.

23. *The leader must play a key role in emphasizing the goals of the group.* Behavior of the leader stimulates enthusiasm for meeting the group's goals or achieving excellent performance.

24. *Qualities desired in leaders become more complex as the responsibilities and scope of operations of the leader expand.*

25. *Asking leaders what they do, asking peers what leaders do, asking subordinates what their leaders do, and asking superiors what the leaders do provide four different sets of answers.*

26. *Subordinate descriptions are most useful in identifying leadership qualities.* However, they do not identify all qualities that are critical.

27. *Best leadership experiences, when self-reported, suggest that leaders do five important things: 1) Challenge the Process, 2) Inspire a Shared Vision, 3) Enable Others to Act, 4) Model the Way, and 5) Encourage the Heart.*

28. *Interviews of top leaders suggest four strategies may be used: 1) Attention through vision, 2) Meaning through communication, 3) Trust through positioning, and 4) Deployment of self through positive self-regard.*

29. *Retired CEOs report that leadership starts with vision, but the skill of a great leader is to give it the appearance of rationality, which provides people a chance to argue, refine the decision, gain commitment, and get it implemented.*

30. *Active corporate CEOs indicate that they create an agenda for change that includes strategies for achieving their vision and building an implementation network strong enough to elicit cooperation, compliance, and teamwork.*

31. *Observing individuals in leadership positions reveals that some lead, while some abdicate their responsibility.* Incredible variations exist.

32. *When adequate leadership is absent for some reason, groups find substitutes.* Groups find ways to overcome or find substitutes for poor leadership, such as resorting to standard operating procedures or accepting and dividing responsibilities to accomplish important objectives.

Leadership and the U.S. Presidency

33. *Presidential leadership in the U.S. is in a class by itself.* The American governmental system with its checks and balances to restrain power fosters conflict requiring endless negotiation for carrying on the business of government. The needs of people are often not served as readily or efficiently as demanded because of the nature of the democratic system.

34. *U.S. presidential leadership depends on the president's ability to persuade*

and to use a gained reputation for action based on prior wise decisions and on the capacity to communicate with clarity.

35. *Human qualities required of a U.S. president are a sense of purpose, a feel for power, and a source of confidence.*

36. *The public most strongly want the following qualities—in descending order of importance—in a U.S. president: 1) Honesty, 2) Compassion, 3) Intelligence, 4) Toughness/Decisiveness, and 5) Decision-Making Ability.*

37. *The charisma of a U.S. president enhances power.* Presidential charisma, defined by behavior, attributions by others, and descriptions by others, correlates highly with cabinet members' level of positive feelings about their role in the administration, frequency of compliance of cabinet members to presidential wishes and orders, and agreement with presidential policies.

38. *The U.S. president's charismatic behavior is strongly and positively related to recorded presidential actions, subjective judgments about presidential performance, presidential economic performance, and presidential social performance.*

39. *The personalities of U.S. presidents are describable in five dimensions, with some presidents portraying more than one dominant dimension.* The dimensions are: 1) Interpersonal, 2) Charismatic, 3) Deliberative, 4) Creative, and 5) Neurotic.

Charismatic and Transformational Leaders

40. *Charismatic leaders set examples by their own behavior and engage in acts to increase their followers' motivation.* Extraordinary performance is obtained when leaders express high self-confidence and strong convictions, spell out an appealing vision, define ideological goals to build follower commitment, set high expectations for performance, and show confidence in the ability of followers to achieve them.

41. *Transformational leaders create greater involvement in work and assure more self-fulfillment for participants by increasing the intellectual and emotional involvement of followers.* A vision is articulated, the reasons for decisions are explained, and goals are set and conveyed to the group so that they are accepted. The leaders, meanwhile, work to engender trust and respect.

42. *School principals who are described as transformational leaders influence the school culture and produce better student performance.*

43. *Better school performance occurs when principals develop a vision, select staff carefully, resolve conflicts and problems in ways that shape values, communicate values and beliefs in daily routines and behaviors, identify and articulate stories that reveal shared values, and nurture the traditions, ceremonies, rituals, and symbols that communicate and reinforce the school culture the leader is constructing.*

44. *Flawed leadership abounds. "Boss stress" is widespread.* Although much of this stress is because of managerial incompetence, a large and unhealthy portion is due to the personality defects of superiors described by some as charismatic leaders.

45. *Transformational and charismatic leaders are seldom found among college and university presidents.* Few presidents attempt to engage faculty, students, and alumni in discussions about the long-range objectives appropriate for their institution.

46. *The charm of charismatic leaders oft obscures fatal flaws that make them poor leaders or ineffective decision makers.*

The Values of Leaders and Organizations

47. *Leaders, by their every statement about the standards of the organization, influence the day-to-day decisions made by all employees.* Explicit company policies affect decisions throughout an organization. Omissions of ethical standards are interpreted to mean that anything furthering the company's interest, regardless of consequences, will be tolerated.

48. *The influence of the leader on a group is not merely in terms of the accomplishment of organizational objectives but extends to standards of conduct as well.* If the group does not hold to high standards, it may produce great damage within the larger community. Leaders must not ignore the responsibility for maintaining high standards.

49. *A clearly defined and well-articulated set of values is essential for every organization.* These values reflect those of the leader and also those of the organization. Stating them is insufficient; they must be built into the fabric of decision making and be adhered to in all components of organizational activities.

50. *Because most problems are messy, leaders must develop guidelines for action that assure integrity, consistency, strength of purpose, and efficacy.*

51. *Ethical leaders of business firms are compromised when business schools teach that "Business corporations are formed solely to make profits for the stockholders: All decisions should be made so as to maximize profits. We will teach you the formulas so that you can make decisions about alternative investments in terms of this ultimate goal."* When organizational morality is thus defined, the only improper behavior is also easily defined: it is any behavior that is not oriented to stockholder benefit.

52. *Ethical leaders must campaign against the philosophical positions that an organization has no "morality" and that decisions made for organizational purposes cannot be considered to have morality.* Leaders have the capability to alter the moral climate and moral destiny of the organization and must choose whether "to become the organization's faceless creature instead of its creator."

53. *Leaders must learn the use of language applied to values and must differentiate among moral values, ethical values, pragmatic values, absolute values, and universal values.*

54. *Different sets of values held by subgroups can either enrich and enhance the larger group or produce differences and dissension.* The effective leader takes advantage of varied talents, but the understanding and support of all followers is required.

Predicting Executive Success

55. *Executive success can be predicted early.* Test batteries predict effectively those among newly employed managers of a company who will end up in the top ranks of an organization.

56. *Components of executive success can be identified.* Predictable components of success include effective leadership, assured independence, intellectual and administrative functioning, effectiveness as a representative of the organization, and competitive drive to improve business.

57. *Assessment of individual qualities in midcareer aid in discriminating between those who will persist in seeking higher positions and those who will not.*

58. *Measurements of the quality of leadership performance of school principals are accurate enough to differentiate principals of high-performing schools and principals of low-performing schools.*

59. *Key leadership behaviors of principals that relate to high-performance schools are problem solving, clarifying, monitoring, motivating, and networking/interfacing.*

60. *Quality of leadership in government agencies can be measured effectively and makes a difference in work output.* Performance increased by 8% for at least a year after a series of training sessions with managers.

61. *Leaders or potential leaders may not know whether they are effective leaders, but those who do know are their subordinates or members of their team.*

62. *Ratings of their superiors by subordinates have been collected without dissension in the workplace. The ratings are useable and relate to important outcome variables.* Subordinates were willing to make the ratings; superiors who were rated high as leaders were managing the most profitable units.

63. *Leadership behaviors described as person-oriented and task-oriented have been shown to be closely related to performance and worker satisfaction in many countries around the world.* The relationship is closer in Japan than in the United States.

64. *Leadership behaviors of young naval officers are related to performance and subordinate satisfaction.* Correlations between scores on transformational leadership and performance varied from modest to very high among the groups studied.

65. *Appointing a new CEO for a major corporation makes a difference.* When major corporations change their CEOs, consistent improvement in the value of the corporation is observed.

Methods of Leadership Training

66. *Investing in selection and training programs for leaders pays off consistently in organizational productivity, reduced absenteeism, higher worker satisfaction, and fewer grievances.*

67. *More than 60% of the nation's largest companies offer leadership training programs.*

68. *Many colleges and universities offer leadership education courses and leadership development courses. The U.S. military academies have intensive leadership training components.*

69. *Programs that encourage goal setting, participation in decision making, and objective feedback to managers consistently lead to improved productivity, increased performance, reduced costs, and average attendance.*

70. *Goal-setting programs are most effective when the leader involves subordinates in setting goals or assigns goals while persuading subordinates of the importance of achieving them.*

71. *Group-level feedback, group goal setting, and incentives increase productivity.*

72. *Persons can learn to be charismatic leaders by projecting a powerful, confident, and dynamic presence as well as a captivating, engaging voice tone, direct eye contact, and animated facial expressions.* Perhaps charisma is not a gift given to a select few but a set of behaviors that can be adopted by many.

73. *Behavior modeling is a key component of successful training methods.* Modeling helps the trainee to see that he or she has the competence to perform the task.

74. *Leadership training programs that use behavior modeling are extremely effective.* Statements must be made in concrete behavioral terms, such as: make

the praise specific; give the praise immediately after the behavior occurs; focus on the issue, rather than the employee; focus on the future, rather than the past.

75. *Teaching methods for leadership development used in college and university courses include innovative features.* Among the most widely used are: journal keeping; oral and written exposition; instruments for self- and other-ratings; observation and critical analysis of meetings and organizational processes; and interviewing persons in leadership positions.

76. *Mentoring programs need review to assure they do not sustain earlier discriminatory practices.* Mentoring has often been a way of preserving a male-dominated upper-level leadership group. Replacing such mentoring programs with informal coaching and tutoring programs can help eliminate exclusive, one-on-one relationships and prevent repeating the unstated "rules" or norms in the organization that favor select insiders.

77. *Leadership training programs that include follow-up training and evaluation and do not rely on single-event training exposure increase the applicability of seminar training to the work setting.*

78. *Leadership training can start early.* Leadership programs and courses now offered on many college and university campuses and in some high school curricula are highly effective.

Experience Counts—Sometimes

79. *Leaders must know how to learn from experience.*

80. *Leaders often experience pain and frustration.* Sustaining motivation and commitment to the institution is often difficult.

81. *Prospective leaders need challenging assignments that teach them important lessons.* Progressive job assignments for career development and learning provide useful learning experiences that seem to teach important lessons.

82. *Experience teaches different things to different people.* Few patterns of learning are the same.

83. *Much of the learning reported by successful executives concerns insights not acquired during earlier education and experience, the absence of which caused problems of every kind.* Much of this was interpersonal: being viewed as self-confident when they were most uncertain, appearing uncaring when their hearts were bleeding, or being perceived as not paying attention during times when they wanted to act but their hands were tied.

84. *Leaders must be able to adapt effectively to changing circumstances.* Candidates for leadership positions include only a minority who can adapt to changed circumstances.

85. *As leaders gain greater responsibility they must be able to expand their geographic horizons and extend their vision into the future.*

86. *Knowledge of the effects of one's actions is required for learning.* Experience per se does *not* teach, but feedback from a given action does provide cues about whether or not to change behavior.

87. *People in powerful positions are shielded from negative information and especially from personal criticism.* Because "kill the messenger" is often a standard response, leaders must take extraordinary measures to assure that they will receive reliable information concerning their own actions and the actions of others.

88. *Subordinates are overwhelmingly willing to provide information about how their superiors are performing and how they are viewed.* Superiors are

usually willing to receive information from their subordinates about their own performance.

89. *Female superiors received higher ratings than male superiors in one large corporation that collected subordinate ratings of superiors.* That finding undercuts one excuse for the presence of so few women in the executive suite.

90. *Worker productivity responds to incentives and disincentives other than money and job security; pay is less a factor in productivity than most persons believe.*

91. *Increasing job satisfaction does not automatically produce improved job performance.*

92. *Persons work better when they have clearly defined goals and when they have good measures of their progress toward these goals.* Goals have more effect when they are specific, when they are difficult but attainable, and when they are attractive.

93. *A leader can stimulate good performance by: 1) structuring work, 2) providing the support for getting it done, 3) attending to the problems of the people who perform the tasks, 4) commending their good work, 5) helping them improve, 6) attending to them as individuals, and 7) settling disputes within the group.*

94. *Leaders can make the work important so that intrinsic interest in tasks develops.*

95. *The role of leaders is critical in increasing commitment among followers and thereby enhancing group performance.* The broad categories used to summarize what leaders do include such words and phrases as "motivated work force," "worker satisfaction," "consideration," "intellectual stimulation," "inspiration," "vision," "commitment," and "extra energy."

96. *If properly conducted and properly interpreted, surveys of worker opinions can provide the leader with good measures of worker satisfaction.*

97. *Many managers and executives find their jobs much less satisfying today.* Increased decentralization, government regulation, and decreased perquisites have increased executive work loads and dimmed their spirits.

Power and Influence

98. *Leadership and the exercise of power go hand in hand.* Working with others to accomplish objectives is essential; it is the appropriate use of power that makes accomplishment possible. Leaders who seek power for self-aggrandizement are doomed to fail eventually; those who use it to achieve desirable objectives are the models to emulate.

99. *Followers expect leaders to exercise power in order to achieve agreed-upon goals.* Leaders are often criticized for failure to use power in legitimate ways. They are also criticized by followers when they use power for self-aggrandizement or for personal perquisites.

100. *The belief that a person has great power influences behavior whether or not that power exists.* Power not exercised is sometimes indistinguishable from the absence of power.

101. *The ideal leader uses power to achieve goals and solve problems, to gather information and make decisions.* Thus described, power can be viewed as a positive, even an essential, force.

102. *In a participative democracy, the potential for exercising power resides in everyone.* People use information to make decisions to further society's goals or abuse information to achieve personal glory.

103. *Leaders at all levels must use power appropriately.* They must attend not only to how they use it but also to how it is distributed, used, and abused among group members.

104. *Leaders must—of necessity—exercise influence and authority.* When resources are limited, someone—preferably the leader—must assure a fair distribution.

105. *Follower loyalty is not guaranteed; it lasts only as long as followers see the leader playing the role properly.* Followers are close observers of every aspect of leader behavior.

106. *A well-structured organization allocates power and authority in ways that encourage accountability.* Without accountability, an organization cannot accomplish goals in keeping with established priorities.

107. *Power is the ability, whether exercised or not, to allocate resources, to assign tasks, and to provide, withhold, or withdraw tangible rewards, including assignment and withdrawal of responsibilities.*

108. *An integral part of the power exercised by the ideal leader includes the award of praise or recognition.* This can produce a strong effect on a follower when the leader is greatly admired.

109. *Leader expertise is required in order to gain the requisite power and authority to promote innovative proposals, gain control over information, control decisions, solve problems, and work with others to do so.* Credibility is attained only if one is perceived as being responsible and loyal to the group.

110. *Successful leaders avoid exercising power in an arrogant, manipulative, or domineering manner, but instead develop influencing tactics to fit the situation.*

111. *Women seeking advancement reportedly prefer to describe power as energy, not control.* A leader does not have to exercise power over others but instead can mobilize power and engage in leadership activities that empower others. These leaders use their position to influence and develop networks that can become powerful agents of change.

112. *Leaders can be too ambitious.*

113. *The exercise of political leadership is less oriented toward well-specified goals and missions than is the exercise of leadership in, for example, business or the military.* Those who succeed in the political arena are people with a high tolerance for conflict, ambiguity, and uncertainty.

Culture, Climate, and Diversity

114. *Corporate climates and images influence the effectiveness and productivity of organizations.*

115. *To benefit from a diversity of cultures, an organization needs to establish common ground and true integration.* When this happens, diversity is no longer discussed in the abstract, challenged, misinterpreted, or viewed as a threat but, instead, is expressed in tangible benefits for employees and their employers. Any such program needs overt and enthusiastic support from the leadership of the organization.

116. *Culture affects the exercise of leadership because it produces distinctive patterns of thinking, feeling, and reacting that vary from group to group.* The leader must take into account the expectations of followers and the culture that produces the expectations.

117. *Work-related values vary substantially depending on national origins of the workers.* Major dimensions on which differences are observed are: individu-

alism versus collectivism, power distance, uncertainty avoidance, and masculinity-femininity. The heterogeneity of corporate cultures and the impact of national and cultural backgrounds on leader and worker expectancies complicate the tasks of multinational organizations.

118. *American workers rank highest in the world on individualism, prefer close personal relations with their superior, are greater risk-takers than their contemporaries in other countries, and get high ratings on masculinity—a measure of ambition, striving, and desire for advancement and success.*

119. *Leadership must be viewed as the management of organizational events and actions within the context of rules and procedures of the organization and the cultural traditions of its members.*

120. *Specific behaviors considered appropriate in one culture may be reprehensible in another.*

121. *Japanese adults respond just as well when another person gets reinforced as when they, themselves, get reinforced.* That is not the case among Americans nor among adolescent Japanese under the age of fifteen.

122. *In most traditional societies the individual is a bundle of roles. One cannot interact "properly" with another without knowing the role relationship.*

123. *An international assignee requires preassignment training.* To function effectively in a new culture, individuals must exhibit behavior that reflects appropriate personal characteristics of both a cognitive and an affective nature.

124. *Many international assignees fail.* Their failures to function effectively in foreign environments result from: the inability of the manager or the manager's spouse to adjust to a different physical and cultural environment; the manager's personal or emotional immaturity; the manager's inability to cope with the larger responsibility posed by overseas work; the manager's lack of technical competence for the assignment; or the manager's lack of motivation to work overseas.

125. *Raising the level of intercultural sensitivity means that the individual becomes more tolerant of other value systems, more accepting of unfamiliar behavior, and more empathic to other beliefs and social norms.*

126. *The increasing diversity of the American work force in the next couple of decades will require changed organizational policies and procedures.*

127. *Leaders help the group unlearn assumptions and learn new assumptions.*

Leaders are responsible for building organizations that help people continually expand their capabilities to understand complexity, clarify vision, and improve shared mental models. In essence, the leader's task is to design the learning processes that enable all people in the organization to deal productively with the critical issues they face.

Leaders heretofore have been selected for high positions because of their decision-making and problem-solving skills, not for their skills in mentoring, coaching, and helping others learn. Effective leaders of the future must inspire dedicated and productive followers; the need for improved leader-follower relationships is immediate and imperative. Faith in the vision and adherence to the goals require the ability to persuade and to explain. The future will be what we make of it. From among great numbers of ready followers, some must choose to lead.

Notes

CHAPTER ONE
Leaders Wanted!

1. William Celis III, "Nation's Top Three School Jobs Open," *Naples Daily News* 21 Feb. 1993: H5.
2. Henry Mintzberg, *The Nature of Managerial Work* (New York: Harper & Row, 1973).
3. Similar findings from other studies include, for example, Morgan W. McCall, Ann M. Morrison, and R. L. Hannan, *Studies of Managerial Work: Results and Methods,* Technical Report No. 9 (Greensboro, NC: Center for Creative Leadership, 1978).
4. James M. Kouzes and Barry Z. Posner, *The Leadership Challenge: How to Get Extraordinary Things Done in Organizations* (San Francisco: Jossey-Bass, 1989).
5. Such a program is in place and has been described in detail in J. A. Conger, *Learning to Lead: The Art of Transforming Managers into Leaders* (San Francisco: Jossey-Bass, 1992).
6. Warren Bennis and B. Nanus, *Leaders: The Strategies for Taking Charge* (New York: Harper & Row, 1985).
7. James Bruce, *The Intuitive Pragmatists* (Greensboro, NC: Center for Creative Leadership, 1986).
8. See note 7, p. 39.
9. John P. Kotter, *The Leadership Factor* (New York: Free Press, 1988).
10. T. J. Peters and R. H. Waterman, *In Search of Excellence: Lessons from America's Best-Run Companies* (New York: Harper & Row, 1982).
11. Robert C. Ginnett, "Airline Cockpit Crews," in *Groups That Work (and Those That Don't)*, ed. Richard Hackman (San Francisco: Jossey-Bass, 1990) 427.
12. Steven Flax, "The Toughest Bosses in America," *Fortune* 6 Aug. 1984: 18.
13. James C. Hyatt and Amal Kumar Naj, "GE Is No Place For Autocrats, Welch Decrees," *Wall Street Journal* 3 Mar. 1992: B1.
14. James MacGregor Burns, *Leadership* (New York: Harper & Row, 1978).
15. James MacGregor Burns, "Leadership in American Politics," in *Proceedings of the Leadership Education Conference*, ed. M. A. Spillett (Richmond, VA: University of Richmond, 1992) 10.
16. Richard E. Neustadt, *Presidential Power and the Modern Presidents* (New York: Free Press, 1990).
17. Thomas E. Cronin, *Evaluating Presidents*, unpublished manuscript, December 1983.
18. See note 17, p. 34.
19. Dean Keith Simonton, "Presidential Style: Personality, Biography, and Performance," *Journal of Personality and Social Psychology* 55 (1988): 928.
20. James S. Hirsch, "To One Xerox Man, Selling Photocopiers is a Gamblers Game," *Wall Street Journal* 24 Sep. 1991: B1.

CHAPTER TWO
Definitions and Dimensions of Leadership

1. John W. Gardner, *On Leadership* (New York: Free Press, 1990) 1.
2. James MacGregor Burns, *Leadership* (New York: Harper & Row, 1978) 425.
3. Francis J. Yammarino and Bernard M. Bass, "Long-Term Forecasting of Transformational Leadership and Its Effects Among Naval Officers: Some Preliminary Findings," in *Measures of Leadership*, eds. K. E. Clark and M. B. Clark (West Orange, NJ: Leadership Library of America, 1990) 152.
4. Abraham Zalesnik, "Managers and Leaders: Are They Different?" *Harvard Business Review* 15 (1977): 67.
5. John P. Kotter, *The Leadership Factor* (New York: Free Press, 1988).

6. T. Richman, "Leadership Expert Ronald Heifetz," *Inc.*, 10 (1988): 37.
7. Gary Yukl, "Managerial Leadership: A Review of Theory and Research," *Journal of Management* 15 (1989): 253.
8. J. C. Rost, *Leadership for the Twenty-First Century* (New York: Praeger, 1991) 102.
9. Owen Jacobs and Elliott Jaques, "Military Executive Leadership," in *Measures of Leadership*, eds. K. E. Clark and M. B. Clark (West Orange, NJ: Leadership Library of America, 1990) 281.
10. Walter F. Ulmer, Jr., personal communication with authors, 11 Nov. 1991.
11. Conversation at the White House reported by Francis B. Carpenter from *Six Months at the White House with Abraham Lincoln* (1866) as reported in J. Bartlett, *Familiar Quotations* (Boston: Little Brown, 1955) 542.
12. John K. Hemphill and Alvin E. Coons, "Development of the Leader Behavior Description Questionnaire," in *Leader Behavior: Its Description and Measurement*, eds. Ralph M. Stogdill and Alvin E. Coons (Columbus, OH: Bureau of Business Research, 1957) 6.
13. Edwin A. Fleishman, "Twenty Years of Consideration and Structure," in *Current Developments in the Study of Leadership*, eds. Edwin A. Fleishman and James G. Hunt (Carbondale: Southern Illinois University Press, 1973) 2.
14. Edwin A. Fleishman, *Leadership Opinion Questionnaire and Examiner's Manual* (Revised) and *Supervisory Behavior Description Questionnaire and Examiner's Manual* (Revised) (Chicago: Science Research, 1989).
15. Jyuji Misumi, *The Behavioral Science of Leadership* (Ann Arbor: University of Michigan Press, 1985).
16. D. G. Bowers and S. E. Seashore, "Predicting Organizational Effectiveness with a Four-Factor Theory of Leadership," *Administrative Science Quarterly* 11 (1966): 238.
17. Gary Yukl, "Managerial Leadership: A Review of Theory and Research," *Journal of Management* 15 (1989): 253.
18. Gary Yukl, Steve Wall, and Richard Lepsinger, "Preliminary Report on Validation of the Managerial Practices Survey," in *Measures of Leadership*, eds. K. E. Clark and M. B. Clark (West Orange, NJ: Leadership Library of America, 1990) 225.
19. P. Hersey and K. Blanchard, *Management of Organizational Behavior: Utilizing Human Resources*, 5th ed. (Englewood Cliffs, NJ: Prentice-Hall, 1988).
20. Douglas MacGregor, *The Human Side of Enterprise* (New York: McGraw-Hill, 1960).
21. R. R. Blake and J. S. Mouton, *The Managerial Grid* (Houston: Gulf Publishing, 1964).

CHAPTER THREE
Charismatic and Transformational Leadership

1. Max Weber, *The Protestant Ethic and Spirit of Capitalism*, trans. A. M. Henderson and T. Parsons (New York: Free Press, 1947) 328.
2. See: Robert J. House, "A 1976 Theory of Charismatic Leadership," in *Leadership: The Cutting Edge*, eds. J. G. Hunt and L. L. Larson (Carbondale: Southern Illinois University Press, 1977) 189. See also: Boas Shamir, Robert J. House, and Michael B. Arthur, "The Transformational Effects of Charismatic Leadership: A Motivational Theory," *Organizational Science* (in press); Robert J. House, Jane M. Howell, Boas Shamir, Brian Smith, and William D. Spangler, "Charismatic Leadership: A 1990 Theory and Five Empirical Tests," working paper (The Reginald Jones Center for Strategic Management, The Wharton School of the University of Pennsylvania, 1990); Robert J. House, William D. Spangler, and James Woyke, "Personality and Charisma in the U.S. Presidency: A Psychological Theory of Leader Effectiveness," *Administrative Science Quarterly* 36 (1991): 364; J. A. Conger and R. N. Kanungo, eds., *Charismatic Leadership: The Elusive Factor in Organizational Effectiveness* (San Francisco: Jossey-Bass, 1988). Robert J. House is the Joseph Frank Bernstein Professor of Organization Studies at The Wharton School of the University of Pennsylvania.
3. R. J. House, W. D. Spangler, and J. Woycke, *Personality and Charisma in the U.S. Presidency: A Psychological Theory of Leader Effectiveness*, unpublished manuscript (Philadelphia: The Wharton School of the University of Pennsylvania, 1990).

4. Dean K. Simonton, "Presidential Style: Personality, Biography, and Performance," *Journal of Personality and Social Psychology* 55 (1988): 928.

5. See note 4.

6. R. J. House and W. D. Spangler, Letter to the Editor, *New York Times* 16 Feb. 1992: E14.

7. Robert Hogan, Robert Raskin, and Dan Fazzini, "The Dark Side of Charisma," in *Measures of Leadership*, eds. K. E. Clark and M. B. Clark (West Orange, NJ: Leadership Library of America, 1990) 343.

8. Manfred F. R. Kets de Vries, "Leaders Who Self-Destruct: The Causes and Cures," *Organizational Dynamics* (1989): 4. See also his book: *Prisoners of Leadership* (New York: Wiley, 1989).

9. James MacGregor Burns, *Leadership* (New York: Harper & Row, 1978).

10. Francis J. Yammarino and Bernard M. Bass, "Long-Term Forecasting of Transformational Leadership and Its Effects Among Naval Officers: Some Preliminary Findings," in *Measures of Leadership*, eds. K. E. Clark and M. B. Clark (West Orange, NJ: Leadership Library of America, 1990) 151.

11. Marshall Sashkin and Warner W. Burke, "Understanding and Assessing Organizational Leadership," in *Measures of Leadership*, eds. K. E. Clark and M. B. Clark (West Orange, NJ: Leadership Library of America, 1990) 297.

12. Terrence E. Deal and K. D. Peterson, *The Principal's Role in Shaping School Culture*, GPO No. 461-D-5 (Washington, DC: U. S. Government Printing Office, 1990).

13. Marshall Sashkin, William E. Rosenbach, Terrence E. Deal, and Kent D. Peterson, "Assessing Transformational Leadership and Its Impact," in *Impact of Leadership*, eds. K. E. Clark, M. B. Clark, and D. P. Campbell (Greensboro, NC: Center for Creative Leadership, 1992) 131.

14. Mansour Javidan, "Developing a Profile of Effective Leaders in Top Management," in *Impact of Leadership*, eds. K. E. Clark, M. B. Clark, and D. P. Campbell (Greensboro, NC: Center for Creative Leadership, 1992) 56.

15. See, for example: D. A. Nadler and M. L. Tushman, "Beyond the Charismatic Leader: Leadership and Organizational Change," *California Management Review*, Winter (1990): 77; R. J. House and Jane M. Howell, "Personality and Charismatic Leadership," *Leadership Quarterly* 3.2 (1992): 81.

16. Steven Lipin and Peter Pae, "Resignation Spurs American Express Shares," *Wall Street Journal* 8 Dec. 1992: A4.

17. G. Christian Hill and Ken Yamada, "Staying Power: Motorola Illustrates How an Aged Giant Can Remain Vibrant," *Wall Street Journal* 9 Dec. 1992: 1.

18. James W. Near, "Wendy's Successful 'Mop Bucket Attitude'," *Wall Street Journal* 22 Apr. 1992: A14.

CHAPTER FOUR
The Leader Sets the Tone

1. M. Loden and J. B. Rosener, *Workforce America! Managing Employee Diversity as a Vital Resource* (Homewood, IL: Business One Irwin, 1991).

2. Elliott Jaques, *Requisite Organization: The CEO's Guide to Creative Structure and Leadership* (USA: Cason Hall, 1989).

3. Max De Pree, *Leadership Is An Art* (New York: Doubleday, 1989) 12.

4. *Looking Glass, Inc.* is a hypothetical firm in the glass manufacturing business. The simulation used here was a 3–1/2 hour "day in the life of" the business. Issues were presented to participants through an in-basket, with documents relating to various aspects of the business. The students played the roles of twenty top managers and then discussed the process. The simulation was developed and is distributed by the Center for Creative Leadership in Greensboro, NC.

5. Karen Gaertner, "The Effects of Ethical Climate on Managers' Decisions," unpublished manuscript (Washington, DC: School of Business Administration, Georgetown University, 1990).

6. Jack N. Behrman, *Essays on Ethics in Business and the Professions* (Englewood Cliffs, NJ: Prentice Hall, 1988).

7. Rebecca Roloff, "Leadership and Ethics in the Real World," in *Leadership Education Conference, 1987*, ed. M. B. Clark (Greensboro, NC: Center for Creative Leadership, 1987) 39.

8. Albert Bandura, "Selective Activation and Disengagement of Moral Control," *Journal of Social Issues* 46 (1990): 27.

9. J. L. Badaracco and R. R. Ellsworth, *Leadership and the Quest for Integrity* (Boston: Harvard Business School Press, 1989).

10. Christopher Hodgkinson, *Towards a Philosophy of Administration* (New York: St. Martin's, 1978) 176.

11. Mark Patinkin, "Helping People to Live, Prosper Where They Are," *Naples Daily News* 19 Aug. 1992: D1.

CHAPTER FIVE
Statistics and Formulas in Leadership Selection

1. Paul E. Meehl, *Clinical Versus Statistical Prediction: A Theoretical Analysis and Review of the Evidence* (Minneapolis: University of Minnesota Press, 1954). A recent review of accumulated evidence is provided by: B. Kleinmuntz, "Why We Still Use Our Heads Instead of Formulas: Toward an Integrative Approach," *Psychological Bulletin* 107 (1990): 296.

2. Adapted from: John C. Flanagan, ed., "The Aviation Psychology Program in the Army Air Forces," in *Army Air Forces Aviation Psychology Program Research Reports* (Washington, DC: U.S. Government Printing Office, 1948).

3. Two of the mathematical characteristics of correlation coefficients are useful to keep in mind. The value of the correlation coefficient provides a direct measure of predictive efficiency. To illustrate this concept, suppose an employer needs twenty new workers. Using a test to select workers will require screening more applicants than needed and picking those with the highest scores. On average, an applicant's later performance (criterion) will be r (the correlation) times the applicant's score on the predictor, expressed in standard scores. Therefore, an r = .70 and an applicant predictor score of +1.0 means a likely performance score of +.70. The direct way to find twenty employees who would be fully satisfactory would be to hire a much larger number, try them out for six months or a year, and then retain only the twenty who had performed best. Obviously, a good test saves a great deal of money.

    The square of the correlation coefficient shows how much of the variance in the criterion has been explained by the predictor. In our cadet study, an r = +.70 means that 49% of the variance in the criterion has been accounted for by the predictor.

4. C. Paul Sparks, "Testing for Management Potential," in *Measures of Leadership*, eds. K. E. Clark and M. B. Clark (West Orange, NJ: Leadership Library of America, 1990) 106.

5. Table 1 reports results as multiple correlations. In this instance, scores on each measure in the battery of tests used to predict success are combined so as to produce the highest correlation with each dimension of success available. The multiple R can be interpreted in the same way as simple correlations. Most of the multiple Rs are quite high and clearly merit attention.

6. V. Jon Bentz, personal communication with authors, 1990.

7. Ann Howard and Douglas W. Bray, "Predictions of Managerial Success Over Long Periods of Time: Lessons From the Management Progress Study," in *Measures of Leadership*, eds. K. E. Clark and M. B. Clark (West Orange, NJ: Leadership Library of America, 1990) 112.

8. For further description of the meaning of these terms, see: K. E. Clark and M. B. Clark, eds., "Validation—The Ultimate Test," in *Measures of Leadership* (West Orange, NJ: Leadership Library of America, 1990) 57.

9. For a detailed view of how one set of scales was developed, see: Gary Yukl, Steve Wall, and Richard Lepsinger, "Preliminary Report on Validation of The Managerial Practices Survey," in *Measures of Leadership*, eds. K. E. Clark and M. B. Clark (West Orange, NJ: Leadership Library of America, 1990) 223.

10. Marshall Sashkin and Warren W. Burke, "Understanding and Assessing Organiza-

tional Leadership," in *Measures of Leadership*, eds. K. E. Clark and M. B. Clark (West Orange, NJ: Leadership Library of America, 1990) 297.

11. See note 10, p. 311.

12. K. D. Major, *Dogmatism, Visionary Leadership, and Effectiveness of Secondary Schools*, unpublished doctoral dissertation (University of La Verne, CA, 1986).

13. Clark L. Wilson, Donal O'Hare, and Frank Shipper, "Task Cycle Theory: The Processes of Influence," in *Measures of Leadership*, eds. K. E. Clark and M. B. Clark (West Orange, NJ: Leadership Library of America, 1990) 185.

14. R. Rosenthal, "How Are We Doing in Soft Psychology?" *American Psychologist* 45 (1990): 775.

CHAPTER SIX
Leadership and Organizational Outcomes

1. For a more detailed description of these methods and their effects, see: K. E. Clark and M. B. Clark, eds., *Measures of Leadership* (West Orange, NJ: Leadership Library of America, 1990) 69–76.

2. Frank Shipper and Clark L. Wilson, "The Impact of Managerial Behaviors on Group Performance, Stress, and Commitment," in *Impact of Leadership*, eds. K. E. Clark, M. B. Clark, and D. P. Campbell (Greensboro, NC: Center for Creative Leadership, 1992) 119.

3. *Variance* is equal to the square of the standard deviation of a distribution of measures of performance. The proportion of variance that is accounted for by a *predictor* variable is determined by squaring the measure of correlation between the predictor and the criterion. The correlation coefficient between two such variables measures the *validity* of the predictor measure.

4. For further discussion of methods of validation, see: K. E. Clark and M. B. Clark, eds., "Validation—The Ultimate Test," in *Measures of Leadership* (West Orange, NJ: Leadership Library of America, 1990) 57.

5. Gary Yukl, Steve Wall, and Richard Lepsinger, "Preliminary Report on Validation of The Managerial Practices Survey," in *Measures of Leadership*, eds. K. E. Clark and M. B. Clark (West Orange, NJ: Leadership Library of America, 1990) 223.

6. See note 5.

7. Jyuji Misumi, *The Behavioral Science of Leadership* (Ann Arbor: University of Michigan Press, 1985).

8. Kwang-kuo Hwang, "The Social Psychology of Chinese People," in *The Psychology of the Chinese People*, ed. Michael Harris Bond (New York: Oxford University Press, 1986) 213.

9. Francis J. Yammarino and Bernard M. Bass, "Long-Term Forecasting of Transformational Leadership and Its Effects Among Naval Officers: Some Preliminary Findings," in *Measures of Leadership*, eds. K. E. Clark and M. B. Clark (West Orange, NJ: Leadership Library of America, 1990) 151.

10. Mansour Javidan, "Developing a Profile of Effective Leaders in Top Management," in *Impact of Leadership*, eds. K. E. Clark, M. B. Clark, and D. P. Campbell (Greensboro, NC: Center for Creative Leadership, 1992) 56.

11. Barry Z. Posner and James M. Kouzes, "Leadership Pactices: An Alternative to the Psychological Perspective," in *Measures of Leadership*, eds. K. E. Clark and M. B. Clark (West Orange, NJ: Leadership Library of America, 1990) 205.

12. See note 11, p. 207.

13. Bruce J. Avolio and Jane M. Howell, "The Impact of Leader Behavior and Leader-Follower Personality Match on Satisfaction and Unit Performance," in *Impact of Leadership*, eds. K. E. Clark, M. B. Clark, and D. P. Campbell (Greensboro NC: Center for Creative Leadership, 1992) 225.

14. Rotter's Locus of Control measure sorts persons into two groups: 1) those who believe that their lives are under their own control and that they can make their own decisions, or 2) those who believe that circumstances beyond their control determine their future. See: Julian B. Rotter, "Generalized Expectancies for Internal Versus

External Locus of Control of Reinforcement," *Psychological Monographs: General and Applied* 80 (Whole Number 609) 1966.

15. Richard S. Tallarigo and Michael A. Rosebush, "An Examination of Leader Behaviors, Organizational Climate, and Subordinate Reactions," in *Impact of Leadership*, eds. K. E. Clark, M. B. Clark, and D. P. Campbell (Greensboro, NC: Center for Creative Leadership, 1992) 196.

16. R. A. Guzzo, R. D. Jette, and R. A. Katzell, "The Effects of Psychologically-Based Intervention Programs on Worker Productivity: A Meta-Analysis," *Personnel Psychology* 38 (1985): 275.

17. Meta-analysis provides a method for combining studies that relate to the same topics in order to 1) determine the consistency of findings in various settings, and 2) provide an estimate of the strength of relations found within the group of studies.

18. Robert Rodgers and John E. Hunter, "Impact of Management by Objectives on Organizational Productivity," *Journal of Applied Psychology* 76 (1991): 322.

19. R. D. Pritchard, S. D. Jones, P. L. Roth, K. K. Stuebing, and S. E. Ekberg, "Effects of Group Feedback, Goal Setting, and Incentives on Organizational Productivity," *Journal of Applied Psychology* 73 (1988): 337.

20. G. P. Latham, M. Erez, and E. A. Locke, "Resolving Scientific Disputes by the Joint Design of Crucial Experiments by the Antagonists: Application to the Dispute Regarding Participation in Goal Setting," *Journal of Applied Psychology* 73 (1988): 753. See also: E. A. Locke and G. P. Latham, *A Theory of Goal Setting and Task Performance* (Englewood Cliffs, NJ: Prentice-Hall, 1990).

21. Stanley Lieberson and James F. O'Connor, "Leadership and Organizational Performance: A Study of Large Corporations," *American Sociological Review* 37 (1985): 117.

22. Alan Berkeley Thomas, "Does Leadership Make a Difference to Organizational Performance?" *Administrative Science Quarterly* 33, (1988): 388.

23. David V. Day and Robert G. Lord, "Executive Leadership and Organizational Performance: Suggestions for a New Theory and Methodology," *Journal of Management* 14 (1988): 453.

24. R. N. Osborn and D. H. Jackson, "Leaders, River-Boat Gamblers, or Purposeful Unintended Consequences in the Management of Complex, Dangerous Technologies," *Academy of Management Journal* 31 (1988): 924.

25. J. M. Howell and P. J. Frost, "A Laboratory Study of Charismatic Leadership," *Organizational Behavior and Human Decision Processes* 43.2 (1989): 243.

CHAPTER SEVEN
A Test Battery Used in a Leadership Development Program

1. The materials presented and the procedures described are those used by the Center for Creative Leadership in Greensboro, North Carolina in its Leadership Development Program offered early in 1992.

CHAPTER NINE
Education and Training for Leaders

1. Dawn Gunsch, "For Your Information—Learning Leadership," *Personnel Journal*, 70.8 (1991): 17.

2. J. S. Russell, K. N. Wexley, and J. E. Hunter, "Questioning the Effectiveness of Behavior-Modeling Training in an Industrial Setting," *Personnel Psychology* 37 (1984): 465.

3. Joseph L. Moses and Richard J. Ritchie, "Supervisory Relationships Training: A Behavioral Evaluation of a Behavior Modeling Program," *Personnel Psychology* 29.3 (1976): 337.

4. G. P. Latham and L. M. Saari, "The Application of Social Learning Theory to Training Supervisors Through Behavior-Modeling," *Journal of Applied Psychology* 64 (1979): 239.

5. Melvin Sorcher and Rod Spence, "The Interface Project: Behavior Modeling as Social Technology in South Africa," *Personnel Psychology* 35 (1982): 557.

6. F. H. Kanfer, "Self-Management Methods," in *Helping People Change: A Textbook of Methods*, eds. F. H. Kanfer and A. P. Goldstein (Elmsford, NY: Pergamon Press, 1980) 334.

7. Colette A. Frayne and Gary P. Latham, "Application of Social Learning Theory to Employee Self-Management of Attendance," *Journal of Applied Psychology* 72 (1987): 387.

8. David P. Campbell, *The Campbell Organizational Survey™ (COS)™* (Minneapolis, MN: National Computer Systems, Inc., P.O. Box 1416, Minneapolis, MN 55440, 1990). Campbell Organizational Survey and COS are trademarks owned by David Campbell, Ph.D. Permission to reprint material has been granted by the author.

9. M. Loden and J. B. Rosener, *Workforce America! Managing Employee Diversity as a Vital Resource* (Homewood, IL: Business One Irwin, 1991) 212.

CHAPTER TEN
Learning Leadership Through Experience

1. James M. Kouzes & Barry Z. Posner, *The Leadership Challenge* (San Francisco: Jossey-Bass, 1987).

2. See note 1, p. 4.

3. Ann Howard and Douglas W. Bray, "Predictions of Managerial Success Over Long Periods of Time: Lessons From the Management Progress Study," in *Measures of Leadership*, eds. K. E. Clark and M. B. Clark (West Orange, NJ: Leadership Library of America, 1990) 113.

4. Morgan W. McCall, Jr., Michael M. Lombardo, and Ann M. Morrison, *The Lessons of Experience* (Lexington, MA: Lexington Books, 1988).

5. See note 4.

6. Information in Tables 1 and 2 is reprinted with the permission of Lexington Books, an imprint of Macmillan, Inc., from *The Lessons of Experience: How Successful Executives Develop on the Job* by Morgan W. McCall, Jr., Michael M. Lombardo, and Ann M. Morrison. Copyright ©1988 by Lexington Books.

7. See note 6, Table 1: p. 7; Table 2, p. 10.

8. See note 6, p. 28.

9. See note 6, p. 33.

10. See note 6, p. 48.

11. Alexander W. Astin, *The College Environment* (Washington, DC: American Council on Education, 1968).

12. Lewis C. Solmon and Paul J. Taubman, eds., *Does College Matter?* (New York: Academic Press, 1973) 18. See also: P. Taubman and T. Wales, *Higher Education and Earnings* (New York: McGraw-Hill, 1974).

13. R. K. Wagner and R. J. Sternberg, "Street Smarts," in *Measures of Leadership*, eds. K. E. Clark and M. B. Clark (West Orange, NJ: Leadership Library of America, 1990) 493.

14. Clark L. Wilson, Donal O'Hare, and Frank Shipper, "Task Cycle Theory: The Processes of Influence," in *Measures of Leadership*, eds. K. E. Clark and M. B. Clark (West Orange, NJ: Leadership Library of America, 1990) 185.

15. See note 3.

16. Joseph L. Moses and Karen S. Lyness, "Leadership Behavior in Ambiguous Environments," in *Measures of Leadership*, eds. K. E. Clark and M. B. Clark (West Orange, NJ: Leadership Library of America, 1990) 327.

17. Robert Hogan, Robert Raskin, and Dan Fazzini, "The Dark Side of Charisma," in *Measures of Leadership*, eds. K. E. Clark and M. B. Clark (West Orange, NJ: Leadership Library of America, 1990) 343.

18. Elliott Jaques, *The Requisite Organization: The CEO's Guide to Creative Structure and Leadership* (USA: Cason Hall, 1989).

CHAPTER ELEVEN
To See Ourselves As Others See Us

1. Brent Bowers, "How to Get Ahead as a Middle Manager by Being Ruthless," *Wall Street Journal* 23 Mar. 1993: 1.

2. Alan Farnham, "The TRUST GAP," *Fortune* 4 Dec. 1989: 56. ©1989 Time Inc. All Rights Reserved.

3. Stanley J. Modic, "Whatever It Is, It's Not Working," *Industry Week* 17 Jul. 1989: 27.

4. "Facts and Figures," *Training* Mar. 1989.

5. C. Emily Feistritzer, "Not Happy Teachers—Better Teachers," *Wall Street Journal* 26 Oct. 1990: B1.

6. Barry Z. Posner and Warren H. Schmidt, "Government Morale and Management: A Survey of Federal Executives," *Public Personnel Management* 17 (Spring 1988): 21.

7. David P. Campbell, *The Campbell Organizational Survey™ (COS)™* (National Computer Systems, Inc., P.O. Box 1416, Minneapolis, MN 55440, 1990).

8. John Wilcox, "In Practice," *Training and Development Journal* (June 1990): 11.

9. R. A. Guzzo, R. D. Jette, and R. A. Katzell, "The Effects of Psychologically-Based Intervention Programs on Worker Productivity: A Meta-Analysis," *Personnel Psychology* 38 (1985): 275.

10. Bernard M. Bass, *Leadership and Performance Beyond Expectations* (New York: Free Press, 1985) 14. See also: Francis J. Yammarino and Bernard M. Bass, "Long-Term Forecasting of Transformational Leadership and Its Effects Among Naval Officers: Some Preliminary Findings," in *Measures of Leadership*, eds. K. E. Clark and M. B. Clark (West Orange, NJ: Leadership Library of America, 1990) 151.

CHAPTER TWELVE
Leadership, Power, and Position

1. Jeffrey Pfeffer, *Managing with Power* (Boston, MA: Harvard Business School Press, 1992) 17.

2. Ian Cunningham, "The Impact of Who Leaders Are and What They Do," in *Impact of Leadership*, eds. K. E. Clark, M. B. Clark, and D. P. Campbell (Greensboro, NC: Center for Creative Leadership, 1992) 249.

3. See note 1, p. 279.

4. Elliott Jaques, *The Requisite Organization: The CEO's Guide to Creative Structure and Leadership* (USA: Cason Hall, 1989).

5. William C. Byham, *Zapp! The Lightning of Empowerment* (Pittsburgh: Development Dimensions International Press, 1989).

6. Fred E. Fiedler, "The Role and Meaning of Leadership Experience," in *Impact of Leadership*, eds. K. E. Clark, M. B. Clark, and D. P. Campbell (Greensboro, NC: Center for Creative Leadership, 1992) 95.

7. Gary Yukl, "Managerial Leadership: A Review of Theory and Research," *Journal of Management* 13 (1989): 251.

8. J. A. Conger and R. N. Kanungo, eds., *Charismatic Leadership: The Elusive Factor in Organizational Effectiveness* (San Francisco: Jossey-Bass, 1988).

9. Helen S. Astin and Carole Leland, *Women of Influence and Women of Vision: A Cross-Generational Study of Leaders and Social Change* (San Francisco: Jossey-Bass, 1991).

10. Robert E. Kaplan, *Beyond Ambition* (San Francisco: Jossey-Bass, 1991).

11. Robert Hogan, "The Dark Side of Charisma," in *Measures of Leadership*, eds. K. E. Clark and M. B. Clark (West Orange, NJ: Leadership Library of America, 1990) 343.

12. D. C. McClelland, *Human Motivation* (Chicago: Scott, Foresman, 1985).

13. See note 5.

14. Arthur S. Goldberg, "On Urban Political Leadership," in proceedings of the *Leadership Education Conference* (Richmond, VA: University of Richmond, 1990).

15. Edwin C. Hargrove, *Jimmy Carter as President: Leadership and the Politics of the Public Good* (Baton Rouge: Louisiana State University Press, 1988).
16. R. J. House, J. M. Howell, B. Shamir, B. Smith, and W. D. Spangler, *Charismatic Leadership: A 1990 Theory and Five Empirical Tests*, unpublished manuscript (Philadelphia: The Wharton School of the University of Pennsylvania, 1990).
17. Dean K. Simonton, "Presidential Style: Personality, Biography and Performance," *Journal of Personality and Social Psychology* 55.6 (1988): 928.
18. R. J. House, W. D. Spangler, and J. Woycke, *Personality and Charisma in the U.S. Presidency: A Psychological Theory of Leader Effectiveness*, unpublished manuscript (Philadelphia: The Wharton School of the University of Pennsylvania, 1990).
19. See note 1.

CHAPTER 13
Leadership and Cultural Differences

1. C. Geertz, *The Interpretation of Cultures* (New York: Basic Books, 1973).
2. Clyde Kluckhohn, "The Study of Culture," in *The Policy Sciences*, eds. D. Lerner and H. D. Lasswell (Stanford, CA: Stanford University Press, 1951).
3. Jyuji Misumi, *The Behavioral Science of Leadership* (Ann Arbor: University of Michigan Press, 1985).
4. Geerte Hofstede, *Culture's Consequences: International Differences in Work-Related Values* (Beverly Hills, CA: Sage, 1980).
5. D. C. McClelland and R. E. Boyatsis, "Leadership, Motive Pattern and Long-Term Success in Management," *Journal of Applied Psychology* 67 (1982): 737.
6. P. B. Smith and M. F. Peterson, *Leadership, Organizations, and Culture* (London: Sage, 1988).
7. See note 6.
8. Harry Triandis, "Individualism and Social Psychological Theory," in *Growth and Progress in Cross-Cultural Psychology*, ed. Çigdem Kagitçibasi (Berwyn, PA: Swets North America, 1987) 78.
9. Simcha Ronen, "Training the International Assignee," in *Training and Development in Organizations: Frontiers of Industrial and Organizational Psychology*, ed. I. L. Goldstein (San Francisco: Jossey-Bass, 1991) 417.
10. D. L. Dotlich, "International and Intra-Cultural Management Development," *Training and Development* 36 (1982): 26.
11. See note 10, p. 28.
12. R. L. Tung, "Selection and Training Procedures of U.S., European, and Japanese Multi-Nationals," *California Management Review* 25 (1982): 57.
13. Max Weber, *The Protestant Ethic and Spirit of Capitalism*, trans. A. M. Henderson and T. Parsons (New York: Free Press, 1947).
14. A. Laurent, *Cultural Dimensions of Managerial Ideologies: National Versus Multi-National Cultures*, paper presented at the Fifth Annual Meeting of The European Business Associates (London: 1979).
15. See note 4.
16. Çigdem Kagitçibasi, "Individual and Group Loyalties: Are They Compatible?" in *Growth and Progress in Cross-Cultural Psychology*, ed. Çigdem Kagitçibasi (Berwyn, PA: Swets North America, 1987) 94.
17. M. Loden and J. B. Rosener, *Workforce America! Managing Employee Diversity as a Vital Resource* (Homewood, IL: Business One Irwin, 1991).
18. Edgar H. Schein, *Organizational Culture and Leadership* (San Francisco: Jossey-Bass, 1985) ix.
19. See note 18, p. 317.
20. Bob Hagerty, "Trainers Help Expatriate Employees Build Bridges to Different Cultures," *Wall Street Journal* 14 Jun. 1993: B1.

CHAPTER FOURTEEN
Translating Knowledge Into Better Practice

1. For further details, see the manuals for the *Campbell Developmental Scales*,™ especially the *Campbell Organizational Survey™ (COS)™* (National Computer Systems, Inc., P.O. Box 1416, Minneapolis, MN 55440, 1990). Campbell Developmental Scales™ and Campbell Organizational Survey™ (COS)™ are trademarks owned by David P. Campbell, Ph.D.
2. Mark Stahlman is president of New Media Associates, Inc., a New York-based media and financial services company.
3. Mark Stahlman, "Creative Destruction at IBM," *Wall Street Journal* 6 Jan. 1993: A10.
4. G. P. Latham and L. M. Saari, "The Application of Social Learning Theory to Training Supervisors Through Behavior-Modeling," *Journal of Applied Psychology* 64 (1979): 239. Latham and Saari studied first-line supervisors at the Weyerhauser Company. They used multiple criteria—which they established before training—for evaluating behavior modeling. They used a control group in a follow-up measure of performance on the job. Subsequent training of individuals in the control group raised their performance to the level of the initially trained groups.
5. Mark Edwards, "In-Situ Evaluation: A New Paradigm for Measuring and Developing Leadership at Work," in *Impact of Leadership*, eds. K. E. Clark, M. B. Clark, and D. P. Campbell (Greensboro, NC: Center for Creative Leadership, 1992) 443.
6. Marian Ruderman, at the Center for Creative Leadership in Greensboro, NC, has examined promotion policies. She observes that even when promotions are distributed fairly among genders, races, and ethnic groups, they are based too frequently on an inadequate examination of past performance, especially with regard to leadership.
7. Peter M. Senge, *The Fifth Discipline* (New York: Doubleday/Currency, 1990).
8. Jon R. Katzenbach and Douglas K. Smith, *The Wisdom of Teams: Creating the High-Performance Organization* (Boston: Harvard Business School Press, 1993).

References and Suggested Readings

Arvey, R. D., & Ivancevich, J. M. (1980). Punishment in organizations: A review, propositions, and research suggestions. *Academy of Management Review, 5,* 123–132.

Astin, A. W. (1968). *The college environment.* Washington, DC: American Council on Education.

Astin, A. W., & Scherrei, R. A. (1980). *Maximizing leadership effectiveness: Impact of administrative style on faculty and students.* San Francisco: Jossey-Bass.

Astin, H. S., & Leland, C. (1991). *Women of influence, women of vision: A cross-generational study of leaders and social change.* San Francisco: Jossey-Bass.

Avolio, B. J., & Howell, J. M. (1992). The impact of leader behavior and leader-follower personality match on satisfaction and unit performance. In K. E. Clark, M. B. Clark, & D. P. Campbell (Eds.), *Impact of leadership* (pp. 225–235). Greensboro, NC: Center for Creative Leadership.

Badaracco, J. L., & Ellsworth, R. R. (1989). *Leadership and the quest for integrity.* Boston: Harvard Business School Press.

Bandura, A. (1977). *Social learning theory.* Englewood Cliffs, NJ: Prentice Hall.

Bandura, A. (1990). Selective activation and disengagement of moral control. *Journal of Social Issues, 46,* 27–46.

Barber, J. D. (1977). *Presidential character: Predicting performance in the White House.* Englewood Cliffs, NJ: Prentice Hall.

Bass, B. M. (1985). *Leadership and performance beyond expectations.* New York: Free Press.

Bass, B. M. (1990). *Bass and Stogdill's Handbook of Leadership: Theory, research, and managerial applications* (3rd ed.). New York: Free Press.

Beekun, R. I. (1989). Assessing the effectiveness of socio-technical intervention: Antidote or fad? *Human Relations, 42,* 877–897.

Behrman, J. N. (1988). *Essays on ethics in business and the professions.* Englewood Cliffs, NJ: Prentice Hall.

Bellingham, R., & Cohen, B. (1990). *Ethical leadership: A competitive edge.* Amherst, MA: Human Resource Development Press.

Bennis, W. G. (1976). *The unconscious conspiracy: Why leaders can't lead.* New York: AMACOM.

Bennis, W. G., & Nanus, B. (1985). *Leaders: The strategies of taking charge.* New York: Harper & Row.

Bentz, V. J. (1990). Contextual issues in predicting high-level leadership performance: Contextual richness as a criterion consideration in personality research with executives. In K. E. Clark & M. B. Clark (Eds.), *Measures of leadership* (pp. 131–143). West Orange, NJ: Leadership Library of America.

Birnbaum, R. (1988). *How colleges work: The cybernetics of academic organization and leadership.* San Francisco: Jossey-Bass.

Blake, R. R., & Mouton, J. S. (1964). *The managerial grid.* Houston: Gulf Publishing.

Bolman, L. G., & Deal, T. E. (1991). *Reframing organizations: Artistry, choice and leadership.* San Francisco: Jossey-Bass.

Bowers, B. (1993, March 23). How to get ahead as a middle manager by being ruthless. *The Wall Street Journal,* p. 1.

Bowers, D. G., & Seashore, S. E. (1966). Predicting organizational effectiveness with a four-factor theory of leadership. *Administrative Science Quarterly, 11,* 238–263.

Bruce, J. (1986). *The intuitive pragmatists: Conversations with chief executive officers.* Greensboro, NC: Center for Creative Leadership.

Burns, J. M. (1978). *Leadership.* New York: Harper & Row.

Burns, J. M. (1992). Leadership in American politics. In M. A. Spillett (Ed.), *Proceedings of the Leadership Education Conference* (pp. 10–15). Richmond, VA: University of Richmond.

Byham, W. C. (1989). *Zapp! The lightning of empowerment*. Pittsburgh: Development Dimensions International Press.

Campbell, D. P. (1990). *The Campbell Organizational Survey™ (COS™)*. Minneapolis, MN: National Computer Systems.

Caskey, F. (1988). *Leadership style and team process: A comparison of the managerial grid and situational leadership*. St. Paul: University of Minnesota, Department of Vocational and Technical Education. (ERIC Document Reproduction No. EDD 296 162).

Celis, W. (1993, February 21). Nation's top three school jobs open. *Naples Daily News*, p. H5.

Clark, K. E., & Clark, M. B. (Eds.). (1990). *Measures of leadership*. West Orange, NJ: Leadership Library of America.

Clark, K. E., Clark, M. B., & Campbell, D. P. (Eds.). (1992). *Impact of leadership*. Greensboro, NC: Center for Creative Leadership.

Clark, M. B., & Freeman, F. H. (Eds.). (1990). *Leadership education 1990: A source book*. West Orange, NJ: Leadership Library of America.

Cohen, W. A. (1990). *The art of the leader*. Englewood Cliffs, NJ: Prentice Hall.

Conger, J. A. (1992). *Learning to lead: The art of transforming managers into leaders*. San Francisco: Jossey-Bass.

Conger, J. A., & Kanungo, R. N. (Eds.). (1988). *Charismatic leadership: The elusive factor in organizational effectiveness*. San Francisco: Jossey-Bass.

Cronin, T. E. (1983). *Evaluating presidents*. Unpublished manuscript.

Cunningham, I. (1992). The impact of who leaders are and what they do. In K. E. Clark, M. B. Clark, & D. P. Campbell (Eds.), *Impact of leadership* (pp. 249–255). Greensboro, NC: Center for Creative Leadership.

Day, D. V., & Lord, R. G. (1988). Executive leadership and organizational performance: Suggestions for a new theory and methodology. *Journal of Management, 14*, 453–464.

Deal, T. E., & Peterson, K. D. (1990). *The principal's role in shaping school culture* (GPO No. 461-D-5). Washington, DC: U.S. Government Printing Office.

Deci, E. L. (1975). *Intrinsic motivation*. New York: Plenum.

Deci, E. L., Connell, J. P., & Ryan, R. M. (1989). Self-determination in a work organization. *Journal of Applied Psychology, 74*, 580–590.

DePree, M. (1989). *Leadership is an art*. New York: Doubleday.

Dotlich, D. L. (1982). International and intra-cultural management development. *Training and Development, 36*, 26–31.

Edwards, M. (1992). In-situ evaluation: A new paradigm for measuring and developing leadership at work. In K. E. Clark, M. B. Clark, & D. P. Campbell (Eds.), *Impact of leadership* (pp. 443–458). Greensboro, NC: Center for Creative Leadership.

Fairholm, G. W. (1991). *Values leadership: Toward a philosophy of leadership*. New York: Praeger.

Farnham, A. (1989, December). The TRUST GAP. *Fortune*, pp. 56–78.

Feistritzer, C. E. (1990, October 26). Not happy teachers—better teachers. *The Wall Street Journal*, p. B1.

Fiedler, F. E. (1992). The role and meaning of leadership experience. In K. E. Clark, M. B. Clark, & D. P. Campbell (Eds.), *Impact of leadership* (pp. 95–105). Greensboro, NC: Center for Creative Leadership.

Fiedler, F. E., Chemers, M. M., & Mahar, L. (1976). *Improving leadership effectiveness: The leader match concept*. New York: Wiley.

Flanagan, J. C. (Ed.). (1948). *Army Air Force aviation psychology program research reports*. Washington, DC: U.S. Government Printing Office.

Flax, S. (1984, August 6). The toughest bosses in America. *Fortune*, p. 18.

Fleishman, E. A. (1953). The measurement of leadership in industry. *Journal of Applied Psychology, 37*, 153–158.

Fleishman, E. A. (1973). Twenty years of consideration and structure. In E. A. Fleishman & J. G. Hunt (Eds.), *Current developments in the study of leadership* (pp. 2–3). Carbondale: Southern Illinois University Press.

Fleishman, E. A. (1989). *Leadership Opinion Questionnaire and examiner's manual* (rev.

ed.), and *Supervisory Behavior Description Questionnaire and examiner's manual* (rev. ed.). Chicago: Science Research Associates.

Fleishman, E. A. (1992). *Handbook of human abilities: Definitions, measurements and job task requirements.* Palo Alto, CA: Consulting Psychologists Press.

Frayne, C. A., & Latham, G. P. (1987). The application of social learning theory to employees' self-management of attendance. *Journal of Applied Psychology, 72,* 387–392.

Freeman, F. H., & King, S. N. (1993). *Leadership education 1992–1993: A source book.* Greensboro, NC: Center for Creative Leadership.

Gaertner, K. (1990). *The effects of ethical climate on managers' decisions.* Unpublished manuscript, School of Business Administration, Georgetown University, Washington, DC.

Gardner, J. W. (1990). *On leadership.* New York: Free Press.

Geertz, C. (1973). *The interpretation of cultures.* New York: Basic Books.

Gellermann, W., Frankel, M. S., & Ladenson, R. F. (1990). *Values and ethics in organizations and human systems development.* San Francisco: Jossey-Bass.

Ginnett, R. C. (1990). Airline cockpit crews. In R. Hackman (Ed.), *Groups that work (and those that don't)* (pp. 427–448). San Francisco: Jossey-Bass.

Goldberg, A. S. (1990, July). *On urban political leadership.* Paper presented at the Leadership Education Conference at the University of Richmond, VA.

Goldstein, I. L., and associates (Eds.). (1989). *Training and development in organizations.* San Francisco: Jossey-Bass.

Graham, J. L., & Sano, Y. (1989). *Smart bargaining: Doing business with the Japanese.* New York: Harper & Row.

Green, M. F. (Ed.). (1988). *Leaders for a new era: Strategies for higher education.* New York: American Council on Education/Macmillan.

Gregory, K. L. (1983). Native-view paradigms: Multi-cultures and culture conflicts in organizations. *Administrative Science Quarterly, 28,* 359–376.

Gunsch, D. (1991). For your information—learning leadership. *Personnel Journal, 70*(8), 17.

Guzzo, R. A., Jette, R. D., & Katzell, R. A. (1985). The effects of psychologically-based intervention programs on worker productivity: A meta-analysis. *Personnel Psychology, 38,* 275–291.

Hackman, J. R. (Ed.). (1990). *Groups that work (and those that don't): Creating conditions for effective teamwork.* San Francisco: Jossey-Bass.

Hagerty, B. (1993, June 14). Trainers help expatriate employees build bridges to different cultures. *The Wall Street Journal,* p. B1.

Halpin, A. W., & Winer, B. J. (1957). A factorial study of the leader behavior description. In R. M. Stogdill & A. E. Coons (Eds.), *Leader behavior: Its description and measurement.* Columbus: Ohio State University Press.

Hannah, M. E., & Midlarsky, E. (1981). *Toward an understanding of power and leadership in the young: A review.* San Rafael, CA: Select Press.

Hargrove, E. C. (1988). *Jimmy Carter as president: Leadership and the politics of the public good.* Baton Rouge: Louisiana State University Press.

Hemphill, J. K., & Coons, A. E. (1957). Development of the Leader Behavior Description Questionnaire. In R. M. Stogdill & A. E. Coons (Eds.), *Leader behavior: Its description and measurement* (p. 6). Columbus, OH: Bureau of Business Research.

Hersey, P., & Blanchard, K. (1988). *Management of organizational behavior: Utilizing human resources* (5th ed.). Englewood Cliffs, NJ: Prentice Hall.

Hickman, C. R. (1990). *Mind of a manager: Soul of a leader.* New York: Wiley.

Hill, G. C., & Yamada, K. (1992, December 9). Staying power: Motorola illustrates how an aged giant can remain vibrant. *The Wall Street Journal,* p. 1.

Hirsch, J. S. (1991, September 24). To one Xerox man, selling photocopiers is a gamblers game. *The Wall Street Journal,* p. B1.

Hodgkinson, C. (1978). *Towards a philosophy of administration.* New York: St. Martin's.

Hodgkinson, C. (1983). *The philosophy of leadership.* New York: St. Martin's.

Hofstede, G. (1980). *Culture's consequences: International differences in work-related values.* Beverly Hills, CA: Sage.

Hogan, R., Raskin, R., & Fazzini, D. (1990). The dark side of charisma. In K. E. Clark & M. B. Clark (Eds.), *Measures of leadership* (pp. 343–354). West Orange, NJ: Leadership Library of America.

Hollander, E. P. (1978). *Leadership dynamics: A practical guide to effective relationships.* New York: Free Press.

House, R. J. (1976). A 1976 theory of charismatic leadership. In J. G. Hunt & L. L. Larson (Eds.), *Leadership: The cutting edge* (pp. 189–207). Carbondale: Southern Illinois University Press.

House, R. J., & Howell, J. M. (1992). Personality and charismatic leadership. *Leadership Quarterly, 3*, 81.

House, R. J., Howell, J. M., Shamir, B., Smith, B., & Spangler, W. D. (1990). *Charismatic leadership: A 1990 theory and five empirical tests.* Working paper, The Reginald Jones Center for Strategic Management, The Wharton School of the University of Pennsylvania.

House, R. J., & Spangler, W. D. (1992, February 16). [Letter to the editor]. *The New York Times*, p. E14.

House, R. J., Spangler, W. D., & Woycke, J. (1991). Personality and charisma in the U.S. presidency: A psychological theory of leader effectiveness. *Administrative Science Quarterly, 36*, 364–396.

Howard, A., & Bray, D. W. (1990). Predictions of managerial success over long periods of time: Lessons from the Management Progress Study. In K. E. Clark & M. B. Clark (Eds.), *Measures of leadership* (pp. 113–130). West Orange, NJ: Leadership Library of America.

Howell, J. M., & Frost, P. J. (1989). A laboratory study of charismatic leadership. *Organizational Behavior and Human Decision Processes, 43*(2), 243–269.

Hui, C. C. H. (1984). *Individualism, collectivism: Theory measurement and its relation to reward allocation.* Doctoral dissertation, Department of Psychology, University of Illinois, Champaign.

Hui, C. C. H., & Triandis, H. C. (1986). Individualism-Collectivism: A study of cross-cultural researchers. *Journal of Cross-Cultural Psychology, 17*, 225–248.

Hunt, J. G. (1991). *Leadership: A new synthesis.* London: Sage.

Hwang, K. (1986). The social psychology of Chinese people. In M. H. Bond (Ed.), *The psychology of the Chinese people* (p. 213). New York: Oxford University Press.

Hyatt, J. C., & Naj, A. K. (1992, March 3). GE is no place for autocrats, Welch decrees. *The Wall Street Journal*, p. B1.

Hyland, M. E. (1988). Motivational control theory: An integrative framework. *Journal of Personality and Social Psychology, 55*, 642–651.

Jacobs, T. O., & Jaques, E. (1990). Military executive leadership. In K. E. Clark & M. B. Clark (Eds.), *Measures of leadership* (pp. 281–295). West Orange, NJ: Leadership Library of America.

Jaques, E. (1989). *Requisite organization: The CEO's guide to creative structure and leadership.* Arlington, VA: Cason Hall.

Jaques, E., & Clement, S. D. (1991). *Executive leadership: A practical guide to managing complexity.* Arlington, VA: Cason Hall.

Javidan, M. (1992). Developing a profile of effective leaders in top management. In K. E. Clark, M. B. Clark, & D. P. Campbell (Eds.), *Impact of leadership* (pp. 47–58). Greensboro, NC: Center for Creative Leadership.

Kagitçibasi, Ç. (1987). Individual and group loyalties: Are they compatible? In Ç. Kagitçibasi (Ed.), *Growth and progress in cross-cultural psychology* (pp. 94–103). Berwyn, PA: Swets North America.

Kagitçibasi, Ç. (Ed.). (1987). *Growth and progress in cross-cultural psychology.* Berwyn, PA: Swets North America.

Kanfer, F. H. (1974). Self-regulations: Research issues and speculations. In C. Neuringer & J. Michael (Eds.), *Behavior modification in clinical psychology* (pp. 397–409). East Norwalk, CT: Appleton Century Crofts.

Kanfer, F. H. (1980). Self-management methods. In F. H. Kanfer & A. P. Goldstein (Eds.), *Helping people change: A textbook of methods* (pp. 309–355). Elmsford, NY: Pergamon Press.

Kaplan, R. E. (1991). *Beyond ambition*. San Francisco: Jossey-Bass.

Katz, D., Maccoby, N., & Morse, N. C. (1950). *Productivity, supervision, and morale in an office situation*. Ann Arbor: University of Michigan, Institute for Social Research.

Katzell, R. A., & Thompson, D. E. (1990). Work motivation: Theory and practice. *American Psychologist, 45,* 144–153.

Katzenbach, J. R., & Smith, D. K. (1993). *The wisdom of teams: Creating the high-performance organization*. Boston: Harvard Business School Press.

Kellerman, B. (Ed.). (1984). *Leadership: Multidisciplinary perspectives*. Englewood Cliffs, NJ: Prentice Hall.

Kerr, C., Dunlop, J. T., Harbison, F., & Myers, C. A. (1961). Industrialism and world society. *Harvard Business Review, 39,* 114–122.

Kets de Vries, M. F. R. (1989). Leaders who self-destruct: The causes and cures. *Organizational Dynamics, 17,* 4–17.

Kets de Vries, M. F. R. (1989). *Prisoners of leadership*. New York: Wiley.

Kleinmuntz, B. (1990). Why we still use our heads instead of formulas: Toward an integrative approach. *Psychological Bulletin, 107,* 296–310.

Kluckhohn, C. (1951). The study of culture. In D. Lerner & H. D. Lasswell (Eds.), *The policy sciences*. Stanford, CA: Stanford University Press.

Kotter, J. P. (1988). *The leadership factor*. New York: Free Press.

Kotter, J. P. (1990). *A force for change: How leadership differs from management*. New York: Free Press.

Kouzes, J. H., & Posner, B. Z. (1987). *The leadership challenge: How to get extraordinary things done in organizations*. San Francisco: Jossey-Bass.

Landis, D., & Brislin, R. W. (1983). *Handbook of inter-cultural training* (Vols. 1–3). Elmsford, NY: Pergamon Press.

Larson, L. L., Hunt, J. G., & Osborn, R. N. (1976). The great Hihi leader behavior myth: A lesson from Occam's Razor. *Academy of Management Journal, 19,* 628–641.

Latham, G. P., Erez, M., & Locke, E. A. (1988). Resolving scientific disputes by the joint design of crucial experiments by the antagonists: Application to the Erez-Latham dispute regarding participating in goal setting. *Journal of Applied Psychology, 73,* 753–772.

Latham, G. P., & Saari, L. M. (1979). The application of social learning theory to training supervisors through behavior modeling. *Journal of Applied Psychology, 64,* 239–246.

Laurent, A. (1979). *Cultural dimensions of managerial ideologies: National versus multi-national cultures*. Paper presented at the Fifth Annual Meeting of the European Business Associates, London.

Leung, K. (1983). *The impact of cultural collectivism on reward allocation*. Unpublished master's thesis, University of Illinois, Department of Psychology, Champaign.

Levinson, H. (1981). *Executive*. Cambridge, MA: Harvard University.

Lieberson, S., & O'Connor, J. F. (1985). Leadership and organizational performance: A study of large corporations. *American Sociological Review, 37,* 117–130.

Lipin, S., & Pae, P. (1992, December 8). Resignation spurs American Express shares. *The Wall Street Journal*, p. A4.

Locke, E. A., & Latham, G. P. (1990). *A theory of goal setting and task performance*. Englewood Cliffs, NJ: Prentice Hall.

Loden, M., & Rosener, J. B. (1991). *Workforce America! Managing employee diversity as a vital resource*. Homewood, IL: Business One Irwin.

MacGregor, D. (1960). *The human side of enterprise*. New York: McGraw-Hill.

Major, K. D. (1986). *Dogmatism, visionary leadership, and effectiveness of secondary schools*. Unpublished doctoral dissertation, University of La Verne, CA.

Manz, C. C., & Sims, H. P., Jr. (1989). *SuperLeadership: Leading others to lead themselves*. New York: Prentice Hall.

McCall, M. W., Jr., Lombardo, M. M., & Morrison, A. M. (1988). *The lessons of experience*. Lexington, MA: Lexington Books.

McCall, M. W., Morrison, A. M., & Hannan, R. L. (1978). *Studies of managerial work: Results and methods*. (Tech. Rep. No. 9). Greensboro, NC: Center for Creative Leadership.

McClelland, D. C. (1985). *Human motivation*. Chicago: Scott, Foresman.

McClelland, D. C., & Boyatzis, R. E. (1982). Leadership, motive pattern and long-term success in management. *Journal of Applied Psychology, 67*, 737–743.

Meehl, P. E. (1954). *Clinical versus statistical prediction: A theoretical analysis and review of the evidence.* Minneapolis: University of Minnesota Press.

Meehl, P. E. (1959). Some ruminations on the validation of clinical procedures. *Canadian Journal of Psychology, 13*, 102–128.

Meindl, J. R., & Ehrlich, S. B. (1987). The romance of leadership and the evaluation of organizational performance. *Academy of Management Journal, 30*, 91–109.

Mintzberg, H. (1973). *The nature of managerial work.* New York: Harper & Row.

Mintzberg, H. (1983). An emerging strategy of "direct" research. In J. Van Maanen (Ed.), *Qualitative methodology* (pp. 105–116). Newbury Park, CA: Sage.

Misumi, J. (1985). *The behavioral science of leadership.* Ann Arbor: University of Michigan Press.

Modic, S. J. (1989, July 17). Whatever it is, it's not working. *Industry Week*, p. 27.

Morrison, A. M., White, R. P., & Van Velsor, E. (1987). *Breaking the glass ceiling.* Reading, MA: Addison-Wesley.

Moses, J. L., & Lyness, K. S. (1990). Leadership behavior in ambiguous environments. In K. E. Clark & M. B. Clark (Eds.), *Measures of leadership* (pp. 327–335). West Orange, NJ: Leadership Library of America.

Moses, J. I., & Ritchie, R. J. (1976). Supervisory relationship training: A behavioral evaluation of a behavior-modeling program. *Personnel Psychology, 29*, 337–343.

Murray, R. K., & Blessing, T. H. (1983). The presidential performance study: A progress report. *Journal of American History, 70*, 535–555.

Nadler, D. A., & Tushman, M. L. (1990). Beyond the charismatic leader: Leadership and organizational change. *California Management Review*, Winter.

Near, J. W. (1992, April 22). Wendy's successful "mop bucket attitude." *The Wall Street Journal*, p. A14.

Neuman, G. A., Edwards, J. E., & Ragu, N. S. (1989). Organization development interventions: A meta-analysis of their effects on satisfaction and other attitudes. *Personnel Psychology, 42*, 461–489.

Neustadt, R. E. (1990). *Presidential power and the modern presidents.* New York: Free Press.

Nystrom, P. C. (1978). Managers and the Hihi leadership myth. *Academy of Management Journal, 21*, 325–331.

Osborn, R. N., & Jackson, D. H. (1988). Leaders, river-boat gamblers, or purposeful unintended consequences in the management of complex, dangerous technologies. *Academy of Management Journal, 31*, 924–947.

Patinkin, M. (1992, August 19). Helping people to live, prosper where they are. *Naples Daily News*, p. D1.

Peters, T. J., & Waterman, R. H. (1982). *In search of excellence: Lessons from America's best-run companies.* New York: Harper & Row.

Pfeffer, J. (1992). *Managing with power.* Boston: Harvard Business School Press.

Phillips, D. T. (1992). *Lincoln on leadership.* New York: Warner Books.

Posner, B. Z., & Kouzes, J. M. (1990). Leadership practices: An alternative to the psychological perspective. In K. E. Clark & M. B. Clark (Eds.), *Measures of leadership* (pp. 205–215). West Orange, NJ: Leadership Library of America.

Posner, B. Z., & Schmidt, W. H. (1988). Government morale and management: A survey of federal executives. *Public Personnel Management, 17*, 21–27.

Pritchard, R. D., Jones, S. D., Roth, P. L., Stuebing, K. K., & Ekeberg, S. E. (1988). Effects of group feedback, goal setting, and incentives on organizational productivity. *Journal of Applied Psychology, 73*, 337–358.

Richman, T. (1988). Leadership expert Ronald Heifetz. *Inc., 10*, 37.

Rodgers, R., & Hunter, J. E. (1991). Impact of management by objectives on organizational productivity. *Journal of Applied Psychology, 76*, 322–336.

Roloff, R. (1987). Leadership and ethics in the real world. In M. B. Clark (Ed.), *Proceedings of the Leadership Education Conference, 1987* (pp. 39–42). Greensboro, NC: Center for Creative Leadership.

Ronen, S. (1991). Training the international assignee. In I. L. Goldstein (Ed.), *Training and development in organizations: Frontiers of industrial and organizational psychology* (pp. 417–453). San Francisco: Jossey-Bass.

Rosenbach, W. E., & Taylor, R. I. (Eds.). (1984). *Contemporary issues in leadership.* Boulder, CO: Westview.

Rosenthal, R. (1990). How are we doing in soft psychology? *The American Psychologist, 45,* 775–776.

Rost, J. C. (1991). *Leadership in the twenty-first century.* New York: Praeger.

Rotter, J. B. (1966). Generalized expectancies for internal versus external locus of control of reinforcement. *Psychological Monographs: General and Applied, 80* (Whole No. 609).

Russell, J. S., Wexley, K. N., & Hunter, J. E. (1984). Questioning the effectiveness of behavior-modeling training in an industrial setting. *Personnel Psychology, 37,* 465–482.

Rustow, D. A. (1970). *Philosophers and kings: Studies in leadership.* New York: George Braziller.

Sashkin, M., & Burke, W. W. (1990). Understanding and assessing organizational leadership. In K. E. Clark & M. B. Clark (Eds.), *Measures of leadership* (pp. 297–325). West Orange, NJ: Leadership Library of America.

Sashkin, M., Rosenbach, W. E., Deal, T. E., & Peterson, K. D. (1992). Assessing transformational leadership and its impact. In K. E. Clark, M. B. Clark, & D. P. Campbell (Eds.), *Impact of leadership* (pp. 131–148). Greensboro, NC: Center for Creative Leadership.

Sayles, L. R. (1989). *Leadership: Managing in real organizations.* New York: McGraw-Hill.

Schein, E. H. (1985). *Organizational culture and leadership.* San Francisco: Jossey-Bass.

Schwartz, B. (1990). The creation and destruction of value. *American Psychologist, 45,* 7–15.

Senge, P. M. (1990). *The fifth discipline: The art and practice of the learning organization.* New York: Doubleday/Currency.

Shamir, B., House, R. J., & Arthur, M. B. (in press). The transformational effects of charismatic leadership: A motivational theory. *Organizational Science.*

Shipper, F., & Wilson, C. L. (1992). The impact of managerial behaviors on group performance, stress, and commitment. In K. E. Clark, M. B. Clark, & D. P. Campbell (Eds.), *Impact of leadership* (pp. 119–129). Greensboro, NC: Center for Creative Leadership.

Simonton, D. K. (1987). *Why presidents succeed: A political psychology of leadership.* New Haven, CT: Yale University Press.

Simonton, D. K. (1988). Presidential style: Personality, biography, and performance. *Journal of Personality and Social Psychology, 55,* 928–936.

Smith, P.B., & Peterson, M. F. (1988). *Leadership, organizations, and culture: An event management model.* London: Sage.

Solmon, L., & Taubman, P. (Eds.). (1973). *Does college matter?* New York: Academic Press.

Sorcher, M., & Spence, R. (1982). The Interface Project: Behavior modeling as social technology in South Africa. *Personnel Psychology, 35,* 557–581.

Spangler, W. D., & House, R. J. (1991). Presidential effectiveness and the Leadership Motive Profile. *Journal of Personality and Social Psychology, 60,* 439–455.

Sparks, P. (1990). Testing for management potential. In K. E. Clark & M. B. Clark (Eds.), *Measures of leadership* (pp. 103–111). West Orange, NJ: Leadership Library of America.

Stahlman, M. (1993, January 6). Creative destruction at IBM. *The Wall Street Journal,* p. A10.

Stumpf, S. A., & Dunbar, R. L. M. (1988). *Using behavioral simulations in teaching strategy implementation.* Paper presented at the meeting of the National Academy of Management, Anaheim, CA.

Tallarigo, R. S., & Rosebush, M. A. (1992). An examination of leader behaviors, organizational climate, and subordinate reactions. In K. E. Clark, M. B. Clark, & D. P. Campbell (Eds.), *Impact of leadership* (pp. 189–198). Greensboro, NC: Center for Creative Leadership.

Taubman, P., & Wales, T. (1974). *Higher education and earnings*. New York: McGraw-Hill.

Taylor, J. C., & Bowers, D. G. (1972). *Survey of organizations*. Ann Arbor: University of Michigan, Institute for Social Research.

Taylor, R. L., & Rosenbach, W. E. (1989). *Leadership: Challenges for today's managers*. New York: Nichols.

Thomas, A. B. (1988). Does leadership make a difference to organizational performance? *Administrative Science Quarterly, 33*, 388–400.

Triandis, H. (1987). Individualism and social psychological theory. In Ç. Kagitçibasi (Ed.), *Growth and progress in cross-cultural psychology* (pp. 78–83). Berwyn, PA: Swets North America.

Tung, R. L. (1982). Selection and training procedures of U.S., European, and Japanese multi-nationals. *California Management Review, 25*, 57–71.

Vogt, J. F., & Murrell, K. L. (1990). *Empowerment in organizations: How to spark exceptional performance*. San Diego: University Associates.

Vroom, V. H., & Jago, A. G. (1988). *The new leadership: Managing participation in organizations*. Englewood Cliffs, NJ: Prentice Hall.

Wagner, R. K., & Sternberg, R. J. (1990). Street smarts. In K. E. Clark & M. B. Clark (Eds.), *Measures of leadership* (pp. 493–504). West Orange, NJ: Leadership Library of America.

Wall, J. A. (1986). *Bosses*. Lexington, MA: Lexington Books.

Webber, R. A. (1969). *Culture and management*. Homewood, IL: Irwin.

Weber, M. (1947). *The Protestant ethic and spirit of capitalism*. A. M. Henderson & T. Parsons (Trans.). New York: Free Press.

Wilcox, J. (1990). In practice. *Training and Development Journal*, June, 11.

Wilson, C. L., O'Hare, D., & Shipper, F. (1990). Task cycle theory: The processes of influence. In K. E. Clark & M. B. Clark (Eds.), *Measures of leadership* (pp. 185–204). West Orange, NJ: Leadership Library of America.

Winter, D. G. (1987). Leader appeal, leader performance, and the motive profile of leaders and followers: A study of American presidents and elections. *Journal of Personality and Social Psychology, 52*, 196–202.

Yammarino, F. J., & Bass, B. M. (1990). Long-term forecasting of transformational leadership and its effects among Naval officers: Some preliminary findings. In K. E. Clark & M. B. Clark (Eds.), *Measures of leadership* (pp. 151–169). West Orange, NJ: Leadership Library of America.

Yukl, G. A. (1989). *Leadership in organizations* (2nd ed.). Englewood Cliffs, NJ: Prentice Hall.

Yukl, G. (1989). Managerial leadership: A review of theory and research. *Journal of Management, 13*, 251–289.

Yukl, G., Wall, S., & Lepsinger, R. (1990). Preliminary report on validation of the Managerial Practices Survey. In K. E. Clark & M. B. Clark (Eds.), *Measures of leadership* (pp. 223–237). West Orange, NJ: Leadership Library of America.

Zalesnik, A. (1977). Managers and leaders: Are they different? *Harvard Business Review, 15*, 67–84.

NAME AND SUBJECT INDEX

Page numbers in italics indicate figures; page numbers followed by t indicate tables.

Authors

KENNETH E. CLARK, Smith Richardson Senior Scientist at the Center for Creative Leadership, Greensboro, North Carolina, was its president from 1981–1985 and its board chairman from 1974–1981.

In 1940, he joined the faculty in psychology at the University of Minnesota after earning his Ph.D. degree at Ohio State University, becoming Chair of the department in 1957–1960. He was dean of the College of Arts and Science at the University of Colorado from 1961–1963 and at the University of Rochester from 1963–1980.

He was president of the American Board in Professional Psychology and the American Psychological Foundation, was appointed by President Kennedy to the National Medal of Science Committee, was chairman of the Association for the Advancement of Psychology and the American Conference of Academic Deans. He wrote *America's Psychologists, The Vocational Interests of Nonprofessional Men*, co-authored *The Graduate Student as Teacher, Psychology, Measures of Leadership*, and *Impact of Leadership*, and edited for ten years the *Journal of Applied Psychology*.

He was consultant to the White House, the Office of Science and Technology, the Central Intelligence Agency, the National Science Foundation, the National Institutes of Health, the Veteran's Administration, the Army, and the Navy. He was awarded Ohio State University's Centennial Achievement Award, the American Personnel and Guidance Association's award for research excellence, and the E. K. Strong, Jr., Gold Medal for contribution to interest measurement. He received the Gold Medal Award of the American Psychological Foundation in 1986 for a lifetime of exceptional contributions to professional psychology.

He is a founding fellow of the American Psychological Society, a fellow of the American Association for the Advancement of Science and the American Psychological Association, and an honorary life fellow of the Canadian Psychological Association.

Clark and his wife, Miriam, reside at 4551 Gulfshore Boulevard North in Naples, Florida.

MIRIAM B. CLARK served as associate dean in the College of Arts and Science at the University of Rochester, retiring in 1980. Her primary responsibilities included undergraduate curriculum, academic advising, and career planning. She has been a member or the president of the board of numerous Rochester, New York, community agencies and civic groups. She is currently chairman of the Board of Trustees of the Seacrest Country Day School of Naples, Florida, and a member of the Board of Directors of the Naples Philharmonic Center for the Arts.

In collaboration with others, her publications include *The Graduate Student as Teacher; Leadership Education: A Source Book* in three editions 1985, 1987, and 1990; *Measures of Leadership*; and *Impact of Leadership*. She resides with her husband, Kenneth, in Naples, Florida.